Knitting Pattern
Essentials

Knitting Pattern Essentials

adapting and drafting
knitting patterns for great knitwear

SALLY MELVILLE

POTTER
CRAFT

NEW YORK

Copyright © 2013 by Sally Melville
Photographs copyright © 2013 by Potter Craft

All rights reserved.
Published in the United States by Potter Craft,
an imprint of the Crown Publishing Group,
a division of Random House, Inc., New York.
www.pottercraft.com
www.crownpublishing.com

POTTER CRAFT and colophon is a registered trademark of Random House, Inc.

Library of Congress Cataloging-in-Publication Data
Melville, Sally.
Knitting pattern essentials : adapting and drafting knitting patterns
for great knitwear / Sally Melville.—1st edition.
Includes index.
1. Knitting—Patterns. 2. Knitwear—Pattern design. I. Title.
TT825.M4543 2015
746.43'2—dc23   2012015715

ISBN 978-0-307-96557-8
eISBN 978-0-307-96558-5

Printed in China

Design by La Tricia Watford
Interior photographs: Rose Callahan
Front cover photographs (clockwise from top): Rose Callahan,
Andrew McCaul/Getty Images, Rose Callahan, Ocean/Corbis
Back cover photographs: Rose Callahan

10 9 8 7 6 5 4 3 2

First Edition

To Robert, who creates beauty
on a large canvas and
personifies vision-to-reality

CONTENTS

Introduction

I believe that whatever level knitter you are, this book is for you.

We don't love what we don't understand. As newer knitters, we often follow published patterns without question—patterns that may not be well written, patterns that may not be appropriate to our skill level, patterns for garments that bear no resemblance to the clothes we actually wear. We finish the garment . . . or not . . . and it looks okay . . . or not. In the latter case, we're not quite sure what's wrong, but—without breaking stride—we're off to the yarn shop for more yarn. (Knitters are unfailingly optimistic!) But, sadly, if this happens often enough, eventually, we decide we weren't meant to make garments and so restrict ourselves to knitting socks and shawls.

I too knit socks and shawls. But I also knit sweaters and coats and dresses and vests—that I wear. And I wish the same for all of you. Because isn't the following dialogue what we want to hear every time we knit what we wear, and wear what we knit?

Other person: Wow, I love your sweater [coat, dress, vest]! Where'd you get it?

You: I knit it myself!

Other person: You made it yourself! I need to learn how to knit!!!

And she's right: she *should* learn to knit! Why not make—and have hours of pleasure doing so—the one sweater that we treasure rather than spending hard-earned cash on the six we don't? Why not revert to the way humans have lived for most of their history—as makers rather than consumers?

One group for whom this book is written is the newer knitter—you who want to continue to knit from published patterns but understand them well enough to knit pieces you are proud to wear. You should read the sections on Essential Measurements and Standard Sizes (page 19), and Standards of Ease (page 27), and then read the section that applies to whatever style you are knitting. As you continue to knit from published patterns, you will use this material to modify them rather than follow blindly, and that's a wonderful thing. (I was once asked "What is the most common mistake knitters make?" The words that flew out of my mouth were "They follow the pattern!" After you read about your essential measurements, you'll understand why I said that, and you'll start adjusting patterns accordingly.) Eventually, you may read the whole book. And then you'll move into the second camp.

The second group for whom this book is intended is those who have been knitting for some time. You want to be liberated from published patterns and given the power to do your own thing. Fabulous! I salute you! I may never sell you another pattern, but I'm so okay with that!

To you, I'd advise the following steps.

- Find a garment you love (something you did not knit) to copy. This step is optional but a great place to start (see How to Copy an Existing Garment, page 15).
- Find appropriate yarn and start swatching—while reading chapter 1 on the basics of drafting, choosing a style, and more.
- Proceed to find the shapes that, when put together, give you the garment you want.
- Read about them, write your pattern, knit your garment . . . and have fun!

For any knitter at any level, the first priority is to have fun. (Why would you want to continue doing something that isn't fun?!?) But what exactly does *have fun* mean? Does it mean to knit with joy and enthusiasm and the expectation of a perfect result? No, it does not. It means to knit with joy and enthusiasm and realistic expectations. If your experience is like mine, you might actually knit each piece of your garment twice (or more) before you get something that works. (One of my favorite garments had pieces that were knit four times before I got it right. And the original sleeves had to be reknit in a different yarn. But the result was worth every moment of rip and reknit.) My mantra comes from the poet Maya Angelou: "You did the best you could until you knew better, and when you knew better you did better."

As we learn more and get better, we sometimes see—while knitting—that something is wrong . . . and that we need to rip. (If you know what the problem is, don't let the sun set before ripping past it: if you're not sure, sleep on it and hope for enlightenment.) But if the thought of ripping makes you anxious . . . well, the truth is that you need to get over it. You *will* rip! I routinely rip (see page 159 on how to reuse yarn), and I've long given up cursing. It's just part of the process. Please do not

think of it as failure. Rather, it's an essential part of the learning process. As Albert Einstein said, "Anyone who never made a mistake never tried anything new." The trick is to recognize mistakes early, learn what you need to not repeat them, then start over.

Sometimes the "mistakes" don't reveal themselves until the garment is done. That's okay, too. Just because it's finished does not mean it's a done-deal disaster. Most "disasters" can still be turned into fabulous pieces. My career is a testament to this, and chapter 8 offers some common solutions that I have learned and used to rescue garments that did not emerge perfectly formed with my first efforts.

As Winston Churchill said, "Creativity is the ability to go from one failure to another with no loss of enthusiasm." With tenacity and optimism, this is exciting stuff! Once you fire your brain cells with the new skills you learn, you will crave a repeat experience. Once you repeat the experience, you'll gain confidence. Once you create something that is entirely your own, your sense of accomplishment will soar . . . and you won't want to work any other way. And once you knit and wear something wonderfully original . . . well, who knows what life may bring?

How This Book Is Written

I do not see pattern drafting as a difficult process. To help you, I kept the writing concise: I don't use more steps or more explanation or more math than I think you need.

For those of you who are experienced knitters, this work will answer many questions. But how should you proceed if you are less experienced? You can keep knitting from published patterns, reading any relevant sections from this book to understand what the pattern asks of you. Or you can decide to draft your own garments by following the material in this book, knowing that its one-step-at-a-time format will soon make wonderful and liberating sense.

You might notice that this book is dedicated only to sweaters—or, more specifically, garments that hang from the shoulders. Why? For several reasons: they are what we knit most often; to have covered everything we could knit (skirts, pants, purses, hats, socks, shawls, scarves, toilet roll covers) would have made the book unwieldy; and, finally, with the exception of pants, most of the other stuff we knit is easier to draft than garments that have to fit around our arms and over our head. If you're interested in drafting other pieces, see the sections on what vertical, horizontal, diagonal, and curved lines mean and how to copy an existing garment (pages 14 and 15): they should give you the skills you need.

In addition, what I say next is obvious . . . but I need to say it anyway. What I've written here is only what I know and use and think is helpful. This is not a stitch dictionary (although I do explain how common stitch patterns behave). And I do not teach basic knitting skills. (A list of the ones I think essential are in the Appendix. The skills themselves are taught in most knitting manuals, including my own.) I also haven't covered every garment shape possible—because you will invent ones I've never dreamed of! And I haven't dealt with ways of working that I don't commonly use (see page 16 for an explanation of my style preferences).

And finally a point of clarification. This is not a design book. Design is different from drafting, and this book is about the latter—the practical mechanics and support material that bring your vision to life. Design is about finding that vision—where to look for inspiration, how to choose yarns, what colors work together, how to envision stitch patterns in combination, and so on. I am not a teacher of design. (But Deborah Newton is, and her

book *Designing Knitwear* is excellent source material.) But I *am* a teacher of drafting and technique. Throughout this book, *you* are the designer, and my job is to offer the know-how that makes your design become a garment. I look forward to the results of your capable hands—a world in which we proudly knit what we wear, wear what we knit, understand what we are doing, and then truly love and honor our craft.

Chapter 1

Preparing to Draft

There are pieces of your puzzle you need in place before you begin the fascinating work of pattern drafting. It's all essential stuff: the basics of measuring, drafting, and swatching; an explanation of how I expect you to use this book; some standards that you need in hand. So please take the time to read through this material before moving on to the shapes you will draft.

Understanding Vertical, Horizontal, Diagonal, and Curved Lines

When developing a new skill, it's helpful to break it down to its components. So here's the simplest expression of what you need to know for pattern drafting: *everything must be expressed in terms of stitches and rows.*

What that means is that when knitting a garment in the traditional manner (up from the hem),

- a horizontal measurement becomes the number of stitches
- a vertical measurement becomes the number of rows

It would be wonderful if horizontals and verticals were all we ever drafted, but in the shapes we want to execute, there are also diagonals and curves.

So how do we produce a diagonal? Remember, everything must be expressed in terms of stitches and rows.

- Never measure a diagonal. Instead, draw perpendiculars: the horizontal measurement becomes the number of stitches; the vertical measurement becomes the number of rows. Then you will do the math—as directed in the pattern drafting that follows. The result of those calculations might mean increases, decreases, short rows, casting on, or binding off. But what makes it a diagonal is that this is all worked as evenly as possible. (The drawing of the diagonal suggests evenly worked decreases.)

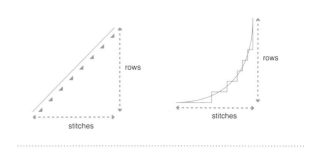

And how do we produce a curve? Remember, everything must be expressed in terms of stitches and rows.

- Never measure a curve. Instead, draw perpendiculars: the horizontal measurement becomes the number of stitches; the vertical measurement becomes the number of rows. Then you will do the math—as directed in the pattern drafting that follows. But for now, you might appreciate that the difference between a curve and a diagonal is the rate at which you do the work: with a diagonal, the work is done at an even rate; with a curve, it is done at an uneven rate. (The drawing above right suggests bind-offs—7 stitches once, 3 stitches once, 2 stitches once, 1 stitch three times—followed with some rows worked straight. Note that you can only bind off at the beginnings of rows, so there is a visible "stair step" between these bind-offs.)

Since curves are more difficult than diagonals (to conceive, to draft, to execute, to seam, and to pick up and knit against), we don't want to use them unless we have to. The good news is that knitting is flexible enough that the much-easier diagonal can often be used instead. This is especially good news for the set-in sleeve (page 43). In fact, there are only two places in knitting where I think curves are necessary: the round neck, and any kind of shirttail. Otherwise, I use diagonals.

How to Copy an Existing Garment

A wonderful place to start pattern drafting is to copy a garment you love. The first step is to measure all its horizontals and verticals. By doing this, you will gain lots of useful information to help you draft a garment of the same shape and style. But here are some words of caution.

- Lay the garment flat, eliminating any wrinkles that might distort your measurements.
- When measuring the width (from side seam to side seam), don't assume the front and back are the same without checking.
- Measure all lengths and widths as you imagine they were knit, not how they might have stretched out. (This is particularly important with respect to the neck.)
- Measure pieces without including finishing. So when measuring the neck depth and width, don't include the neck band. And when measuring finished length, don't include the neck band.
- When measuring the armhole depth, be careful with the flat "shelf" at the underarm, because it often droops with wear. This shelf occurs in the modified drop shoulder, the set-in sleeve, and the raglan. Measure your armhole depth with that shelf perpendicular to the side seam. (Otherwise, you will assume a larger armhole depth, and this is an area where small measurements have great impact.)
- Often we plan to duplicate all the stylistic elements of a garment we like but in a yarn that is heavier than the original. (Most hand-knitting yarns are heavier than most commercially knit garments.) So once you have chosen your yarn, you will want to check the ease suggestions on page 27. If your yarn is heavier, add a little more width to the garment and a little more depth to your armhole.

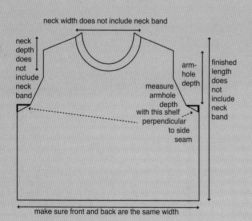

neck width does not include neck band

neck depth does not include neck band

armhole depth

measure armhole depth with this shelf perpendicular to side seam

finished length does not include neck band

make sure front and back are the same width

Sweaters That Are Knit Flat

The pattern drafting that follows is dedicated to garments knit flat—separate front and separate back, sleeves knit flat—all requiring seams. I do appreciate that, in our world, not all garments are worked this way, but before addressing the exceptions I'll tell you why the following patterns are written to be knit flat.

First, I believe the seams of the garment are its skeleton, holding it to shape. I've seen (and probably produced one or two myself) knit-in-the-round garments with sides that have drooped. And I feel so strongly about this that I will put extra seams into the center back of a coat or dress so it will not *seat* (or "go butt-sprung," as knitters like to say).

Think about this. The commercial garment you are copying has side seams, so why shouldn't the piece you are knitting? You don't own a coat without a center back seam—and they're mostly made in firmer fabrics—so why would you knit one? If your objection is that you don't like sewing seams, then rethink! All you are avoiding are the row-to-row side seams, the easiest and usually most invisible of our seams. (Look for the mattress stitch in my book *The Purl Stitch* or almost any knitting manual.)

Second, flat pieces are the way most knitting—hand or commercial—is worked. If you are copying an existing garment (which is a great place to start), then it only made sense to write the following shapes the way most knitting is offered—with selvedges and seams.

Third, if you avoid side seams and knit in the round below the armhole, what will you do above the armhole? Our knitting can look different when we knit back and forth. And, yes, we can sew and cut our tubular knitting to give it armholes and a neck, but how is this easier than knitting flat with side seams?

Finally, if you knit the front and back separately, you can employ the rescue techniques I offer in chapter 8. If you knit in the round, what you knit is what you get . . . or you rip.

I do realize that there are garments knit without seams for their own good reasons.

- Color-stranded knitting (referred to in this book as *fairisle*) is often knit in the round to avoid purling with two colors. Even so, I prefer to knit flat (page 189).

- In some very complex stitch patterns (with long repeats) a side seam where you need it (for your size) might interrupt the stitch pattern (that is, it might be right in the middle of a cable). In this rare situation, allowing the stitch pattern to continue around the garment, eliminating side seams, may be the solution.

Sweaters That Are Knit Bottom-Up

I understand that many knitters like top-down sweaters: after all, you can stop knitting when you achieve your length or run out of yarn!

For a number of reasons, I have not developed this preference—not even for the sleeves. Although my objections are not as forceful as those I voiced in the previous section, here they are:

- For most garments, the complex stuff happens above the armhole: below the armhole is generally straight yardage. I like to work that yardage first, getting familiar with my yarn and stitch pattern before executing armholes and necks.

- I use the fabric from hem to underarm as a really large gauge swatch. If I'm surprised, I can make adjustments for girth before the armhole (see page 156).

- I know the appropriate lengths for my garments (see pages 22–25), so I don't need the security of knitting down. And making my garment the right length is much more important than knitting until I run out of yarn. Plus, I know how to shorten or lengthen my garments (see page 158) in case a fabric behaves unexpectedly.

- I don't like sleeves knit down combined with garments knit up: the stitches going the opposite way bother me (especially with any kind of color or stitch pattern).

In addition, I have not covered side-to-side garments for the following reasons:

- I think their usage is limited, best used in garments with stripes (either the stripes of different colors or the textured stripes of garter stitch).

- Except in garter stitch, I'm not thrilled with how the fabric hangs.

- To have all the shapes of this book also cover side-to-side garments would have made it unwieldy.

A Clarification of the Shapes Covered

Here are the shapes covered in the book, and here's what you need to know about these sketches.

- The shapes are shown as schematics with the relevant areas highlighted in bold.
- In three cases—the gathered, puffed, and cap sleeves—the schematics don't quite tell the story, so I've included "as worn" drawings.
- Because I work the cap sleeve out from the armhole edge, the drawing is shown that way.

basic shapes (and their sleeves)

the drop shoulder + its sleeve   the modified drop shoulder + its sleeve   the set-in sleeve + its sleeve   the raglan + its sleeve

shoulder shaping, back and front neck shaping

shoulder shaping   back neck shaping   straight (boat) neck   funnel neck

square neck   V-neck   round neck

hems

diagonal hem   standard shirttail   reverse shirttail

side shaping

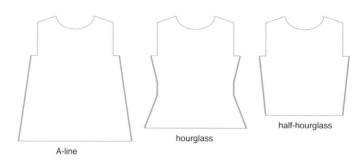

A-line

hourglass

half-hourglass

sleeve alternatives

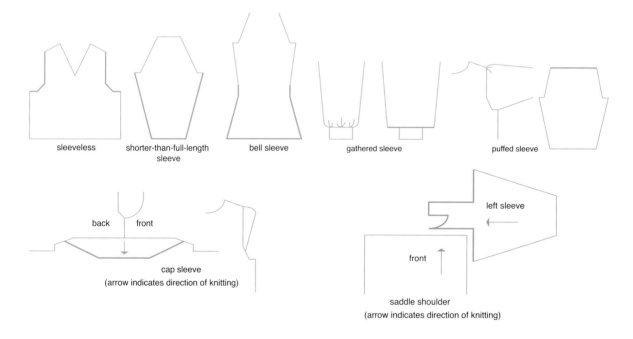

sleeveless

shorter-than-full-length sleeve

bell sleeve

gathered sleeve

puffed sleeve

back   front

cap sleeve
(arrow indicates direction of knitting)

left sleeve

front

saddle shoulder
(arrow indicates direction of knitting)

cardigan styles

no front overlap

overlapping front bands

overlapping front pieces

How to Use the Shapes in This Book

There are three points to consider here: choosing the shapes you want to combine, which shapes combine well, and shaping versus finishing.

Choosing the Shapes You Want to Combine

This book doesn't teach you how to draft a shape by offering completed pieces—perhaps an hourglass garment with a set-in, saddle sleeve and a round neck. There is no way to anticipate all the combinations you might envision, and that's not how designers work.

What this book does is offer chapters dedicated to the following shapes:

- basic (side and sleeve) shapes
- shoulder and neck shapes
- hem alternatives
- side shaping
- sleeve alternatives
- cardigan styles

You choose what you wish to combine. Finding and executing your own combinations is left to you—as it should be.

Please don't think that finding and executing your own combinations is difficult. If you are new at this, chapter 2 presents basic shapes in their simplest forms (with a straight hem and straight sides and standard sleeves) but without their necks: you'll go to chapter 3 to choose the neck shape that will complete your garment. Chapters 2 and 3 alone will give you a tremendous variety of garment shapes to knit.

If you are more advanced and want a shaped hem or shaped sides or an alternative sleeve or a cardigan, go to those chapters. There you will find the modifications that need to be made to the basic shapes specified in chapter 2. For the most part, shape-combining is straightforward because each shape can be independent of the others. Consider this: for a set-in sleeve garment front, an hourglass shape doesn't need to start until after you've shaped the hem; the armhole shaping doesn't start until after the side shaping; and the neck shaping doesn't need to start until after the armhole is shaped.

Of course there are exceptions: not all shapes can always be independent of all others. But you'll be alerted to these exceptions—where you may have to

do two things at once—in the drafting directions. And it will always make sense for you to read through any shape you plan to use before beginning—because that's what a designer would do!

Which Shapes Combine Well

Having said that you will combine shapes, every possibility is not always feasible. I know that you'll go places I couldn't imagine, so all I can say here is that, in my experience, there are combinations that work and combinations that may not. See the chart on page 20.

Shaping Versus Finishing

You might have noticed that these shapes are all about garment pieces: there is no mention of collars, hoods, or front bands. While these additions are essential to the style of your garment, they all occur in the final part of sweater construction—the finishing. The directions for these are found in chapter 8—where all manner of finishing is discussed.

Essential Measurements and Standard Sizes

Before discussing and calculating your pattern, we must determine some measurements that the garments need: some are taken from your body, some are taken from an existing garment, and some we'll get from standards in place.

You won't need to take as many measurements from your body as you may think. Here are the only five measurements that require a tape measure against your body:

- girth
- length
- waist length
- sleeve length
- shoulder width

Truly, that's all you need. Yes, there are other sweater dimensions you'll determine for your pattern: armhole depth, shoulder shaping depth, neck depth, neck width, and sleeve widths. But these are more easily taken from a sweater of the same weight and style or from standards already in place. And all of this will be clarified within each individual pattern section.

Shape Combinations

✓ go for it

〰 with some qualifications *(which will be clarified in the drafting directions that follow)*

✗ not in my experience   N/A not applicable

	drop shoulder	modified drop shoulder	set-in sleeve	raglan	drop shoulder with saddle	set-in sleeve with saddle	modified drop shoulder with saddle
straight neck	✓	✓	✓	✓	〰	〰	〰
funnel neck	✓	✓	✓	✓	〰	〰	〰
square neck	✓	✓	✓	✓	✓	✓	✓
V-neck	✓	✓	✓	✓	✗	✗	✗
round neck	✓	✓	✓	✓	✓	✓	✓
diagonal hem	✓	✓	✓	✓	✓	✓	✓
standard shirttail	✓	✓	✓	✓	✓	✓	✓
reverse shirttail	✓	✓	✓	✓	✓	✓	✓
A-line	✗	〰	✓	✓	〰	✓	✓
hourglass	✗	〰	✓	✓	〰	✓	✓
half-hourglass	✗	✓	✓	✓	✓	✓	✓
sleeveless	✓	✓	✓	✓	N/A	N/A	N/A
shorter-than full-length sleeves	✓	✓	✓	✓	✓	✓	✓
gathered sleeve	✓	✓	✓	✓	✓	✓	✓
bell sleeve	✓	✓	✓	✓	✓	✓	✓
puffed sleeve	✗	✗	✓	✗	✗	✗	✗
cap sleeve	✗	✓	✓	〰	✗	✗	✗
cardigan	✓	✓	✓	✓	✓	✓	✓

Girth

To determine your girth measurement, put a tape measure around the widest part of your body that the garment will cover. (Because this widest part is not always the bust, we call it *girth* rather than the usual bust measurement.) In the chart below, specifying standard women's sizes, you can see that the hips are larger than the bust . . . which is larger than the waist. If these standards apply to you,

- to make a short sweater that ends before your hips, you'll need your bust measurement.
- to make a long sweater that reaches or passes the widest part of your hips, you'll need your hip measurement.

But some of us aren't so standard: the waist could be bigger than the bust, the bust could be bigger than the hips. Again, we need the measurement of the widest part of your body that the garment will cover.

women's sizing chart/standard body measurements (in inches)

Size	Bust	Waist	Hips
XS	28–30	20–22	30–32
S	32–34	24–26	34–36
M	36–38	28–30	38–40
L	40–42	32–34	42–44
1X	44–46	36–38	46–48
2X	48–50	40–42	50–52

This chart of standard women's sizes is what our knitting books and magazines generally adhere to, and it is what we use to choose our size when following a pattern.

But a curious situation may occur. What about those whose measurements fall between sizes? What if you have a 39″ (99cm) bust? Are you a medium or a large? Between every size there are gaps, and maybe you've been puzzled by this. It has certainly puzzled me. But the good news is that this book "fills the gap." Once we understand how to draft, that gap will concern us no more. We can deal with it by writing our own pattern. Or—if you're following a published pattern—you'll understand how to combine sizes (a L front plus a M back) for a garment that fits.

How to Measure

Wrap the tape measure around the widest part of your bust, then your hips, and record these measurements. If your waist is standard (8″ [20cm] smaller than your bust), we don't need that measurement (because sweaters with waist shaping rarely fit tight to the waist). But if your waist is larger than standard for your size, record that measurement, too.

Keep a record of these measurements. But do understand that rarely are your garments knit to them. Ease, as clarified on page 27, must be added. And different styles and weights of yarn require different ease, so these measurements are only the base on which you will build.

Garment Length

As much as it matters that we knit our garment to the right girth, it is equally as important that we knit to the right length. Unfortunately, not as much attention is commonly paid to length as I think it deserves. Let's redress that here.

How to Measure Length While Knitting

Before discussing appropriate sweater lengths, let's talk about measuring the length of the knitting itself. (How to do this is a question I am asked often enough that I know it's important.)

As much as we know what length we're aiming for, it isn't always the length we get. Knitting can stretch. So here are my tips to ensure that you get the length you want.

Some yarns stretch more than others. Heavy yarns (not bulky so much as dense) tend to stretch. And yarns with little elasticity (plant fibers especially) tend to stretch. But gravity can cause any knitting to stretch, so I always measure length with my knitting hanging, not laid flat.

And if I am concerned that my fabric may stretch with washing, I will put my knitting onto a thread and wash it as I would wash the garment before I reach its armhole. (Even with a drop shoulder that has no defined armhole, there is a theoretical one—where the lower edge of the sleeve attaches to the body. This spot is half the upper sleeve width from the end of the front or back.) If this washing causes the piece to stretch in length, you can now rip back—before having gone past the armhole. If this washing causes the piece to stretch

sweater too short,
worn with a longer layer

sweater too long

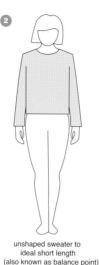

unshaped sweater to
ideal short length
(also known as balance point)

unshaped sweater

unshaped sweater,
too long for a short sweater,
too short for a long sweater

in width, there are rescue techniques you can employ that may not require ripping: see chapter 8.

I also suggest measuring in the following manner and so all pieces match: when you've knit to the length you need (say, to the underarm), count that number of rows, then knit matching pieces to that number of rows.

If you are concerned about the finished length, always block or wash your pieces after sewing the shoulder seams and finishing the neck but before sewing the side seams or adding front bands. With the shoulders and neck finished, you can try it on. And it's a lot easier to shorten or lengthen when you don't have to undo side seams and front bands.

That said, I'm more likely to knit my garments an inch (2.5cm) too short rather than an inch (2.5cm) too long, because much of our knitting stretches over time. But if it doesn't, and it's a little too short, I can get creative by layering it over something that is the right length—sometimes a belt, sometimes a blouse or a T-shirt. This is a better look than a garment that is too long—making us look like, oh, Mrs. Doubtfire .

Okay, so how do you find the best length to knit your garment?

You can always find your sweater's best length from a sweater of the same style and weight—even if it's too long (because you can fold it up). Be sure to wear the sweater with the appropriate skirt or pants, then record the length that seems right.

Most of us can just *see* what looks like the right

measurement. But if you aren't sure, what follows is what my experience has told me works best with the styles of sweaters we are likely to make.

The Ideal Length for a Short, Straight-Sided Sweater: Your Balance Point

Look at our boxy, unshaped sweater . Its best length is what I call your *balance point*. This length is a function of your height. But it's important to see that your balance point is not where you would expect— half your height. It's less than that, because we automatically give weight to the head. Your balance point measurement puts your upper and lower body

short, unshaped sweater
with A-line skirt

short, unshaped sweater
with wide pants

into balance, as you can see in the drawing: the one on the right is at half her height and looks top-heavy, the one in the middle is too short, and the one on the left looks balanced. In addition, this measurement usually lands mid-belly—which is a good thing, because it's a famous design principle that the best way to make something look smaller is to cut it in half.

Because the garment is small on top, it looks better with something wider on the bottom—like an A-line skirt or wide pants ❸. I think the hips look too exposed if it's worn alone over slimmer pants ❹.

How to Measure for a Short, Straight-Sided Sweater: Balance Point

- Record your height, without shoes.
- Divide by 2.
- Subtract 2½″ (6cm).
- Find the height of your head and neck (by holding something rigid on your head and having someone measure from the top of your head to the top of your shoulder, 2″ [5cm] out from the base of your neck), then subtract this measurement from the previous number.
- Add extra length (to accommodate girth) as follows: for size XS (S, M, L, 1X, 2X), add 0 (½, 1, 1½, 2, 2½)″ (0 [1.5, 2.5, 4, 5, 6]cm).

For this last step, you may need to refer to the chart of standard women's sizes (page 21). (I stopped at 2X,

because this is where most knitting patterns usually stop. But if you are larger, add 2½″ [6cm] plus ½″ [1.5cm] for every size larger than 2X.)

Note that the heading for this section refers to the balance point. Even if you never knit a short, straight-sided sweater, this measurement is important. Do the math, and record this length. You'll see why it's important in the following sections.

The Ideal Length for a Midlength, Shaped Sweater

If you don't like the boyishness of the previous garment, this longer, hourglass-shaped sweater is for you. But the length of this sweater entirely depends on what you're going to wear with it.

- If you plan to wear a shaped sweater with straight pants ❹, it will look too short if it's knit to your balance point, plus your hips will look exposed. To minimize hip width, find the widest point of your hips as revealed by these pants, and make the garment to this length. (Again, remember that the best way to make something look smaller is to divide it in half.)
- If you plan to wear a shaped sweater with a skirt, make it land at your balance point (as calculated in the previous section): if it's knit to the widest point of the hips, it might look too long ❺.

But wait! These length suggestions of the previous

short, unshaped sweater with straight pants

shaped sweater with straight pants knit to balance point (looks too short)

shaped sweater with straight pants knit to widest point of hips as revealed by pants

shaped sweater with A-line skirt knit to balance point

shaped sweater with A-line skirt knit to widest point of the hips (looks too long)

too long sweater improved
with shorter layer

too long sweater improved
with built-in balance point

too short vest worn with
longer layer beneath

sweater with
knit-in balance point

section assume that we need to knit garments to different lengths depending on what we are planning to wear with them. How do we solve this?

- If a garment looks too long, raise the eye to the balance point—by wearing a shorter layer on top. Or knit a garment with a built-in balance point (like a change of stitch pattern) ⑥.
- If a garment looks too short, the solution is to have something land at the widest point of the hips—by wearing a longer layer underneath. Or knit a longer garment with a built-in balance point ⑦.

I did say earlier that the balance point measurement would be useful: as you can see, drawing the eye's attention there is a good look. And it can solve a problem by allowing us to wear the same garment with different bottoms.

How to Measure for a Midlength, Shaped Sweater

Since this garment works best if it lands at the widest point of the hips, put on a pair of pants that reveals this place and that you might wear with the sweater. Place a tape measure on the top of your shoulder (2″ [5cm] out from the base of your neck), let the tape measure fall over the bust and down to that length, and record it.

long A-line sweater with slim pants
(and crotch of pants revealed)

long, unshaped sweater
with leggings

long, unshaped sweater with
shorter layer at balance point

long, unshaped sweater with change
of stitch pattern at balance point

The Ideal Length for a Long Sweater (Usually Straight-Sided or A-Line)

The length for this sweater is, again, entirely dependent on what you're going to wear with it.

- Try on the pants you are likely to wear with it—slim pants or leggings **8**. Find the point on your leg where you like what is revealed and where everything you want covered is covered.
- There is a design principle that says that if we can see the crotch of your pants, you will look taller. But some pants—skinny jeans or leggings—might not look good at this length, so don't let this be a firm rule.
- Remember that any long sweater can be improved by a shorter, top layer or a change of stitch pattern—both of which would land at your balance point **9**.

How to Measure for a Long Sweater

Wearing the pants you would wear with the sweater, mark the spot on your leg below which you still like what is revealed of your legs. Place a tape measure on the top of your shoulder (2″ [5cm] out from the base of your neck), let the tape measure fall over the bust and down to that length, and record it.

The Ideal Length for a Sweater with an Uneven Hem

I make a lot of these—usually with longer backs than fronts. And here's what I find most successful.

- Make the shortest point of the front to your balance point.
- Make the back to where you like what is revealed and everything you want covered is covered. (Remembering that the best way to make something look smaller is to cut it in half, perhaps you'd want the hem to fall mid-backside.

- Sometimes these garments have a curved back hem: it's okay if the center of it cuts your backside in half: you may not wish the curve to sit above and "frame" it.

The Ideal Length for a Dress

Ideally, it would be the length of a dress you already love.

Otherwise, put on your pantyhose or tights, and find the point at which you like what would be revealed.

Waist Length

This only applies to hourglass garments—a shape that is narrowed at the waist. And for them to look wonderful, the waist needs to fall at the right place.

- In garments with waist shaping, there is usually a straight, unshaped area: see the bolded area below. The bottom of that area should sit at your waist; the bolded area will sit above your waist—accentuating the slimness between waist and bust.
- What you don't want is for the bold area in the diagram to fall below your waist, onto your hips, because that will just make your waist look . . . bigger.

How to Measure for Waist Length

Have someone find the bone at the top of your spine that sits across from what would be the inside edge of your garment's shoulder seam. (We start there because that's equal to the top of the schematic's waist measurement.) Measure down your back to your waist (which you can find by placing your index finger on the place at your waist that "breaks" when you bend backward). Take the measurement standing straight.

waist length

bold line shows length worked even

This is your back waist length. But what about an adjustment for your girth? You may do the same thing you did to find your balance point: for a size XS (S, M, L, 1X, 2X), add 0 (½, 1, 1½, 2, 2½)″ (0 [1.5, 2.5, 3.75, 5, 6]cm) to your back waist length. But do measure against another garment to make sure this adjusted waist length is not too long.

Sleeve Length

Sleeve length is a tailoring term that is *not* the length of the sleeve to its armhole. It is better described as a "half-body" measurement, because it starts at the spine and ends at the cuff. But this measurement is called *sleeve length* because it tells us how to find the length of the sleeve for all styles of sweaters: for a drop shoulder where the sleeve lands somewhere on the upper arm; for the modified drop shoulder and set-in sleeve, where the sleeves end at the shoulder; and for the raglan, where the sleeve ends at the neck.

How to Measure for Sleeve Length

Stand with a bent arm, with your wrist at your belly. Have someone measure you, tight to your body, from your spine to one shoulder, down your arm to that elbow,

then around that elbow to where you want your sleeve to end—to the "break" of your wrist for a long-sleeved garment, to something shorter (where you still like what is revealed of your arm) for a short-sleeved garment. This is your sleeve length: it will not be the length of the sleeve from cuff to armhole. But the latter will be calculated from this measurement.

How to Work with Sleeve Length

In the drafting that follows, you will work with this number to find the length of your sleeve to its armhole. But even after you get this measurement, you may choose to change it for individual styles.

- If your yarn is heavy and your sleeve is loose, the sleeve may pull the garment off your shoulders: make the garment's sleeve length 1–2″ (2.5–5cm) shorter than your sleeve-length measurement.
- If your yarn is light and your upper sleeve is tight, the sleeve will not pull the garment off your shoulders, so work to your sleeve length measurement.
- If you have a tight cuff, above which a wide sleeve will blouse, add 1″ (2.5cm) to your sleeve length, because blousing will eat up an inch (2.5cm) of length.

sleeve length

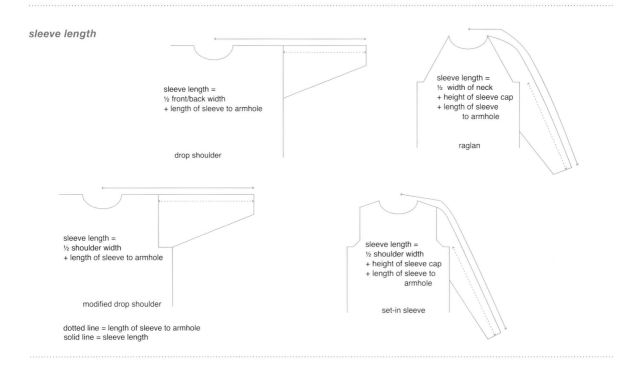

sleeve length =
½ front/back width
+ length of sleeve to armhole

drop shoulder

sleeve length =
½ width of neck
+ height of sleeve cap
+ length of sleeve
to armhole

raglan

sleeve length =
½ shoulder width
+ length of sleeve to armhole

modified drop shoulder

dotted line = length of sleeve to armhole
solid line = sleeve length

sleeve length =
½ shoulder width
+ height of sleeve cap
+ length of sleeve to
armhole

set-in sleeve

Sleeve length is something you always want to check against a garment of the same weight and style.

Shoulder Width

It would be both attractive and comfortable if our garments fit us on our shoulders. But oh so often, whether we buy or knit them, they do not. How wonderful that we can change this and knit garments that fit.

How to Measure for Shoulder Width

Have someone measure you across the back, between the seams of a garment where you like how the seams sit. If you don't have such a garment, take the measurement across your back and between the slight depressions (that hurt if you press on them) that sit just outside the top edges of your collarbone. (Note that this measurement is not to the outside edge of your shoulders nor straight up from your armpit.)

How to Work with Shoulder Width

You don't always knit to this measurement: it can be changed for practical or stylistic considerations.

- For a sleeveless garment, you may knit your garment to this measurement.
- For a sleeveless garment, you may knit your shoulders 1″ (2.5cm) wider than this measurement—to give yourself a wide shoulder, knowing that the garment doesn't have sleeves pulling this garment off your shoulders.
- For a sleeveless garment, you may knit your garment narrower than this measurement (as you might for a tank top).
- For a set-in-sleeve garment in a light yarn and with a tight upper sleeve, you may knit your garment to this measurement.
- For a set-in sleeve or modified-drop-shoulder garment in a heavier yarn and with a loose upper sleeve, you may knit your garment to 1″ (2.5cm) narrower than this measurement—knowing that your heavy and loose sleeves may pull the garment off your shoulders.

Standards of Ease

Ease is the difference between the circumference of your body and the circumference of your garment, and it is applied to the largest part of you that the garment body (not the sleeves) will cover. The chart below specifies standard terms and measurements plus very loose guidelines as to how I think they are best applied (which will be repeated in more detail in the drafting sections). But always remember that these are only guidelines: you are the designer, so you make your own rules!

very close fit

- actual bust (or hip) minus as much as 2″ (5cm)
- used in light yarns
- used in fitted styles
- used in stretchy stitch patterns

close fit

- actual bust (or hip) plus 0–2″ (0–5cm)
- used in light yarns
- used in fitted styles

standard fit

- actual bust (or hip) plus 2–4″ (5–10cm)
- used in light or medium yarns
- used in fitted styles

loose fit

- actual bust (or hip) plus 4–6″ (10–15cm)
- used in medium or bulky yarns
- used in fitted styles for outerwear garments
- used in nonfitted styles

oversized

- actual bust (or hip) plus more than 6″ (15cm)
- used in medium or bulky yarns
- used in fitted styles and heavy yarns for outerwear garments
- used in nonfitted styles

In case you need more help interpreting yarn weights and style terms, here are their explanations.

Standard Yarn Gauges (see page 217)

These are the standards applied by our industry—gauges are what you would get if you knit a closely woven fabric.

In the suggestions for standards of ease, I did not repeat all yarn-weight terms. If I wrote *light,* I meant weight 3 or anything finer: if I wrote *bulky,* I meant weight 5: if I wrote *medium,* I meant weight 4.

Style Terms

By *fitted styles* I mean a style with a defined armhole and/or shoulder width—most often a set-in sleeve or raglan. By *nonfitted styles,* I mean a style without a defined armhole and/or shoulder width—most often a loose-fitting raglan or any form of drop shoulder.

Can you see why I always suggest checking your plan against a garment of the same style and weight? There is a great deal of latitude as to how ease can be applied. And different styles and weights work best with different amounts of ease: a fine garment doesn't need too much ease, but a heavy garment will add weight if it fits too closely to your body.

Swatching

Okay, so you've got your measurements, you understand ease, and you've considered your garment's shape. What's missing? Oh yes, the swatch—that small piece of knitting on which everything depends!

I don't want to influence you with my preferences or lack of experience with all the yarns at your disposal, so all I am going to say is this: find the yarn you think you want to use. (And if you really want to know about yarns and fibers and how they behave, Clara Parkes's *The Knitter's Book of Yarn* will serve you well.)

Once you choose your yarn, do the following. (Yes, there are six steps. Please believe that I am not suggesting that you do any more work than needed—I know how much you just want to start knitting. But this is the most important knitting you will do for your garment to succeed.)

1. Start with your best guess of needle size—from experience or the label's recommendation—and knit a 4″ × 4″ (10cm × 10cm) square in your stitch pattern.
2. Block the swatch as the fabric allows. (Ideally, this means you'll wash it as you would wash the garment. But for some yarns and stitch patterns, you may steam-press.) Do you like the feel of the fabric? Does it feel as if it would hold shape without being too stiff? If you can answer yes, go to step 5.
3. If the fabric feels too loose, knit a new swatch on smaller needles. If the fabric feels too tight, knit a new swatch on larger needles.
4. Repeat step 2. Keep repeating until you can answer yes to the questions. When you can, you know the needle size you like and can go to step 5. (If you

are planning to combine stitch patterns, read the following section before working step 5.)

5. Ideally, you should now knit a much larger swatch in your stitch pattern—at least 6″ × 6″ (15cm × 15cm). What this larger swatch will give you is a really accurate gauge, plus a bigger swatch with which you will estimate how much yarn you need. (It's amazing how often a small swatch will tell you one gauge but a larger swatch will give you another!) I'll be honest and tell you that I don't always make this larger swatch. I think my reasoning is that the garment itself functions as this larger swatch. But my frequent use of the rescue techniques of chapter 8 is directly proportional to my not taking the time to make that larger swatch! If you make this larger swatch, block it (as in step 2).
6. Measure for gauge as follows:
   - Not including cast-on, bind-off, or selvedge stitches, lay a tape measure horizontally across 4″ (10cm) at the center of your piece: put pins at each end of this 4″ (10cm).
   - Do the same vertically.
   - Now count stitches and rows between the pins: do not round up or down (that is, if you get 17½ stitches × 22½ rows, record this as your gauge). #stitches in 4″ (10cm) ÷ 4 = #stitches/inch (cm) =

     _____

     #rows in 4″ (10cm) ÷ 4 = #rows/inch (cm) =

     _____

Combining Stitch Patterns

Different stitch patterns behave differently—in terms of gauge and topography (rolling or not). Does this mean they cannot be combined? Of course not! But some questions need to be asked and answered.

- Will you use the same size needles for each section? (Work a separate swatch in each stitch pattern on the same needles. Are you happy with the result? If not, work a separate swatch on different needles for any that don't feel right.)
- Will there be a change in gauge? (Measure stitch and row gauge in each swatch and compare.)
- If there is a change in stitch gauge, how will you move from one stitch pattern to another? (This is not about increases or decreases; obviously, those will happen. It's more about a boundary between the two stitch patterns so those increases and decreases

won't be obvious. My favorite boundaries are a few rows of garter or reverse stockinette. Both these choices are best begun and ended with a RS knit row.)

- Now work step 5 in the swatch sequence, working a swatch in which you move from one stitch pattern to another, working with different needle sizes (if necessary) and practicing your increases or decreases and your boundary.

Using the Swatch to Estimate How Much Yarn You Need

Not everyone does what follows here. Sometimes you're just willing to guess and purchase a little extra. Or you have a yarn on hand that you believe will be enough. (Many of us buy yarn on spec, figuring that someday it'll tell us what it wants to be and that we'll have what we need. Didn't I say knitters were unfailingly optimistic?)

I wish I could tell you how much yarn you'll need. You'd think, after hundreds of garments, I'd know. But I don't. Too many factors intrude. How long? How much ease? Sleeves or not? How tightly knit is the fabric? How complex is the stitch pattern? How stiff is the yarn? What I sometimes do is check an existing pattern and make a generous estimate.

But if you are willing to do the math, and if you know the approximate sizes of the pieces you want to make, here's how you calculate how much yarn you will need from your swatch:

1. Measure how many yards (meters) remain in the ball from which you knit the swatch _____
2. Subtract that number of yards (meters) from the number of yards (meters) in a ball = number of yards (meters) per swatch _____
   (Instead of steps 1–2, you could rip out your swatch, stretch the yarn straight, and measure the yards

[meters] you used. But most prefer to keep the swatch intact.)

3. Multiply the width by the height of your swatch = square inches (cm^2) in your swatch _____
4. Estimate the width and height of your front, then multiply the width by the height = square inches (cm^2) in front _____
5. Estimate the width and height of your back, then multiply the width by the height = square inches (cm^2) in back _____
6. Divide the square inches (cm^2) in your front and back by the square inches (cm^2) in your swatch = number of "swatches" in front and back _____
7. Multiply this number of "swatches" by the number of yards (meters) per swatch (step 2) = **number of yards (meters) in front and back _____**
8. Estimate the width of your lower sleeve; estimate the width at the widest point of your upper sleeve; add the two widths, then divide by 2 = average width of sleeve _____
9. Multiply average width of sleeve by length of sleeve = square inches (cm^2) in each sleeve _____
10. Divide the square inches (cm^2) in your sleeve by the square inches (cm^2) in your swatch = number of "swatches" in sleeve _____
11. Multiply this number of "swatches" by the number of yards (meters) per swatch (step 2) = number of yards (meters) in one sleeve _____
12. Multiply by 2 = **number of yards (meters) in two sleeves _____**
13. Add the results of steps 7 and 12, then divide by the number of yards (meters) in one ball = number of balls you need before adding bands _____
14. If you are adding bands, add 1 or 2 more balls for bands and for fudging (fudging being a technical term in knitting). This will give you a good estimate of the number of balls you need.

Chapter 2

Basic Shapes

Now we've come to the exciting stuff—the number crunching that is the marriage of your swatch to your vision, where you draft a garment that fits your body. This chapter gets you started by covering the four basic shapes of our knit garments, moving from simplest to most complex.

- drop shoulder
- modified drop shoulder
- set-in sleeve
- raglan

Everything you draft from this book will start with one of these. In this chapter, the drafting and patterns are offered in their simplest forms—with straight hems, straight sides, and long sleeves. You'll finish with neck shaping after you choose your neck from the following chapter.

A Short Math Lesson

You will need to "do the math" to draft a pattern. I know some of you don't love the subject of math. But here's what I would say by way of encouragement. Read the following to make sure you understand basic terminology and symbols. Then read about fudging, so weird results don't scare you. (And it helps if you approach that section with an understanding that knitting is wonderfully flexible). You will then read about your shape before working it out, one comprehensible step at a time. Above all, know that with a positive mind-set, and moving as slowly as you need to, it will all become familiar and comfortable very soon—and you'll wonder why you ever thought it mysterious!

Standard Symbols and Terminology

You probably know all these, but I want to clarify the mathematical operation signs used throughout this book.

+ plus

− minus

× multiplied by

÷ divided by

= equals

/ per

\# number

If given this equation, $(8 \times 2) - 1 = 15$, do what's inside the parentheses before doing what's outside the parentheses.

What you see most often through the drafting process is something like this: (desired circumference of garment × #stitches/inch [cm]) ÷ 2 = #stitches in front/back. It means the following:

1. Take the desired circumference of the garment (which will be a number of inches [cm]), multiply it by the number of stitches per inch (2.5cm).

2. Then divide the result of that multiplication by 2 to get the number of stitches in the front and back.

Fudging—Rounding Up or Down, Finding Appropriate Multiples

Most of the time, when you do the math, you won't get an answer you can work with: more work might be required, and you'll fudge. Here's how.

- If the result of your calculations is a whole number with stuff after the decimal, consider the whole numbers on either side. ($21 \times 4.75 = 99.75$. Consider 99 or 100.)

- Your first consideration is whether you have a stitch or row repeat that you need to work with. If so, then you'll need to alter the number to suit your repeat. And you will be asked to do so in every garment piece in which it is appropriate. (In the previous example, you got 99.75 stitches. You could have chosen 99 or 100. But let's say your stitch repeat is 7. We know that 100 is not a multiple of 7 because $100 \div 7 = 14.286$. Since the result was between 14 and 15, try both and choose the one you prefer. $14 \times 7 = 98$. $15 \times 7 = 105$.)

- We care about a stitch or row repeat when we are setting up our piece and when we have long and straight borders that will be visible. But we don't care about either if we are going to continue to disrupt them or they won't be visible.

- Another consideration is whether or not you want odd or even numbers. If you already have odd or even established, then stick with that choice. (If we are increasing (or decreasing), we prefer to do so on RS rows, so we usually want the rate of increase (or decrease) to be an even number. The following three bullets address this.

- If the result of a division gives you a rate of increase (or decrease) that is closest to an even, whole number, dump the stuff after the decimal and go with the even, whole number. (#rows = 118. #stitches to be increased = 14. $118 \div 14 = 8.428$. Make your rate of increase 8.) The missing numbers after the decimal represent some rows that you will work even after completing your increases.

- If the result of a division gives you a rate of increase (or decrease) that is closest to an odd whole number, you can try to get an even, whole number by changing either the #rows or #stitches involved in the shaping. (# rows = 118. #stitches to be increased = 15. $118 \div 15 = 7.866$. But if you went up to 120 rows, $120 \div 15 = 8$.) Or you can drop down to the nearest even whole number. (In this example, you'd go from 7.866 to 6.) This just means more rows are worked even after shaping—perfectly okay in most situations.

- If the result of a division gives you a rate of increase (or decrease) that is closest to an odd whole number, and you can't fudge your numbers, you can dump the stuff after the decimal and go with the odd number. (You can increase every 7 rows, but it's not fun because this means increasing on a RS row, then on a WS row. What you can do instead is *increase on row 6, then row 8; repeat from *. The result is the same as increasing every 7 rows.)

How to Work with These Calculations and Patterns

If you have never done this work before, it does help to know how things are set up.

- Each shape's discussion includes a generic schematic: this is what you should photocopy to use as your worksheet as you read through the discussion and then work through your calculations and pattern. You can enter your measurements—and even numbers of stitches and rows—onto this photocopy. At the very least, it will become the schematic to keep with your pattern.
- All numbers that you need before you start any calculations will be listed at the top of that section. These should be entered before beginning.
- Because you may need to fudge, I recommend working all calculations in pencil until you are sure you have your final version.
- All calculations are numbered, and you will work them in order.
- The sleeve's calculations and patterns are in the section following the body's. (Separating them makes the work more manageable.)

And now, with all that in place, let's get started!

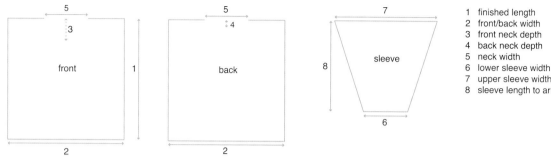

1 finished length
2 front/back width
3 front neck depth
4 back neck depth
5 neck width
6 lower sleeve width
7 upper sleeve width
8 sleeve length to armhole

Drop Shoulder

This style—with its straight sides from hem to neck and with its straight-across upper sleeve—is one of the easiest to draft and knit because it has so little shaping. And that makes it the style of choice for learning to draft or for a garment with complications of color or texture. (You might notice that most traditional garments—with their explorations of color or texture—are drop shoulders.)

I definitely feel that the drop shoulder has its place—for kids, for guys, for large garments, and for the other reasons mentioned. But I also understand why some women find it unflattering: it has no defined shoulder, its lack of shaping demands that it be loose, and this looseness means lots of unwanted fabric—especially at the underarm. So if you are ready for the challenge, see the modified drop shoulder (page 38) or the saddle shoulder (page 114): they have modifications that might be more appealing to you.

Measurements You Have

You have the results of your swatch (stitches and rows), and you have these essential measurements (pages 19–27) which you will record in the following calculations:

- your girth
- your garment's finished length
- your sleeve length.

And here's what is assumed about your garment.

- Front and back are the same width.
- Front and back are the same length. (If not, work separate calculations for each whenever length is part of the equation.)
- It has full-length sleeves.

Appropriate Ease

Since this is a nonfitted style (with no shaped armhole and no defined shoulder width), to be comfortable it is usually knit quite generously. And since it is usually knit quite generously, it is usually knit in medium-bulky yarns (or in the case of *fairisle,* two light yarns that combine for a bulkier fabric). The following are suggestions for appropriate garment circumferences for this style. Generous ease is added to your girth for your garment's circumference.

- bust + 6–8″ (15–20.5cm) for a short pullover
- hips + 6–8″ (15–20.5cm) for a long pullover
- bust + 8–10″ (20–25.5cm) for a short jacket
- hips + 10–12″ (25.5–30.5cm) for a heavy coat

Can you see how ease varies with the length to which the garment is knit or with how the garment is worn? Long garments need ease that covers the (usually) wider hips, and jackets and coats need ease added because they are often worked in heavier yarns and worn over other garments.

Measurements You Need

There are measurements you still need (and we need to discuss): neck dimensions and sleeve dimensions. And we also need to discuss shoulder shaping.

Neck Dimensions

You don't know your neck width or neck depth until you determine the neck shape you want. But you'll need your *neck depth* for this pattern, because the calculations require it. So here's what I suggest:

- Go to the relevant pages of chapter 3 and choose your front neck depth. (It's possible that your neck shape has no depth—for the boat neck or funnel neck. Don't let that confuse you: you'll just insert 0 at that point in your calculations.)
- If you have a front neck depth greater than 0, your back neck depth may be a standard 1″ (2.5cm). But if your front neck depth is 0, your back neck depth will also be 0.

Don't worry about your neck width for now: it can wait until you are ready to draft and knit that part of the garment.

Sleeve Dimensions

A standard sleeve is tapered from the narrow lower sleeve to the wider upper sleeve. You don't yet know either of these widths, nor do you know the length of the sleeve to the armhole. Here's how you'll work these out.

The drop shoulder is not shaped to the joints of the body: it has no shaped armhole or defined shoulder width, and it has a sleeve that doesn't follow the shape of the upper arm (from underarm to shoulder). So in order to be comfortable, it is made to a generous upper sleeve width. (Many drop shoulder garments will have upper sleeve widths greater than what I suggest here.) Because I know that the volume of fabric at the underarm is what we don't love about this style, here are the narrowest possibilities for a drop shoulder *upper sleeve width*.

- For sizes XS (S, M, L, 1X, 2X), try 16 (17, 18, 19, 20, 21)″ (40.5 [43, 45.5, 48, 51, 53.5] cm) in a light–medium yarn
- For larger sizes, extrapolate from what you see here.
- For a heavy yarn, add 1″ (2.5cm).

Choose an upper sleeve width based on your size and your yarn: you'll need it for your calculations. And remember that the ones offered here are minimums. (Don't be surprised if a garment you measure is wider.) But enough ease was added to the body of the garment to bring the armhole seam far enough down the arm that these upper sleeve widths will work. And this should have you realizing that if you make a larger body, your armhole seam will travel farther down the arm, which would allow you an even narrower upper sleeve width.

To determine the *minimum number of stitches to cast on for your sleeve*, do the following: knit the front or back first; wrap a cast-on edge from the garment around your fist; record this number of stitches as the minimum that allow your hand to pass through. (If you haven't done the knitting that allows you to do this, perhaps you can extrapolate from your swatch.) The added bonus to a number of stitches that fits your wrist is that when you push your sleeves up (to expose the slim part of your arm), the sleeve will stay.

This number of stitches is what you will want to cast on. If you have no cuff, this is your *lower sleeve width*. If you have a cuff, you may increase stitches after the cuff, and the calculations allow for this.

Your *sleeve length to armhole* is part of the following calculations. But because the bind-off row at the end of the sleeve is one long straight line, you may do the work to make sure you end with a full row repeat (if you have one). You will see this in the calculations.

Shoulder Shaping (and Front / Back Droop)

A drop shoulder has no defined shoulder width (and its shoulder seam extends far down the arm), so we don't need your shoulder width, and we don't do shoulder shaping.

Because we do no shoulder shaping, the bind-off row at the shoulders is one straight line. Because it is one straight line, we do the work to make sure that we end at a reasonable place in our row repeat (if we have one): this will make the top of the sleeve ever-so-much more attractive. You will see this in the calculations.

You do need to know that because we do no shoulder shaping, the garment will droop at the sides—and be shorter at the center back. The wider the garment is, the more it will fall down the arm, and the more the sides will droop. This can be corrected by a tight bottom band (which holds the garment straight at the hem). But I'm not a huge fan of tight bottom bands, and I don't mind the droop at the sides. I consider it a feature of this garment's style that can be highlighted—perhaps with a longer back and with open side seams at the hem.

Drop Shoulder Front / Back, Hem to Neck
Calculations

#stitches/inch (2.5cm) = _____

#rows/inch (2.5cm) = _____

your girth + appropriate ease = circumference of garment _____ inches (cm)

finished length = _____ inches (cm)

height of bottom band (if there is one) = _____ inches (cm)

front neck depth = _____ inches (cm)

back neck depth = _____ inches (cm) (If front neck depth is greater than 0 back neck depth may be 1″ [2.5cm].)

1. circumference of garment ÷ 2 = front/back width _____ inches(cm)
2. (front/back width × #stitches/inch [2.5cm]) = #stitches in front/back _____
3. Do you need to fudge for a stitch pattern repeat?
4. Do you need to add selvedge stitches?
5. revised #stitches in front/back = _____

6. finished length – height of bottom band = front/back length (above band) _____ inches (cm) (Use this length for all following calculations.)
   Do you have a stitch pattern that needs to end with a full row repeat (assumed to be an even number)? If not, skip steps 7–10.
7. front/back length x #rows/inch (2.5cm) = #rows in front/back length _____
8. #rows in front/back length ÷ #rows in full repeat = #row repeats in front/back _____ (Fudge to achieve a whole number.)
9. #row repeats x #rows in repeat = revised #rows in front/back length _____
10. revised #rows in front/back length ÷ #rows/inch (2.5cm) = revised front/back length _____ inches (cm)
11. front/back length – front neck depth = length to front neck _____ inches (cm)
12. front/back length – back neck depth = length to back neck _____ inches (cm)

Pattern

- If there is no bottom band, cast on #stitches in front/back width (step 5), and ignore bottom band references.
- If you're starting with a bottom band, you may cast on fewer stitches and with smaller needles (see page 145). You may need to change to larger needles and increase stitches at the end of the band. End with #stitches in front/back (step 5).
- After bottom band, work front to neck (step 11). End after working a WS row.
- After bottom band, work back to neck (step 12). End after working a WS row.
- Finish the garment with front and back neck shaping, then bind off each shoulder's stitches on a RS row.

Drop Shoulder, Long Sleeves
Calculations

#stitches/inch (2.5cm) = _____
#rows/inch (2.5cm) = _____
minimum #stitches that allow your hand to pass through
= _____
lower sleeve width (if different from above) = _____
inches (cm)
upper sleeve width = _____ inches (cm)
your sleeve length = _____ inches (cm)
height of cuff (if there is one) = _____ inches (cm)
front/back width (step 1, from front/back) = _____
inches (cm)

1. upper sleeve width × #stitches/inch (2.5cm) =
   #stitches in upper sleeve _____.
2. Do you need to add selvedge stitches?
3. revised #stitches in upper sleeve = _____ (This
   may be even or odd, but #stitches in lower sleeve—
   step 4—must be the same choice.)
4. *With no cuff:* minimum #stitches that allow hand to
   pass through = minimum #stitches in lower sleeve
   _____ (You may add to this if you want a looser
   lower sleeve.)
   With a cuff: desired width of lower sleeve above
   cuff × #stitches/inch (2.5cm) = #stitches in lower
   sleeve _____

5. Do you need to fudge #stitches in the lower sleeve so
   you can start with a full stitch pattern repeat?
6. Do you need to add selvedge stitches?
7. revised #stitches in lower sleeve = _____
8. (#stitches in upper sleeve – #stitches in lower sleeve)
   ÷ 2 = #stitches to be increased at each side for
   length of sleeve _____
9. your sleeve length – (front/back width ÷ 2) – height
   of cuff = length of sleeve _____ inches (cm). Do
   you have a stitch pattern that needs to end with a full
   row repeat? (If not, skip steps 10–12.)
10. length of sleeve x #rows/inch (2.5cm) = #rows in
    sleeve _____
11. #rows in sleeve ÷ #rows in full repeat = #row repeats
    in sleeve _____ (Fudge to achieve a whole number.)
12. #row repeats x #rows in repeat = revised #rows in
    sleeve _____
13. #rows in sleeve ÷ #stitches to be increased (step 8)
    = 1 stitch should be increased at each side every
    _____ rows (Fudge, or round down, to a whole
    number, preferably even. If your result is less than 4,
    your lower sleeve width may be too narrow for this
    style.)

Pattern

- If there is no cuff, cast on #stitches in the lower sleeve
  (step 7) and ignore cuff references.
- If you're starting with a cuff, cast on #stitches that
  allow your hand to pass through. You may also have
  cast on with smaller needles. At the end of the cuff,
  work any increases to lower sleeve width before
  changing to larger needles. End with #stitches in lower
  sleeve (step 7).

- After cuff, work to length of sleeve (step 9, or step
  12 if you're working to a row repeat), *at the same
  time* increasing as determined in step 13. End with
  #stitches for upper sleeve (step 3).
- Bind off all stitches on a RS row.

Modified Drop Shoulder

This style is a kind of hybrid—combining the armhole and shoulder definition of the set-in sleeve with the simplicity of the drop shoulder. It's essentially a drop shoulder but with a slot into which the sleeve will fit. But these slight alterations to the drop shoulder have big-bang-for-your-buck results—a more attractive style that isn't difficult and may still easily accommodate complications of color and texture.

Measurements You Have

You have the results of your swatch (stitches and rows). And you have these essential measurements (pages 19–27), which you will record in the following calculations:

- your girth
- your garment's finished length
- your shoulder width
- your sleeve length.

Here's what is assumed about your garment.

- Front and back are the same width.
- Front and back are the same length. (If not, work separate calculations for each whenever length is part of the equation.)
- It has full-length sleeves.

Appropriate Ease

Since this is a semifitted style (with both a defined armhole and shoulder depth but without a sleeve that follows the shape of the upper arm), it is knit less generously than the unfitted drop shoulder but more generously than the form-following set-in sleeve. What follows are suggestions for appropriate garment circumferences for this style. Somewhat generous ease is added to your girth for your garment's circumference. (Again, note how ease varies with length and how the garment will be worn.)

- bust + 4–6″ (10–15cm) for a short pullover
- hips + 4–6″ (10–15cm) for a long pullover
- bust + 6–8″ (15–20.5cm) for a short jacket
- hips + 8–10″ (20.5–25.5cm) for a heavy coat

Measurements You Need

There are measurements you still need: neck dimensions, armhole depth, shoulder-shaping depth, and sleeve dimensions. And there's one measurement that demands a little more discussion: shoulder width.

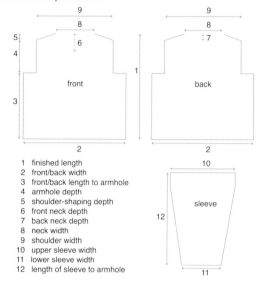

modified drop shoulder

1. finished length
2. front/back width
3. front/back length to armhole
4. armhole depth
5. shoulder-shaping depth
6. front neck depth
7. back neck depth
8. neck width
9. shoulder width
10. upper sleeve width
11. lower sleeve width
12. length of sleeve to armhole

Neck Dimensions

You don't know your neck width or neck depth until you determine the neck shape you want. But you'll need your *neck depth* for this pattern, because the calculations require it. So here's what I suggest.

- Go to the relevant pages of chapter 3 and choose your front neck depth. (It's possible that your neck shape has no depth—for the boat or funnel neck. Don't let that confuse you: you'll just insert 0 at that point in your calculations.)
- If you have a front neck depth greater than 0, your back neck depth may be a standard 1″ (2.5cm). But if your front neck depth is 0, your back neck depth will also be 0.

Don't worry about your neck width for now: that can wait until you are ready to draft and knit that part of the garment.

Armhole Depth

Armhole depth is the length between the outside edge of your garment's shoulder and its underarm. It's not a measurement I recommend trying to get from your body. (How far down from your shoulder should you extend your tape measure?) In addition, you may not have a garment to measure. But the good news is that the modified drop shoulder offers a tidy relationship between the armhole depth and the sleeve, because the armhole depth should be exactly half the upper sleeve width. So *armhole depth* will be figured out in the section on upper sleeve width.

Shoulder-Shaping Depth

This depth is the "drop" between the garment at your neck and the garment at the outside edge of its shoulder. And it is applied to styles—like this one—in which the shoulder width is defined by a seam. If we don't work shoulder shaping, the garment won't fit well at the shoulders and will droop at its sides.

But this depth is also not something I suggest measuring from the body. Here's why. In our culture, we like straight shoulders with a standard 1″ (2.5cm) depth. If your shoulders slope more than standard, you usually don't want to accentuate this by shaping to it (and may wear shoulder pads to fill the space).

So, rather than attempting to measure your body, measure a garment of the same style or use the following suggestions for *shoulder-shaping depth*.

- If a garment's shoulder seam ends at the shoulder (as measured on page 27), allow a standard 1″ (2.5cm) for shoulder depth.

- If the garment's shoulder seam extends past the edge of the shoulder, allow 1½–2″ (4–5cm) for shoulder depth.
- If the garment's shoulder seam is narrower than the shoulder, allow only ½–¾″ (1.5–2cm) for shoulder depth.

For now, all we have to know is how deep your shoulder shaping must be: you'll need that information, because your pattern requires you to knit to shoulder shaping. Whenever you wish, you may go to chapter 3 to finish both your shoulders and your neck.

However, I need to alert you to a common error: that is to not see that armhole depth is complete before shoulder-shaping depth occurs. They are entirely independent of each other, and the drawing should make that relationship clear.

Shoulder Width

You know this measurement (from chapter 1), but let's see how it is applied to this shape. At your armhole depth (discussed next in Sleeve Dimensions), you will bind off stitches on each side to bring your front/back width to your shoulder width. It happens all at once, as shown in the schematic, and nothing could be simpler.

Sometimes we choose to have shoulder width work to a full stitch repeat (and the calculations allow for this). But it's more important that the garment fit the way you want at the shoulders.

Sleeve Dimensions

A standard sleeve is tapered from a narrow lower sleeve width to a wider upper sleeve width. You don't yet know either of these widths, nor do you know the length of the sleeve to the armhole. Here's how you'll work those out.

Because this style has a defined armhole, it conforms more to the joints of the body than the standard drop shoulder, so its upper sleeve width can be narrower. But its sleeve does not follow the shape of the upper arm (from armhole to shoulder), so it still needs extra space (more than a fitted style) to be comfortable. Again, like the drop shoulder, this style has a wide range of possibilities for *upper sleeve width*. Here are its narrowest possibilities.

- For sizes XS (S, M, L, 1X, 2X), try 14 (15, 16, 17, 18, 19)″ (35.5 [38, 40.5, 43, 45.5, 48])cm in a light-medium yarn.

shoulder-shaping + armhole depths

shoulder-shaping depth

armhole depth

shoulder-shaping depths

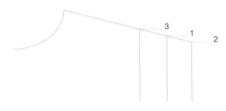

3 1
2

1 seam ends at shoulder: shoulder depth = 1″
2 seam extends past shoulder: shoulder depth = 1½ – 2″
3 seam ends inside shoulder: shoulder depth = ½ – ¾″

- For larger sizes, extrapolate from what you see here.
- For a heavy yarn, add 1″ (2.5cm).

Choose an upper sleeve width based on your size and your yarn: you'll need it for your calculations. And remember: these are minimums. This style could have a much wider upper sleeve width.

For the pieces to fit together, your *armhole depth* needs to be exactly half your upper sleeve width (you'll work this out in your calculations).

To determine the *minimum number of stitches to cast on for your sleeve*, do the following: knit the front or back first; whether or not your garment has a cuff, wrap a cast-on edge from the garment around your fist; record this number of stitches as the minimum that allow your hand to pass through. (If you haven't done the knitting that allows you to do this, perhaps you can extrapolate from your swatch.) The added bonus to a number of stitches that fits your wrist is that when you push your sleeves up (to expose the slim part of your arm), the sleeve will stay.

This number of stitches is what you will want to cast on. If you have no cuff, this is your *lower sleeve width*. If you have a cuff, you may increase stitches after the cuff, and the calculations allow for this.

Your *sleeve length to armhole* is part of the following calculations. But you will notice that because the bind-off row at the end of the sleeve is one long straight line, you may do the work to end with a full row repeat (if you have one). You will see this in the calculations.

Modified Drop Shoulder Front/Back, Hem to Neck Calculations

#stitches/inch (2.5cm) = _____

#rows/inch (2.5cm) = _____

your girth + appropriate ease = circumference of garment below armhole _____ inches (cm)

finished length = _____ inches (cm)

garment's shoulder width = _____ inches (cm)

upper sleeve width = _____ inches (cm)

armhole depth (½ upper sleeve width) = _____ inches (cm)

front neck depth = _____ inches (cm)

shoulder-shaping depth = _____ inches (cm)

back neck depth = _____ inches (cm) (If front neck depth is greater than 0, back neck depth may be 1″ [2.5cm].)

note If your front neck depth is lower than your armhole depth, that will complicate the following calculations (requiring you to shape your neck at the same time as your armhole). Because that is a rare occurrence, I have assumed neck depth to be shallower than armhole depth.

1. circumference of garment ÷ 2 = front/back width _____ inches (cm)

2. (front/back width × #stitches/inch [2.5cm]) = #stitches in front/back _____

3. Do you need to fudge for a stitch pattern repeat?

4. Do you need to add selvedge stitches?

5. revised #stitches in front/back = _____ (This may be even or odd, but #stitches above armhole—step 10—must be the same choice.)

6. finished length – armhole depth – shoulder-shaping depth = length of front/back to armhole _____ inches (cm)

7. garment's shoulder width × #stitches/inch (2.5cm) = #stitches above armhole _____

8. Do you need to fudge for a stitch pattern repeat?

9. Do you need to add selvedge stitches?

10. revised #stitches above armhole (shoulder width) = _____

11. (#stitches in front/back – #stitches above armhole) ÷ 2 = #stitches to be bound off at each armhole _____

12. finished length – front neck depth = length of front to neck _____ inches (cm)

13. finished length – back neck depth or shoulder-shaping depth (whichever is greater) = length of back to neck or shoulder _____ inches (cm)

Pattern

- If there is no bottom band, cast on #stitches in front/back (step 5).
- If you're starting with a bottom band, you may have cast on fewer stitches and with smaller needles (page 145). You may need to change to larger needles and increase stitches at the end of the band. End with #stitches in front/back width (step 5).
- Work length to armhole (step 6). End after working a WS row.

- Bind off #stitches for armhole (step 11) at the beginning of the next 2 rows—#stitches in shoulder width (step 10) remain.
- Work front to neck (step 12). End after working a WS row.
- Work back to neck (step 13). End after working a WS row.
- Finish the garment with back and front neck shaping and with shoulder shaping.

Modified Drop Shoulder, Long Sleeves
Calculations

#stitches/inch (2.5cm) = _____
#rows/inch (2.5cm) = _____
minimum #stitches that allow your hand to pass through
= _____
lower sleeve width (if different from above) = _____
inches (cm)
upper sleeve width = _____ inches (cm)
your sleeve length = _____ inches (cm)
front/back width (step 1, above) = _____ inches (cm)
garment's shoulder width = _____ inches (cm)
height of cuff (if there is one) = _____ inches (cm)

1. upper sleeve width × #stitches/inch (2.5cm) =
   #stitches in upper sleeve _____
2. Do you need to add selvedge stitches?
3. revised #stitches in upper sleeve = _____ (This
   may be even or odd, but #stitches in lower sleeve—
   step 7—must be the same choice.)
4. *With no cuff:* #stitches that allow hand to pass
   through = minimum #stitches in lower sleeve
   _____ (You may add to this if you want a looser
   lower sleeve.)
   With a cuff: desired width of lower sleeve above cuff
   × #stitches/inch (2.5cm) = #stitches in lower sleeve
   _____
5. Do you need to fudge #stitches in lower sleeve so
   you can start with a full stitch pattern repeat?

6. Do you need to add selvedge stitches?
7. revised #stitches in lower sleeve = _____
8. (#stitches in upper sleeve – #stitches in lower sleeve)
   ÷ 2 = #stitches to be increased at each side through
   length of sleeve _____
9. your sleeve length – (front/back width ÷ 2) – height
   of cuff = length of sleeve for increases _____
   inches (cm)
10. #rows/inch (2.5cm) × length of sleeve for increases =
    #rows for increases _____
11. your sleeve length – (shoulder width ÷ 2) – height
    of cuff = full length of sleeve above cuff_____
    inches (cm)
    Do you have a stitch pattern that needs to end with a
    full row repeat (assumed to be an even number)? (If
    not, skip steps 12–14.)
12. full length of sleeve × #rows/inches (2.5cm) = #rows
    in sleeve _____
13. #rows in sleeve ÷ #rows in full repeat = #row repeats
    in sleeve _____ (Fudge to achieve a whole
    number.)
14. #row repeats × #rows in repeat + revised #rows in
    full length of sleeve above cuff = _____
15. #rows for increases (step 10) ÷ #stitches to be
    increased (step 8) = 1 stitch should be increased at
    each side every _____ rows (Fudge or round down
    to a whole number, preferably even.)

Pattern

- If there is no cuff, cast on #stitches for lower sleeve
  (step 7), and ignore cuff references.
- If you're starting with a cuff, cast on #stitches that
  allow your hand to pass through. You may also have
  cast on with smaller needles. At the end of the cuff,
  work any increases to #stitches in the lower sleeve
  (step 7) before changing to larger needles.

- After the cuff, work to length for increases (step 9) *at
  the same time* increasing as determined in step 15.
  End with #stitches for upper sleeve (step 3).
- Work to full length of sleeve (step 11, or step 14 if
  you're working to a row repeat).
- Bind off all stitches on a RS row.

Set-in Sleeve

The set-in sleeve is our most form-following garment. And it is universally attractive, as long as it fits. What we're going to do is make it fit. Oh, yes, and let's also make it easy.

You'll notice that the discussion of this style is rather lengthy, but I spend a lot of time here for two reasons: first, this is a universally attractive style so it behooves us to understand it well; second, many find it difficult—to both execute and assemble—and we need to change that by challenging some basic assumptions.

Here's where I need to tell you the big secret of my professional life. I did not go to fashion or design or art school! And you will soon see that that is a very good thing! Why? Because fashion school is dedicated to shaping with fabric—rigid fabric without the forgiving flexibility of our knits but in which it's easy to execute a curve; all you need is a pair of scissors.

Okay, so what we've seen (and probably cursed) are directions for set-in sleeves that are shaped with those curves so easily executed in fabric pieces—the underarm of the front and back and the cap of the sleeve. And what do we know about knit curves (as opposed to diagonals)? That they are

- difficult to draft
- difficult to seam
- difficult to pick up and knit against.

Because I didn't absorb fashion school's fondness for curves, I have always drafted set-in sleeves with diagonal lines. (This is probably a result of studying math, a subject in which two sides of an equation

had to be equal. You'll see the beauty of this played out shortly.) As you can imagine from the drawing, executing this shape with the decreases of diagonals rather than the bind-offs of curves has made it simpler. And—because of knitting's flexibility—it has always worked beautifully. To execute the set-in sleeve with diagonals, here's what I do.

At the front/back underarm
- bind off for the shelf,
- work decreases to bring the garment into shoulder width.

And at the sleeve cap
- bind off for the shelf,
- work decreases to bring the sleeve down to its final sleeve cap width.

Here's what I hear from most of my students: "Guaranteed! Easiest sleeve cap I have ever made or sewed in. And it fits perfectly!!!" And what I hope to hear from you pattern drafters is this: "Wow! Who knew the set-in sleeve could be so easy?"

Measurements You Have

You have the results of your swatch (stitches and rows). And you have these essential measurements (pages 19–27) which you will record in the following calculations:
- your girth
- your garment's finished length
- your shoulder width
- your sleeve length.

And here's what is assumed about your garment.
- Front and back are the same width.
- Front and back are the same length. (If not, work separate calculations for each whenever length is part of the equation.)
- It has full-length sleeves.

Appropriate Ease

Since this is our most form-following style, it's most comfortable with the least amount of ease—usually within the range of close fit, to standard ease. (You can also work with very close fit, but it's rare enough that I don't enter it here.) Minimal ease is added to your girth for your garment's circumference.
- bust + 0–4" (0–10cm) for a short pullover
- hips + 0–4" (0–10cm) for a long pullover
- bust + 2–4" (5–10cm) for a short cardigan
- hips + 4–8" (10–20.5cm) for a heavy coat

set-in sleeve diagonal vs. curves

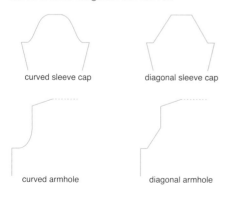

curved sleeve cap   diagonal sleeve cap

curved armhole   diagonal armhole

You will use less ease with a light yarn or a garment worn alone; you will use more ease with a medium or bulky yarn or with a garment worn over other clothing. As noted before, it's always a good idea to measure an existing garment of the same weight and style.

Measurements You Need

But there are measurements you still need: neck dimensions, armhole depth, shoulder-shaping depth, and sleeve dimensions. And there's one measurement that demands a little more discussion: shoulder width.

Shoulder Width

I said earlier that this shape is universally attractive as long as it fits. And where it most needs to fit is across the shoulders. While you already know this measurement, let's make sure you see how it is worked within this shape.

At your armhole depth (discussed shortly), you will bind off some stitches (for the underarm shelf) and then decrease down to your *shoulder width*. Here's how easy it is to do both those things.

- For sizes XS–S (M, L, 1X, 2X or larger), bind off approximately ½ (1, 1–1½, 1½–2, 2)" (1.5 [2.5,

2.5–4, 4–5, 5]cm) for the underarm shelf.
- Decrease at each end of every RS row until you reach your shoulder width.

Sometimes we choose to have shoulder width work to a full stitch repeat (and the calculations allow for this). But it is more important that the garment fit the way you want at the shoulders.

Neck Dimensions

You don't know your neck width or neck depth until you determine the neck shape you want. But you'll need your *neck depth* for this pattern, because the calculations require it. So here's what I suggest.

- Go to chapter 3 and choose your front neck depth. (It's possible that your neck shape has no depth—for the boat or funnel neck. Don't let that confuse you: you'll just insert 0 at that point in your calculations.)
- If you have a front neck depth greater than 0, your back neck depth may be a standard 1" (2.5cm). But if your front neck depth is 0, your back neck depth will also be 0.

Don't worry about your neck width for now: that can wait until you are ready to draft and knit that part of the garment.

Armhole Depth

Armhole depth is the length between the outside edge of your garment's shoulder and its underarm. The set-in sleeve is the style that best conforms to the joints of the body (with a defined armhole depth and shoulder width and a sleeve that follows the shape of the upper arm). So it can be knit to the shallowest possible armhole depth. Here are some important features.

- If the armhole is too deep, it is uncomfortable.
- Since there is a direct relationship between armhole depth and upper sleeve width, the shallower the armhole depth, the tighter the upper sleeve.
- The tighter the upper sleeve, the slimmer you look.

But armhole depth is not a measurement I recommend trying to get from your body: how far down from your shoulder should you extend that tape measure? Since this is a style you will have in your closet, go measure a few pieces you like to see the range of possibilities. Here are my suggestions for the shallowest *armhole depth*.

set-in sleeve

1 finished length
2 front/back width
3 front/back length to armhole
4 armhole depth
5 shoulder-shaping depth
6 front neck depth
7 back neck depth
8 neck width
9 shoulder width
10 final sleeve cap width
11 sleeve cap height
12 upper sleeve width
13 lower sleeve width
14 length of sleeve to armhole

shoulder-shaping + armhole depths

shoulder-shaping depth

armhole depth

shoulder-shaping depths

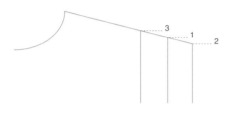

1 seam ends at shoulder: shoulder depth = 1"
2 seam extends past shoulder: shoulder depth = 1½ – 2"
3 seam ends inside shoulder: shoulder depth = ½ – ¾"

- For sizes XS (S, M, L, 1X, 2X), 5½ (6, 6½, 7, 7½, 8)″ (14 [15, 16.5, 18, 19, 20.5]cm) for a pullover in a light yarn.
  - For sizes larger than 2X, extrapolate from what you see here.
  - For a pullover in a medium yarn, add ½″ (1.5cm).
  - For a cardigan in a medium yarn or a pullover in a heavy yarn, add 1″ (2.5cm).
  - For a cardigan in a heavy yarn, add 1½″ (4cm).

Note that we add more depth for cardigans because we might wear cardigans over another layer. And a heavy coat can be deeper still.

Before proceeding, look at the accompanying drawing, notice that the armhole depth does not include shoulder-shaping depth: armhole depth is complete before shoulder shaping begins.

Shoulder-Shaping Depth

This depth is the "drop" between the base of your neck and the outside edge of your garment's shoulder, and it is applied to styles—like this one—in which the shoulder width is defined by a seam.

But this depth is also not something I suggest measuring from the body. Here's why. In our culture, we like straight shoulders with a standard 1″ (2.5cm) depth.

If your shoulders slope more than standard, you usually don't want to accentuate this by shaping to it (and may wear shoulder pads to fill the space).

So, rather than attempting to measure your body, measure a garment of the same style or work from the following suggestions for *shoulder-shaping depth*:

- If a garment's shoulder seam ends right at the shoulder (as measured on page 27), allow a standard 1″ (2.5cm) shoulder depth.
- If the garment's shoulder seam extends past the edge of the shoulder, allow 1½–2″ (4–5cm) for shoulder depth.
- If the garment's shoulder seam is narrower than the shoulder, allow only ½–¾″ (1.5–2cm) for shoulder depth.

For the following calculations, we need to know your shoulder-shaping depth. You'll knit to that place and then finish your garment with neck and shoulder shaping, all worked out in chapter 3.

Sleeve Dimensions

A standard sleeve is tapered from a narrower lower sleeve width to a wider upper sleeve width. You don't yet know either of these widths, nor do you know the length of the sleeve to the armhole. And for this particular style you also need the height of the cap and the final sleeve cap width—neither of which you know.

Wow, that's a lot of unknowns! But maybe there is something we can establish as standard, and then maybe there's something we can learn.

First, the *final sleeve cap width*—the width at which the sleeve cap is finished—can be established as a standard 5–6″ (12.5–15cm).

Second, we know that we want to begin our sleeve with the same shelf as our front/back armhole.

- For sizes XS–S (M, L, 1X, 2X or larger), bind off approximately ½ (1, 1–1½, 1½–2, 2)″ (1.5 [2.5, 2.5–4, 4–5, 5]cm).

So what can we learn from what we already know? Let's say we have already established an armhole depth. And we know that we are going to end our sleeve with a standard 5–6″ (12.5–15cm) final sleeve cap width. And we know that the final sleeve cap width is going to seam to front/back, centered over the shoulder seam. From this, we should be able to figure out the *height of our sleeve's cap*. That would be expressed as follows:

- sleeve cap height = armhole depth − (½ final sleeve cap width).

But let's make this clearer by looking at sample garment pieces and inserting actual numbers.

- Let's assume an 8″ (20.5cm) armhole depth.
- Let's assume a 6″ (15cm) final sleeve cap width.
- That means that we have 8 − (6 ÷ 2) = 5″ (12.5cm) of the armhole depth untouched by the final sleeve cap width. (See the bold vertical arrow.)
- And this means that a 5″ (12.5cm) tall sleeve cap would seam perfectly into this armhole.

Okay, but we still don't know the number of stitches in the upper sleeve width (the ? in the drawing below) nor how to decrease that larger number of stitches down to the number of stitches in the final sleeve cap. We need one more piece of information, and it's a huge piece of the puzzle!

Remember when I said up front that this shape is easily accomplished by replacing curves with diagonals? Here is where that becomes significant. Instead of the bind-offs that curves demand, we are going to decrease as diagonals allow. To see how we ought to be decreasing, we can look at a series of diagonals that are produced by decreases in stockinette. (What follows is entirely dependent on getting something like a standard stockinette gauge—and that's why I write the standard decrease row in stockinette. See page 50 for how to work with other gauges.)

Look at the set-in sleeve caps (below right). If we decrease at each end of every row, we get a very flat sleeve cap (drawing on left). If we decrease at each end of every alternate RS row, we get a very tall sleeve cap (drawing on right). But if we decrease at each end of every RS row, we get a sleeve cap that is just right (drawing in center).

What gives us the shape we like is the standard RS decrease row: k1, skp or ssk, knit to the last 3 stitches, k2tog, k1. You may not realize it, but that was huge! Because (Take a deep breath and be prepared to be amazed!) . . . if we decrease at each end of each RS row, how many stitches are we decreasing on RS rows? Two! How many stitches are we decreasing on WS rows? None! So how many stitches are we decreasing every 2 rows? Two! How many stitches every 4 rows? Four! (Stay with me here!) How many stitches every 10 rows? Ten! How many stitches every 34 rows? Thirty-four!

See the pattern? The number of stitches we can decrease is the same as the number of rows over which we are doing the decreasing! (No, stitches did not become rows: we simply saw two sides of an equation match up. Isn't math beautiful!?!)

So, the perfect number of stitches for our *upper sleeve width* is the following 3 added together:

- the number of stitches bound off at each underarm shelf
- plus the number of stitches in the final sleeve cap width
- plus the number of rows between the underarm bind-off and the final sleeve cap (which you figured out earlier as armhole depth minus half the width of the upper sleeve cap).

Let's make this clearer by looking again at those sample garment pieces and inserting actual numbers.

- Let's assume a gauge of 5 stitches × 7 rows = 1″ (2.5cm).
- Let's assume an underarm bind-off of 5 stitches: 5 stitches × 2 = **10** stitches bound off in total.
- Let's assume a 6″ (15cm) final sleeve cap width: 6″ × 5 stitches/inch (2.5cm) = **30** stitches.

sleeve cap height

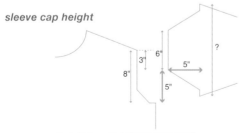

6″   3″   5″   ?
8″   5″

the bold lines should be the same length

set-in sleeve caps

2 decreases every row   2 decreases every RS row   2 decreases every alternate RS row

set-in sleeve sample

back front
3" 8"

5s 6" = 30s 5s

5" = 34r

5s 5s

10 + 30 + 34 = 74s

s = stitches   gauge is 5 stitches x 7 rows = 1"
r = rows   bold lines = standard decrease rows

- Let's assume an 8" (20.5cm) armhole depth.
- Therefore, #inches (cm) between underarm bind-off and sleeve cap = 8 − (6 ÷ 2) = 5" (12.5cm).
- 7 rows/inch (2.5cm) × 5" (12.5cm) = 35: but let's make this an even number: **34** rows.
- Therefore, there are 34 rows between underarm bind-off and sleeve cap—which is the same as the number of stitches we can decrease over those rows.
- So the perfect #stitches in the upper sleeve width are the three boldface numbers added together: 10 + 30 + 34 = 74 stitches.

Can you see how this is going to be a beautiful thing to seam? Five stitches will seam to 5 stitches at the underarm, 34 rows will seam to 34 rows as we seam the sleeve cap into the armhole, and the stitches of the final 6" (15cm) sleeve cap will seam over 6" (15cm) of rows, centered over the shoulder seam.

One thing that very clever students have asked is the following: with sewing, we use multiple pins to ease the sleeve cap into the armhole. What happened to the need for those pins? And the answer is that the diagonal lines of the 5" (12.5cm) sleeve cap (bold in the drawing above) are longer than 5" (12.5cm). (It's Pythagorean Theorem. Don't you love it when ninth-grade geometry finally applies to something meaningful?) But by seaming the 34 rows of the diagonal sleeve cap to the 34 rows of the more-or-less straight armhole edge, we fulfill the function of all those pins!

Let's take a moment to look at the result of this math. The finished upper sleeve width is 74 stitches. Now let's divide this by our gauge (5 stitches/inch [2.5cm]):

74 ÷ 5 = 15" (37.5cm). This math is telling us that a 15" (37.5cm) sleeve will fit perfectly into our 8" (20.5cm) armhole.

You'll see all this as you work out the following calculations. But what you need to appreciate is that this math will give you a perfect sleeve-to-armhole relationship. Here's how this usually works out.

- For sizes XS–M, upper sleeve width may be ½–1" (1.5–2.5cm) smaller than twice the armhole depth.
- For sizes L–2X, upper sleeve width may be the same as or ½–1" (1.5cm–2.5cm) larger than twice the armhole depth.

Larger sizes get a larger sleeve by virtue of the larger underarm shelf. And it only makes sense that larger sizes need both a larger shelf and a larger sleeve. The point is that everyone gets a sleeve that seams like a dream.

Please make sure you understand what we just did. Because once you "get it," it'll become second nature. And you'll appreciate the beauty of not using curves. Not only is the shape now really simple to draft and knit and seam, but it works!

One more thing (it doesn't affect the calculations you've made, but it does make the cap turn a nice corner at the top): Once I get to the final sleeve cap's stitches, I always bind off in small stair steps—to create a tiny curve that softens the cap's top corners—and you'll be asked to do this at the end of the following pattern.

To determine the *minimum number of stitches to cast on for your sleeve*, do the following: knit the front or back first; whether or not your garment has a cuff, wrap a cast-on edge from the garment around your fist; record this number of stitches as the minimum that allow your hand to pass through. (If you haven't done the knitting that allows you to do this, perhaps you can extrapolate from your swatch.) The added bonus to a number of stitches that fits your wrist is that when you push your sleeves up (to expose the slim part of your arm), the sleeve will stay.

This number of stitches is what you will want to cast on. If you have no cuff, this is your *lower sleeve width*. If you have a cuff, you may increase stitches after the cuff, and the calculations allow for this.

Your *sleeve length to armhole* is part of the following calculations.

Set-in Sleeve Front/Back, Hem to Neck

Calculations

note These calculations are based on a stockinette gauge. For other gauges, see page 50.

#stitches/inch (2.5cm) = _____
#rows/inch (2.5cm) = _____
your girth + appropriate ease = circumference of garment below armhole _____ inches (cm)
finished length = _____ inches (cm)
garment's shoulder width = _____ inches (cm)
armhole depth = _____ inches (cm)
#stitches bound off at each underarm shelf = _____
front neck depth = _____ inches (cm)
shoulder-shaping depth = _____ inches (cm)
back neck depth = _____ inches (cm) (If front neck depth is greater than 0, back neck depth may be 1″ [2.5cm].)

notes If your front neck depth is lower than your armhole depth, that will complicate the following calculations (requiring you to shape your neck at the same time as armhole shaping). Because that is a rare occurrence, I have assumed neck depth to be shallower than armhole depth.

1. circumference of garment ÷ 2 = front/back width _____ inches (cm)
2. (front/back width × #stitches/inch or cm) = #stitches in front/back _____.
3. Do you need to fudge for a stitch pattern repeat?
4. Do you need to add 2 selvedge stitches? (They are assumed in the following pattern.)
5. revised #stitches in front/back = _____ (This may be even or odd, but the #stitches in shoulder width—step 10—must be the same choice.)
6. finished length – armhole depth – shoulder-shaping depth = length of front/back to armhole _____ inches (cm)
7. shoulder width × #stitches/inch (2.5cm) = #stitches in shoulder width _____
8. Do you need to fudge for a stitch pattern repeat?
9. Do you need to add selvedge stitches?
10. revised #stitches in shoulder width = _____
11. #stitches in step 5 – #stitches in step 10 – (#stitches in underarm shelf × 2) = #stitches to be decreased _____
12. finished length – front neck depth = length of front to neck _____ inches (cm)
13. finished length – back neck depth *or* shoulder-shaping depth (whichever is greater) = length of back to neck or shoulder _____ inches (cm)

Pattern

- If there is no bottom band, cast on #stitches in front/back (step 5).
- If you're starting with a bottom band, you may have cast on fewer stitches and with smaller needles (page 145). You may need to change to larger needles and increase stitches at the end of the band. End with #stitches in front/back width (step 5).
- Work length to armhole (step 6). End after working a WS row.
- Bind off #stitches for underarm shelf at the beginning of the next 2 rows.

- Work the following RS decrease row until #stitches for shoulder width (step 10) remain: k1, skp or ssk, work to the last 3 stitches, k2tog, k1.
- Work front to neck (step 12). End after working a WS row.
- Work back to neck (step 13). End after working a WS row.
- Finish the garment with back neck, front neck, and shoulder shaping.

note These calculations are based on a stockinette gauge. For other gauges, see page 50.

#stitches/inch (2.5cm) = _____
#rows/inch (2.5cm) = _____
minimum #stitches that allow your hand to pass through = _____
lower sleeve width (if different from above) = _____ inches (cm)
height of cuff (if there is one) = _____ inches (cm)
armhole depth = _____ inches (cm)
#stitches bound off at each underarm shelf = _____
final sleeve cap width = _____ inches (cm) (usually 5–6″ [12.5–15cm])
your sleeve length = _____ inches (cm)
garment's shoulder width = _____ inches (cm)

1. armhole depth – ½ final sleeve cap width = height of sleeve cap _____ inches (cm)
2. height of sleeve cap × #rows/inch (2.5cm) = #rows for sleeve cap but also #stitches to be decreased over sleeve cap _____ (Make this an even number.)
3. final sleeve cap width × #stitches/inch (2.5cm) = #stitches in final sleeve cap _____ (This may be even or odd, but #stitches in lower sleeve—step 8—must be the same choice.)
4. (#stitches bound off at each underarm shelf × 2) + #stitches to be decreased over sleeve cap (step 2) + #stitches in final sleeve cap (step 3) = #stitches in upper sleeve _____

5. *With no cuff:* #stitches that allow hand to pass through = #stitches in lower sleeve _____. (You may add to this if you want a looser lower sleeve.)
   With a cuff: desired width of lower sleeve above cuff × #stitches/inch (2.5cm) = #stitches in lower sleeve _____
6. Do you need to fudge for a stitch pattern repeat?
7. Do you need to add 2 selvedge stitches? (They are assumed in the following pattern.)
8. revised #stitches in lower sleeve = _____
9. (#stitches in upper sleeve [step 4] – #stitches in lower sleeve [step 8]) ÷ 2 = #stitches to be increased at each side of sleeve _____
10. your sleeve length – (garment's shoulder width ÷ 2) – height of sleeve cap (step 1) = length of sleeve to armhole _____ inches (cm)
11. *With no cuff:* length of sleeve to armhole × #rows/inches (2.5cm) = #rows for sleeve increases _____ inches (cm). Skip to step 13.
    With a cuff: length of sleeve to armhole (step 10) – height of cuff = length of sleeve above cuff _____ inches (cm)
12. length of sleeve above cuff × #rows/inches (2.5cm) = #rows for sleeve increases _____
13. #rows for sleeve increases ÷ #stitches to be increased (step 9) = 1 stitch should be increased at each side every _____ rows (Fudge or round down to a whole number, preferably even.)

Pattern

- If there is no cuff, cast on #stitches for lower sleeve (step 8).
- If you're starting with a cuff, cast on #stitches that allow your hand to pass through (step 5). You may also cast on with smaller needles. At the end of the cuff, work any increases to #stitches in lower sleeve (step 8) before changing to larger needles.
- Work to armhole (step 10), *at the same time* increasing as determined in step 13. End with #stitches for upper sleeve (step 4). End after working a WS row.

- Bind off #stitches for underarm shelf at the beginning of the next 2 rows.
- Work the following RS decrease row for #rows for sleeve cap (step 2) until #stitches in final sleeve cap (step 3) remain: k1, skp or ssk, work to the last 3 stitches, k2tog, k1. End after working a WS row.
- Bind off 2 stitches at the beginning of the next 2 rows.
- Bind off 4 stitches at the beginning of the next 2 rows.
- Bind off remaining stitches.

Set-in Sleeve Using Gauges Other Than Stockinette

I said earlier that this work was based on the stitch-to-row proportions of stockinette. And that's because that proportion gives us the perfect slope when we decrease on RS rows. If you are working with other stitches—like garter, with many more rows—or if you don't get a standard stitch-to-row gauge in stockinette, you'll need to make adjustments. Here's how I would estimate your upper sleeve width.

- For sizes XS–M, upper sleeve width may be ½–1″ (1.5–2.5cm) smaller than twice the armhole depth.
- For sizes L–2X, upper sleeve width may be the same as or ½–1″ (1.5cm–2.5cm) larger than twice the armhole depth.

Work the calculations and pattern for the sleeves as specified, but with the following changes.

- Step 2—Delete "but also #stitches to be decreased over sleeve cap."
- Step 4—Enter your own #stitches in the upper sleeve (based on the estimate above).

Add the following 2 steps at the end of the your set-in sleeve calculations.

- (#stitches in upper sleeve – #stitches bound off at underarm – #stitches in final sleeve cap) ÷ 2 = #stitches to be decreased on each side of sleeve cap _____.
- Now you have to sort out how you are going to decrease the #stitches to be decreased (previous step) over the #rows in the sleeve cap (step 2).

Your pattern will be different, because it won't use the standard decrease row. You may choose different selvedges and/or work different decreases. And your decreasing will probably involve skipping some RS row decreases (since most alternative row gauges are denser than stockinette). Use the chart of Ratios for Decreasing (page 218) to calculate how often you will decrease.

Raglan

The raglan is an interesting style: it has a defined armhole depth and a sleeve that somewhat follows the shape of the upper arm, but it has no shoulder seam so it doesn't define the shoulder width. Therefore, it is comfortable worn snug (like a set-in sleeve) or generous (like a drop shoulder).

Its shape is accomplished with diagonals: at the armhole, it has a small underarm shelf and then decreases—down to the neck width for the front and back, and to almost nothing for the sleeves.

But despite its flexibility and its diagonals, I am not a huge fan of this style. Those diagonals may draw attention to narrow shoulders, may frame a larger bust, and may accentuate a pear shape. And through the fronts and backs of raglans, we are often required to do two things at once—shape the armholes while shaping the neck. Finally, it can be difficult to make the puzzle pieces fit together properly.

This last statement may seem odd to you, since you may have been exposed to the raglan as an easy, perhaps top-down, probably seamless garment, all of which is purported to make knitting easier. Whether it does or not, you already know that I'm no fan of top-down or seamless knitting. But here is my real issue with raglans. If the armholes and front and back are all decreased at the same rate (as these easy sweaters are, with decreases at each end of each piece's right-side rows), they often don't fit well: sleeves to deep sleeves to narrow, puckered seams. And deep armholes tend to make us look heavy.

What follows is a more complex raglan than you may have seen before. It makes the calculations a little more involved, but it improves the fit.

Measurements You Have

You have the results of your swatch (stitches and rows). And you have these essential measurements (pages 19–27), which you will record in the following calculations:
- your girth
- your garment's finished length
- your sleeve length.

Here's what is assumed about your garment.
- Front and back are the same width.
- Front and back are the same length. (If not, work separate calculations for each whenever length is part of the equation.)
- It has full-length sleeves.

raglan

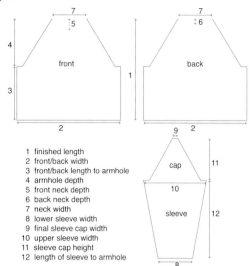

1 finished length
2 front/back width
3 front/back length to armhole
4 armhole depth
5 front neck depth
6 back neck depth
7 neck width
8 lower sleeve width
9 final sleeve cap width
10 upper sleeve width
11 sleeve cap height
12 length of sleeve to armhole

Appropriate Ease

Since this is a style with a wide range of possibilities, it's comfortable with any amount of ease. The least amount of ease would be within the range of close fit to standard ease: bust or hips + 0–4″ (0–10cm). But this garment is also comfortable within the range of loose fit: bust or hips + 4–6″ (10–15cm). Or it could be oversized: bust or hips + more than 6″ (15cm). This ease will be added to your girth for your garment's circumference. You will use less ease with a light yarn or a garment worn alone: you will use more ease with a medium or heavy yarn or with a garment worn over other clothing.

Measurements You Still Need

But there are measurements still you need: neck dimensions, armhole depth, and sleeve dimensions.

Neck Dimensions

You don't know your neck width or depth until you determine the neck shape you want. But you need these dimensions for this style, because the calculations require them. The front and back are reduced to neck width as you work the slope from the armhole to the end of the garment, so we need the measurement of your neck width to calculate the front/back above the armhole. You can still draft your neck's pattern later, but here is what I suggest for now.

- Go to the relevant pages of chapter 3 and choose your front neck depth. (It's possible that your neck shape has no depth—for the boat or funnel neck. Don't let that confuse you: you'll just insert 0 at that point in your calculations.)
  - If you have a front neck depth greater than 0, your back neck depth may be a standard 1″ (2.5cm). But if your front neck width is 0, your back neck width will also be 0.
  - Go to the relevant pages of chapter 3 and choose your neck width.

In the calculations, you will be required to convert your neck width to stitches, and then you'll be asked to add a few more—at least 4 and maybe 6. Here's why. At each side of the front, you need stitches remaining after you finish your decreases: 1 stitch on each side will go into the seam allowance for the sleeve, 1 stitch on each side will go into the allowance for the neck edging. This brings us to 4 extra stitches. If you want another stitch on each side—to remain on the right side of the work—that means 6 extra stitches.

raglan front/back

Armhole Depth

This garment's flexibility means that it can be knit to the shallowest possible armhole depth (like the set-in sleeve) or to a deeper armhole (like the drop shoulder). Like all styles with armhole definition, there is a direct relationship between armhole depth and upper sleeve width. So the shallower the armhole depth, the tighter the upper sleeve. (And the tighter the upper sleeve, the slimmer you look.)

But this is not a measurement I recommend trying to get from your body: how far down from your shoulder should you extend that tape measure? If you own garments of this style, measure a few to see the range of possibilities. It can have a shallow *armhole depth*—like a lightweight set-in sleeve:
- For sizes XS (S, M, L, 1X, 2X), 5½ (6, 6½, 7, 7½, 8)″ (14 [15, 16.5, 18, 19, 20.5]cm) for a pullover in a light yarn.

But it can also have a deep armhole length—like a drop shoulder:
- For sizes XS (S, M, L, 1X, 2X), 8 (8½, 9, 9½, 10, 10½)″ (20.5 [21.5, 23, 24, 25.5, 26.5]cm) in a heavy yarn.

It could, of course, be anywhere in between. Or it could be deeper still (like the garment upon which I modeled the Uptown Jacket, page 177). As I said earlier, the raglan can be worked in a wide range of styles.

You'll be asked to establish your armhole depth before making the following calculations. And then you'll also be asked for your underarm shelf, which will be figured as follows.
- For sizes XS–M (L–1X, 2X or larger), bind off ½ (1, 1½)″ (1.5 [2.5, 4]cm).

Then you'll decrease, over the length of your armhole depth, to neck width plus those 4–6 extra stitches.

Sleeve Dimensions

A standard sleeve is tapered from a narrower lower sleeve width to a wider upper sleeve width. You don't yet know either of these widths, nor do you know the length of the sleeve to armhole. And for this particular style you also need to know the height of the sleeve cap and the final sleeve cap width.

Wow, that's a lot of unknowns! But you do know that you want to begin your sleeve with the same small underarm shelf as the front/back.
- For sizes XS–M (L–1X, 2X or larger), bind off ½ (1, 1½)″ (1.5 [2.5, 4]cm).

Now you need to narrow the sleeve down—but to what? Traditionally, you decrease to a *final sleeve cap width* of 2 or 3 stitches as mentioned earlier in Neck Dimensions.

Decreasing to 2 or 3 stitches remaining at the end of the sleeve is the easiest way to execute this shape because a sleeve cap with no width means it doesn't include neck shaping. If you choose to decrease to a wider final sleeve cap width (perhaps 2″ [5cm]), you may have to work neck shaping into this piece.

But a *final sleeve cap width* of 2″ (5cm) is not difficult. Here's what will happen:
- If your neck has no back neck shaping, this 2″ (5cm) piece will be finished along with your neck— bound off for a straight neck, worked as part of the funnel of a funnel neck (see center drawing below).

- If your neck has shaping, you will split that 2″ (2.5cm) in half. One inch (2.5cm) will go to the front neck and the same to the back (below right). The front piece can be bound off in one step, because—as you will see in the square, round, and V-necks of chapter 3—the final 1″ (2.5cm) of these front neck shapes is straight. The back bit will require a little back neck shaping. (By the way, note that this neck shaping made it the left—and not the right—sleeve.)

So what about the sleeve's dimensions can we learn from what we already know? After we establish our front/back armhole depth, we will establish that depth as a number of rows. We know that we want our sleeve to fit into that armhole, so that means that the *height of the sleeve cap* should have the same number of rows as the front/back's armhole depth.

But we don't know yet what *upper sleeve width* will f it into this armhole depth. And here's where I can explain why the math of the raglan is more complicated than that of other styles. (You don't need to read this explanation: if you just want the answer to suggested upper sleeve width, skip the next six paragraphs.)

Let's start by wondering what would happen if we decrease at each end of every RS row to bring our upper sleeve width down to our final sleeve cap width. (This standard decrease row means decreasing 2 stitches on RS rows and 0 stitches on WS rows. That means we decrease 2 stitches every 2 rows, 4 stitches every 4 rows, 20 stitches every 20 rows, etc.) So, like the cap of the set-in sleeve, the number of stitches we are decreasing is the same as the number of rows over which we are doing the decreasing.

If we decreased this way, we could calculate the narrowest upper sleeve width that would fit into this armhole by adding the following three together:

- the number of stitches bound off at each underarm
- plus the number of stitches in the final sleeve cap width
- plus the number of rows in the front/back armhole depth.

But let's study this by looking at sample garment pieces and inserting actual numbers. (Note that this sample is assuming a stockinette gauge. Different gauges—with different stitch-to-row ratios—will yield different results.)

raglan sample

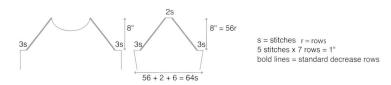

s = stitches   r = rows
5 stitches x 7 rows = 1″
bold lines = standard decrease rows

raglan sleeve caps

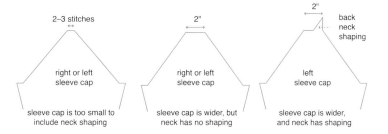

- Let's assume a gauge of 5 stitches × 7 rows = 1″ (2.5cm).
- Let's assume an 8″ (20.5cm) armhole depth: 8″ (20.5cm) × 7 rows/inch (2.5cm) = **56** rows (which is the same as the number of stitches we can decrease with our standard decrease row).
- Let's assume the **2**-stitch final sleeve cap width.
- Let's assume an underarm shelf of 3 stitches: 3 × 2 = **6** stitches.
- That means that, working with the standard decrease row, the narrowest sleeve we can put into an 8″ (20.5cm) armhole is the 3 bold numbers added together: 56 + 2 + 6 = 64 stitches.

But after seaming, the circumference at its upper sleeve will be 64 − 2 = 62 stitches. 62 ÷ 5 = 12½″ (32cm). This means putting a 12½″ (32cm) sleeve into an 8″ (20.5cm) armhole. That's a very small sleeve!

We learned when we worked out the example of the set-in sleeve—pages 45–47—that the smallest sleeve for our sample 8″ (20.5cm) armhole was 15″ (37.5cm). And it's not reasonable to assume that this style would want an upper sleeve width 2″ (5cm) narrower. Clearly, this sleeve is too small to be comfortable. So how do we find an appropriate upper sleeve width?

For the raglan, a style with a wide range of armhole depths, here's what I suggest for an appropriate *upper sleeve width*:

- For a shallow armhole depth, make your upper sleeve width twice the armhole depth minus ½–1″ (1.5–2.5cm).
- For a medium-depth armhole, make your upper sleeve width twice the armhole depth minus 1–2″ (2.5–5cm).
- For a deep armhole depth, make your upper sleeve width twice the armhole depth minus 2–4″ (5–10cm).

- For a really deep armhole, make your upper sleeve width twice the armhole depth minus 4–6″ (10–15cm) or more.

Whether you decrease to a minimal sleeve cap of 4–6 stitches of the wider sleeve cap of 2″ (5cm)—into which neck shaping might be worked (see page 53)—these suggestions will give you an upper sleeve width that's neither too tight nor too full.

Again, it's always a good idea to measure an existing garment. When you do, measure both its armhole depth and its upper sleeve width.

What you will probably find yourself making is a raglan that requires something other than our standard decrease row (in which we decrease at each end of RS rows), and this is covered in the following calculations and pattern.

To determine the *minimum number of stitches to cast on for your sleeve*, do the following: knit the front or back first; whether or not your garment has a cuff, wrap a cast-on edge from the garment around your fist; record this number of stitches as the minimum that allow your hand to pass through. (If you haven't done the knitting that allows you to do this, perhaps you can extrapolate from your swatch.) The added bonus to a number of stitches that fits your wrist is that when you push your sleeves up (to expose the slim part of your arm), the sleeve will stay.

This number of stitches is what you will want to cast on. If you have no cuff, this is *your lower sleeve width*. If you have a cuff, you may increase stitches after the cuff, and the calculations allow for this.

Your *sleeve length to armhole* is part of the following calculations.

Raglan Front/Back, Hem to Neck
Calculations

#stitches/inch (2.5cm) = _____
#rows/inch (2.5cm) = _____
your girth + appropriate ease = circumference of garment below armhole _____ inches (cm)
finished length = _____ inches (cm)
armhole depth = _____ inches (cm)
#stitches bound off at each underarm shelf = _____ stitches
front neck depth = _____ inches (cm)
back neck depth = _____ inches (cm) (If front neck depth is greater than 0, back neck depth may be 1″ [2.5cm].)
neck width = _____ inches (cm)

1. circumference of garment ÷ 2 = front/back width _____ inches (cm).
2. (#stitches/inch [2.5cm] × front/back width) = #stitches in front/back _____
3. Do you need to fudge for a stitch pattern repeat?
4. Do you need to add selvedge stitches?
5. revised #stitches in front/back = _____ (This may be even or odd, but the #stitches in neck width—step 8—must be the same choice.)
6. finished length – armhole depth = length of front/back to armhole _____ inches (cm)

7. #stitches in front/back – (#stitches bound off at each underarm shelf × 2) = #stitches remaining after underarm bind-offs _____
8. #stitches/inch (2.5cm) × neck width = #stitches in neck _____
9. #stitches in neck width + 4 or 6 stitches = #stitches remaining in front/back (for neck + selvedges) _____
10. #stitches remaining after underarm bind-offs (step 7) – #stitches remaining in front/back (step 9) = #stitches to be decreased between underarm and end of front/back _____
11. #rows/inch (2.5cm) × armhole depth = #rows for decreasing over armhole depth _____
12. #stitches to be decreased (step 10) ÷ #rows for decreasing (step 11) = _____ Go to the chart of Ratios for Decreasing (page 218) to find the number closest to your result. This will tell you how to decrease between underarm and end of front/back. You may revise the #rows in armhole depth—step 11—so your division gives you one of the options offered.
13. finished length – front neck depth = length of front to neck _____ inches (cm)
14. finished length – back neck depth = length of back to neck _____ inches (cm)

Pattern

- If there is no bottom band, cast on #stitches in front/back (step 5).
- If you're starting with a bottom band, you may cast on fewer stitches and with smaller needles (page 145). You may need to change to larger needles and increase stitches at the end of the band. End with #stitches in front/back width (step 5).
- Work length to armhole (step 6). End after working a WS row.

- Bind off #stitches for underarm shelf at the beginning of the next 2 rows.
- Work to neck (step 13 for front, step 14 for back), *at the same time* decreasing as determined in step 12. End after working a WS row.
- Finish the garment with back and front neck shaping, *at the same time* continuing armhole decreases as established.

#stitches/inch (2.5cm) = _____
#rows/inch (2.5cm) = _____
upper sleeve width = _____ inches (cm)
minimum #stitches that allow your hand to pass through
= _____
lower sleeve width (if different from above) = _____
inches (cm)
height of cuff (if there is one) = _____ inches (cm)
armhole depth = _____ inches (cm)
#stitches bound off at each underarm shelf = _____
your sleeve length = _____ inches (cm)
neck width = _____ inches (cm)

1. #stitches/inch (2.5cm) × upper sleeve width =
   #stitches in upper sleeve _____
2. Do you need to add selvedge stitches?
3. revised #stitches in upper sleeve = _____ (This
   may be even or odd, but #stitches in final sleeve
   cap—step 4—and in lower sleeve width—step10—
   must be the same choice.)
4. #stitches in final sleeve cap = _____
5. #stitches in upper sleeve − (#stitches bound off at
   each underarm shelf × 2) = #stitches to be decreased
   over sleeve cap _____
6. #stitches to be decreased over sleeve cap ÷ #rows
   in armhole depth for decreasing (step 11 from front/
   back) = _____ Go to the chart of Ratios for
   Decreasing (page 218) to find the number closest
   to your result. This will tell you how to decrease
   between underarm and end of front/back. If your
   rate is 1.2 or higher, your seam may pucker. To avoid

puckering, subtract up to 1″ (2.5cm) from the upper
sleeve width. Go back to the chart with your new
numbers. You can continue to adjust #stitches so
your division gives you a rate of decrease less than
1.2.

7. *With no cuff:* #stitches that allow hand to pass
   through = #stitches in lower sleeve _____ (You
   may add to this if you want a looser lower sleeve.)
   With a cuff: desired width of lower sleeve above cuff
   × #stitches/inch (2.5cm) = #stitches in lower sleeve
   _____
8. Do you need to fudge for a stitch pattern repeat?
9. Do you need to add selvedge stitches?
10. revised #stitches in lower sleeve = _____
11. (#stitches in upper sleeve [step 3] − #stitches in lower
    sleeve [step 10]) ÷ 2 = #stitches to be increased at
    each side of sleeve _____
12. your sleeve length − (neck width ÷ 2) − armhole depth
    = length of sleeve to armhole _____ inches (cm)
13. *With no cuff:* length of sleeve to armhole (step 12)
    × #rows/inch (2.5cm) = #rows for sleeve increases
    _____. Skip to step 15.
    With a cuff: length of sleeve to armhole (step
    12) − height of cuff = length of sleeve above cuff
    _____ inches (cm)
14. length of sleeve above cuff × #rows/inch (2.5cm) =
    #rows for sleeve increases _____
15. #rows for sleeve increases ÷ #stitches to be
    increased (step 11) = 1 stitch should be increased at
    each side every _____ rows (Fudge or round down
    to a whole number, preferably even.)

Pattern

- If there is no cuff, cast on #stitches for lower sleeve (step 10).
- If you're starting with a cuff, cast on #stitches that allow your hand to pass through. You may also cast on with smaller needles. At the end of the cuff, work any increases to #stitches in lower sleeve (step 10) before changing to larger needles.
- Work to armhole (step 12), *at the same time* increasing as determined in step 15. End with #stitches for upper sleeve (step 3). End after working a WS row.
- Bind off #stitches for the underarm shelf at the beginning of the next 2 rows.
- Work #rows for decreasing armhole depth, *at the same time* decreasing as determined by step 6, ending with #stitches in final sleeve cap (step 4).
- Bind off (if you have only 2 or 3 stitches in the final sleeve cap) or leave stitches live (if you have more stitches into which you must work neck shaping).
- If you adjusted the #rows for decreasing to make them smaller for the sleeve than the front/back, go to the chart of Ratios for Seaming (page 219) to seam sleeve into armhole.

Chapter 3

Shoulder Shaping, Back and Front Neck Shaping

The work of this chapter is small but mighty: it sits front and center on our garment, framing the face. So a lot of important stuff happens in a relatively little—but very important—part of the garment.

Shoulder shaping and neck shaping are in the same chapter, because when they happen, they happen at the same time. This chapter begins with shoulder and back neck shaping (because they are generic and worked the same through whatever front neck you choose) and ends with the choices for neck shapes.

What makes this chapter a little different than the others is that these garment parts are interdependent, and you'll often be doing two things at once. So this chapter will involve some back-and-forth work because you need your neck's width before you can work shoulder or back neck shaping, and you don't know your neck's width until you choose your front neck's style. Here's how I suggest you work.

- If you wish to just read and understand shoulder and back neck shaping, insert an arbitrary value of 8″ (20.5cm) for neck width.
- If you are ready to work out your neck pattern, go to the different styles, choose yours, read about and choose a neck width, come back and work your shoulder and back neck shaping, then carry this work forward and use it for your neck's pattern.

We can save space by clarifying and establishing one piece of information that carries over from the previous chapter and applies to all the shapes in this chapter; that is, the number of stitches remaining in the front/back when it's time to shape the neck.

- For the drop shoulder, it's the #stitches in front/back (because no shaping has altered that #stitches).
- For the modified drop shoulder or set-in sleeve, it is the #stitches for shoulder width (after armhole shaping is completed). However, if the front neck is deep, and armhole shaping is not completed, it is the #stitches on the needles when front neck shaping needs to begin.
- For the raglan, it is the #stitches on the needles when neck shaping needs to begin (because we are still shaping the armhole as we work the neck).

Another thing to make clear again is that the shapes of this chapter are shapes that are drafted into the garment pieces: any other work (like adding a neck band, or making a shawl collar from a V-neck, or turning a round neck into a turtleneck) is all part of finishing, which is addressed in chapter 8.

Shoulder Shaping

If your garment defines the width of the shoulders—either with a finished edge or with a seam—your garment should have shoulder shaping. Otherwise, your garment will droop at the sides (see an explanation for this on page 35), or not fit the shoulders well, or have "wings" at the shoulders if it's sleeveless. Which styles would need shoulder shaping?

- modified drop shoulder
- set-in sleeve
- anything sleeveless (discussed in chapter 6)

What appears below is generic shoulder shaping, with its even sequence of bind-offs. (No, I do not recommend short rows or the three-needle bind-off: the whole weight of the garment hangs from these seams, so I prefer the firmness of bound-off edges sewn together. One exception is a decorative shoulder seam, which sits on the right side of the garment: then I'll work a three-needle bind-off from live stitches. But this is rare.)

Measurements You Have

As you read in the previous chapter, your shoulder-shaping depth is one of the following:

shoulder-shaping depths

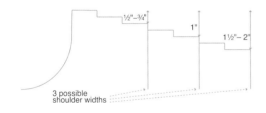

- If shoulder seams end right at the edge of the shoulder, allow a standard 1″ (2.5cm) shoulder depth.
- If shoulder seams extend past the edge of the shoulder, allow 1½–2″ (4–5cm) for shoulder depth.
- If shoulder seams are narrower than the shoulder, allow only ½–¾″ (1.5–2cm) for shoulder depth.

We also know (from the work of the previous chapter) our garment's finished length and the #stitches remaining in the front/back as we approach shoulder shaping.

Measurements You Need

What you still need to do is determine how many stitches you have for each shoulder and what to do with them. But you can't know how many stitches remain for each shoulder until you know how many will be taken by the neck. So what is specified below requires you to choose your neck width before completing the garment. You will then carry your shoulder-shaping pattern forward to your neck's pattern.

Shoulder Shaping

Calculations

#stitches/inch (2.5cm) = _____
#rows/inch (2.5cm) = _____
#stitches remaining in front/back = _____
neck width = _____ inches (cm)
shoulder-shaping depth = _____ inches (cm)
front/back finished length = _____ inches (cm)

1. #stitches/inch (2.5cm) × neck width = #stitches in neck _____ (This should be odd or even, whichever matches the #stitches in front/back.)
2. (#stitches remaining in front/back − #stitches in neck) ÷ 2 = #stitches in each shoulder _____
3. #rows/inch (2.5cm) × shoulder-shaping depth = #rows for shoulder shaping _____ (Make this an even number.)
4. #rows for shoulder shaping ÷ 2 = #opportunities to bind off shoulder stitches on each side _____
5. Write a series that describes how to bind off #stitches in step 2 as evenly as possible over #opportunities in step 4 _____ (For example, with 19 stitches you might bind off 5, 5, 4, and 5.)
6. finished length − shoulder-shaping depth = length to shoulder _____ inches (cm)

Pattern

notes

1. For necks without front or back neck shaping (the boat or funnel), the following instructions will complete your garment.
2. For necks with front or back neck shaping (the square, round, or V-neck), your shoulder shaping will be interrupted by your neck shaping. You will work shoulder shaping *at the same time* as neck shaping, and this will be included in the following neck patterns.

- Work to shoulder (step 6). End after working a WS row.
- Bind off stitches for each shoulder, at beginnings of rows and as indicated by the series in step 5.

Back Neck Shaping

For necks with front shaping (the square, round, or V-neck), you will also work back neck shaping. And while it's obvious why we'd shape a front neck, why do we also shape the back? The answer is that we have a slight protuberance at the top of our spine, and the back of our garment doesn't want to climb that hill. So it will

- offer a lump of fabric at the back neck
- force the shoulder seams to slide down the back.

We need to shape around that place in your spine, getting rid of the fabric that wants to lump or slide. For a V-neck, we'll shape with decreases. For a round neck, we'll shape with bind-offs. For a square neck, you may choose either of these.

For straight necks without front or back neck shaping (the boat or funnel), this lumping or sliding will occur. But, as you'll read in each of these sections, we accept this as part of their style.

Measurements You Have

We've already established a standard back neck depth for styles with back neck shaping as 1″ (2.5cm).

If you have shoulder shaping, you already have the number of rows and the series of stitches to be bound off (from steps 3 and 5, page 62).

back neck shaping

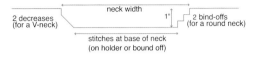

back neck shaping

What you also know (from the work of the previous chapter) is your garment's finished length and the #stitches remaining in the back as you approach the back neck.

Measurements You Need

What you need to determine is how many stitches you have for the back neck, and what to do with them. This requires you to choose your neck width before completing the garment—and this is done by choosing which front neck shape you want. (We do this first because, while back neck shaping is the same for all styles, front neck widths vary slightly with different styles.)

Back Neck Shaping
Calculations

#stitches/inch (2.5cm) = _____
#rows/inch (2.5cm) = _____
#stitches remaining in back = _____
neck width = _____ inches (cm)
front/back finished length = _____ inches (cm)
back neck depth = 1″ (2.5cm)
(if applicable) #rows for shoulder shaping (step 3, page 62) = _____
(if applicable) shoulder shaping bind-off series (step 5, page 62) = _____

1. #rows in 1″ (2.5cm) = #rows for back neck shaping _____ (Make this an even number.)
2. #stitches/inch (2.5cm) × neck width = #stitches in neck _____ (This should be odd or even, whichever matches the #stitches in front/back.)
3. #stitches in neck – 4 = #stitches in base of back neck _____
4. (#stitches remaining in back – #stitches in base of back neck) ÷ 2 = #stitches from side edge to base of neck _____
5. finished length – 1″ (2.5cm) = length to back to neck _____ inches (cm)

Pattern

notes I bind off for round necks and decrease for V-necks so the shaping on both front and back necks match. For square necks, you can make either choice.

You may or may not be doing shoulder shaping at the same time, so work with the appropriate section.

With No Shoulder Shaping
for right back shoulder
- Work to back neck (step 5). End after working a WS row.
- Work a RS row over #stitches of step 4.
- *If shaping a round neck:* Bind off 1 stitch at next 2 WS neck edges while working RS rows even. At finished length, bind off all stitches for right shoulder on following RS row.
- *If shaping a V-neck:* Decrease 1 stitch at next 2 RS neck edges while working WS rows even. At finished length, bind off all stitches for right shoulder on following RS row.
- Make one of the previous choices for a square neck.

for center back neck
- For a pullover, put #stitches of step 3 onto a holder; for a cardigan, bind off #stitches in step 3.

for left back shoulder
- Work 1 RS and 1 WS row (without neck shaping) over remaining stitches, then work as follows.
- *If shaping a round neck:* Bind off 1 stitch at next 2 RS neck edges while working WS rows even. At finished length, bind off all stitches for left shoulder on following RS row.

- *If shaping a V-neck:* Decrease 1 stitch at next 2 RS neck edges while working WS rows even. At finished length, bind off all stitches for left shoulder on following RS row.
- Make one of the previous choices for a square neck.

With Shoulder Shaping
- You need to know when to begin shoulder shaping and how that relates to back neck shaping. So compare the #rows for shoulder-shaping depth to the #rows for back neck shaping to determine if shoulder shaping starts before, at the same time as, or after the beginning of back neck shaping.
- If back neck shaping starts first, just work as for garments with no shoulder shaping and introduce shoulder shaping when appropriate.
- If shoulder shaping starts before or at the same time as back neck shaping, the #stitches in step 4 will have changed, and you will need to know when to turn and begin the back neck work. To establish this, sometime before you begin shoulder shaping, place markers on either side of the stitches of step 3 by working a row as follows: Work #stitches in step 4, place markers; work #stitches in step 3, place markers.
- Proceed to work back neck shaping and shoulder shaping *at the same time,* working back neck shaping through the steps specified for garments with no shoulder shaping, except that the second bullet should read "Work a RS row to marker."

Neck Shapes and the Rule of 10

What follows are choices for front neck shaping: straight (or boat) neck, funnel (a version of straight), square, V-, or round necks. And they all share one common characteristic: when made as pullovers, they have to fit over your head.

To accomplish this, I apply the rule of 10, stated as follows.

- To fit over an adult head, neck width + front neck depth should add up to 10″ (25.5cm) or greater before any neck band is applied.

So, for example, a round neck might be 7½″ (19cm) wide and 3″ (7.5cm) deep, and because the two parameters add up to 10 or more, it will fit over the head. A shallower round neck might be 8″ (20.5cm) wide and 2″ (5cm) deep, and that will also fit over the head.

You might, of course, ask about an edging that may be added. Wouldn't that fill the space and tighten the fit? No, because the number of stitches we pick up and knit for the edging (as discussed in chapter 8, page 153) is appropriate for the outside boundaries of the neck shape (which follows the rule of 10), and we don't decrease as we work the round neck band. So as long as you don't bind off too tightly, the garment will fit over your head.

I've applied this rule to the round neck, but what about other neck shapes?

- The V-neck, with its extra depth, easily meets this criterion.
- The square neck has to meet this criterion, just as the round neck did. And, yes, we do decrease stitches while working the (mitered) edging, but these decreases are minimal: not binding off too tightly will solve the problem.

- The rule suggests that a boat or funnel neck needs to be 10″ (25.5cm) wide, because it has no depth. But that produces a really wide neck. My experience is that we can make these necks smaller (as small as 8″ [20.5cm]) as long as we give it a really loose and stretchy bind-off.
- Cardigans do not need to fit over the head, and they tend to pull wide, so they are usually made narrower—6–6½″ (15–16.5cm) wide—and perhaps slightly shallower—2½″ (6.5cm) deep.

This rule doesn't apply to pieces knit for babies or children or adults with unusually large heads. Measure an existing garment and, if in doubt, err on the side of being generous.

Straight (Boat) Neck

A straight (boat) neck has no front or back neck shaping. Because of this, the fabric may bunch a little at both the front and back neck. We just accept that as part of its style.

It's a great style for anyone with a long neck (who can afford the neck-shortening of this style) and with straight shoulders (because this style accentuates the shoulders). Those with shorter necks and sloping shoulders are not flattered by this style. Also, if you have a fuller bust, you may not love the large expanse of fabric accentuating the area between the neck and the bust.

Measurements You Have

You know (from the work of the previous chapter) your garment's finished length and the #stitches remaining in the front/back as you approach the neck.

And if you are working shoulder shaping, you already have that number of rows and the series of stitches to be bound off (steps 3 and 5, page 62).

---

the rule of 10 / round neck samples

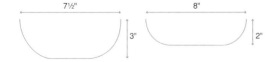

straight (or boat) neck

Measurements You Need

You still need your neck dimensions—your front (and back) neck depth and neck width.

This neck has no depth, so both front and back neck depth = 0.

You need enough width to go over your head, and since there is no depth that would give extra space, the neck width for this style has to be more generous than most. I would allow a minimum of 8″ (20.5cm) and a maximum of 10″ (25.5cm), only working with the narrower neck width if you are willing to bind off very loosely.

· ●

Straight (Boat) Neck
Calculations

#stitches/inch (2.5cm) = _____
#rows/inch (2.5cm) = _____
#stitches remaining in front/back = _____
neck width = _____ inches (cm)
front/back finished length = _____ inches (cm)
(if applicable) #rows for shoulder shaping (step 3, page 62) = _____
(if applicable) shoulder-shaping bind-off series (step 5, page 62) = _____

1. #stitches/inch (2.5cm) × neck width = #stitches in neck _____ (This should be odd or even, whichever matches the #stitches in front/back.)
2. (#stitches remaining in front/back – #stitches in neck) ÷ 2 = #stitches in each shoulder _____
3. *With shoulder shaping:* finished length – shoulder-shaping depth = length to shoulder _____ inches (cm)

Pattern

With No Shoulder Shaping

• If you plan to just bind off the neck's stitches, work to finished length. End after working a WS row. Bind off all stitches over the next RS row. Seam #stitches in each shoulder, front to back, leaving #stitches for neck un-seamed at center.
• If you plan to add an edging, work to finished length. End after working a WS row. Bind off #stitches in each shoulder (step 2) at the beginning of the next 2 rows. What remains are #stitches for the neck, for you to treat as you wish.

With Shoulder Shaping

• Work to shoulder (step 3). End after working a WS row.
• Work shoulder shaping.
• What remains after shoulder shaping are #stitches for neck (step 1). Bind them off or add an edging.

· ●

Funnel Neck

The funnel neck is like a turtleneck (or mock turtleneck) but—like the straight neck—it has no front or back neck shaping. Therefore, it can be knit as an extension of the garment front and back (after the shoulders are completed) or it can be added after the front and back are seamed: both possibilities are included in what follows.

Since it is a straight neck with a funnel knit up from it, we can draft it like a straight neck.

- Apply measurements as for the straight neck.
- Work all calculations as for the straight neck.
- Work your pattern as follows.

funnel neck

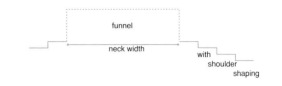

Funnel Neck Pattern

With No Shoulder Shaping

- Work to finished length. End after working a WS row.
- Bind off #stitches in each shoulder (step 2) at the beginning of the next 2 rows—#stitches in neck remain.
- Work to desired height of funnel, adding a final edging if you wish, and be sure to bind off loosely. Or sew shoulder seams, put the stitches for both the front and back necks onto one circular needle, then knit the funnel as one piece. (This avoids side seams in the funnel. But to neaten this, on row 1 decrease 1 stitch right before and right after each shoulder seam.)

With Shoulder Shaping

- Work to shoulder (step 3). End after working a WS row.
- Work shoulder shaping.
- What remains after shoulder shaping is #stitches for neck. Treat them as the third bullet in With No Shoulder Shaping above.

Square Neck

This neck shape is simple to execute but rather uncommon—probably because its finishing is complex. We might need to miter our neck band at the corners (directions for this are on page 149). But if there is no neck band, or the neck band is minimal, this shape is simpler.

square neck

bold line = neck band mitering

Measurements You Have

You know (from the work of the previous chapter) your garment's finished length and the #stitches remaining in the front as you approach the neck.

And if you are working shoulder shaping, you already have that number of rows and the series of stitches to be bound off (steps 3 and 5, page 62).

Measurements You Need

You still need your neck dimensions—your front neck depth and your neck width.

The square neck doesn't have standard parameters: it just needs to be wide enough so it doesn't fall off your shoulders and high enough so as not to defy modesty. Here are my suggestions.
  • neck width = 7–9″ (18–23cm)
  • neck depth = 5–1″ (12.5–2.5cm)

I deliberately specified the neck depth in descending order because when the square neck is made wider, it is usually made shallower. The smallest possible neck you could make—to follow the rule of 10—might be 7″ (18cm) by 3″ (7.5cm). But this neck shape is usually drafted more generously than it needs to be to fit over the head.

This pattern is available through my website.

Square Neck
Calculations

#stitches/inch (2.5cm) = _____
#rows/inch (2.5cm) = _____
#stitches remaining in front = _____
neck width = _____ inches (cm)
front/back finished length = _____ inches (cm)
front neck depth = _____ inches (cm)
(if applicable) #rows for shoulder shaping (step 3, page 62) = _____
(if applicable) shoulder-shaping bind-off series (step 5, page 62) = _____

1. neck width × #stitches/inch (2.5cm) = #stitches in neck _____ (This should be odd or even, whichever matches the #stitches in front/back.)
2. (#stitches remaining in front − #stitches in neck) ÷ 2 = #stitches from side to base of neck _____
3. finished length − neck depth = length to front neck _____ inches (cm)

Pattern

note If garment is a raglan, you will be working armhole decreases at the same time.
- Work to neck (step 3). End after working a WS row.
- Work a RS row over #stitches in step 2; turn.
- *With no shoulder shaping:* Work to finished length. End after working a WS row. On next RS row, bind off remaining stitches (for shoulder).
- *With shoulder shaping:* Work to finished length minus shoulder-shaping depth, then work shoulder shaping over #rows for shoulder shaping—0 stitches remain.*

- Return to remaining stitches, RS facing.
- Put #stitches for neck onto a holder or bind them off.
- Over remaining stitches of right front, work right front neck as from * to *, left.

V-Neck

A V-neck is easier than the universally attractive round neck that follows because—and, yes, you've heard this before—diagonals are easier than curves! And why else might we love a V-neck? It slims and elongates the neck and cuts the bust in half, so it's great on anyone with a larger neck, a shorter neck, or a full bust.

Despite its advantages, there aren't a lot of V-neck patterns out there. I think the reasons might be that we think of them as a "guy" thing (which does not have to be true), we think of them as dated (which also does not have to be true), we find them uncomfortable (which they are when they're shaped too wide), and we think their finishing is difficult (because the band must be mitered: read page 150). Having said all that, I'm gaining an appreciation for them—especially because my neck has gotten wider with age and they show off the tight skin you may have between your neck and bust.

Measurements You Have

You know (from the work of the previous chapter) your garment's finished length. And you know the #stitches remaining in the front as you approach the neck—although you may still be working armhole shaping (for a deep V in a set-in sleeve or for a raglan).

And if you're working shoulder shaping, you already have that number of rows and the series of stitches to be bound off (steps 3 and 5, page 62).

Measurements You Need

You still need your neck dimensions—your front neck depth and your neck width.

A V-neck can have any neck depth: it can be quite short or it can plunge to your waist. The only thing you need to be aware of is that a 1″ (2.5cm) neck band can fill in up to 2″ (5cm) of the neck's depth, as shown in the base of the drawing below.

This neck band will need to be mitered if the V is more than 5″ (12.5cm) deep. To prepare for this, I advise leaving 1 or 2 stitches at the base of the neck for the center of the mitering—and I've built this into the calculations. (Directions for the mitering itself are on page 150.)

A V-neck is quite uncomfortable if shaped too wide: a shirt may bunch under it, or bra straps may show, or it may fall off your shoulders. Here are my suggestions for neck width.

- 6–6½″ (15–16.5cm) if it is to be worn over a shirt
- no more than 8″ (20.5cm) if it is to be worn alone

You'll also notice that I ask you to work some rows unshaped at the end of your neck's diagonal. This makes room for shoulder shaping (so you don't have to do two things at once) and softens the upper corners of the V (making it a friendlier space for the neck band to circumnavigate).

V-neck

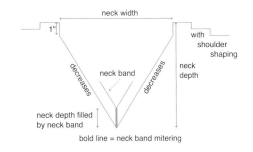

V-Neck
Calculations

#stitches/inch (2.5cm) = _____
#rows/inch (2.5cm) = _____
front/back finished length = _____ inches (cm)
neck width = _____ inches (cm)
front neck depth = _____ inches (cm)
#stitches remaining in front = _____
(if applicable) #rows for shoulder shaping (step 3, page 62) = _____
(if applicable) shoulder shaping bind-off series (step 5, page 62) = _____

1. #stitches/inch (2.5cm) × neck width = #stitches in neck _____ (This should be odd or even, whichever matches the #stitches in front/back.)
2. *If you are adding a neck band that needs to be mitered:* If #stitches in neck is even, subtract 2 stitches = #stitches to shape for neck _____. If #stitches in neck is odd, subtract 1 stitch = #stitches to shape for neck _____. (The stitches subtracted are the stitches left at the base of the neck for the mitering, which is done if the V is more than 5″ [12.5cm] deep.)
3. #stitches to shape for neck (step 1 or 2) ÷ 2 = #stitches to be shaped at each side of neck _____
4. #rows/inch (2.5cm) × front neck depth = #rows in neck depth _____

5. *With shoulder shaping:* #rows in neck depth − #rows for shoulder shaping *or* #rows in 1″ (2.5cm)— whichever is greater = #rows for shaping neck _____
   With no shoulder shaping: #rows in neck depth − #rows in 1″ (2.5cm) = #rows for shaping neck _____
6. *If the result of step 5 is greater than that of step 3, you will work decreases:* #rows for shaping (step 5) ÷ #stitches to be shaped at each side (step 3) = 1 stitch should be decreased at neck edge every _____ rows (Fudge to make this a whole number, preferably even.)
   If the result of step 5 is less than that of step 3, you will bind off: #stitches to be shaped at each side (step 3) ÷ #rows for shaping (step 5) = _____ stitches should be bound off at neck edge each time (Fudge to make this a whole number [for example, 3 stitches] or a half [for example, 2.5, which would mean *binding off 2 stitches once, 3 stitches once, repeat from *].)
7. finished length − front neck depth = length to front neck _____ inches (cm)
8. (#stitches remaining in front/back before neck − any stitches to be put on hold for mitering [from step 2]) ÷ 2 = #stitches from side of garment to base of neck _____

Pattern

note Depending on your style or neck depth, you might be working armhole shaping *at the same time* as neck shaping.

- Work to neck (step 7). End after working a WS row.
- Work #stitches in step 8.

For Left Front

- Put center stitch(es) onto a holder (if you allowed for them in step 2).
- Turn, and work 1 WS row over stitches of left front.
- Shape left front neck as indicated in step 6. After neck shaping is complete, #stitches in left shoulder remain.

- **With no shoulder shaping:* Work straight to finished length. End after working a WS row. On the next RS row, bind off remaining stitches (for shoulder).
- *With shoulder shaping:* Work shoulder shaping over #rows for shoulder shaping—0 stitches remain.*

For Right Front

- Return to remaining stitches.
- Work 1 RS and 1 WS row over stitches of right front.
- Shape right front neck as indicated in step 6. After neck shaping is complete, stitches in right shoulder remain.
- Finish by working from * to * above.

Round Neck

The round neck is considered universally attractive, as long as it is shaped appropriately—not so narrow as to make our necks look larger and not so deep that we can't bend over without immodesty.

As its name applies, it's a curve. And curves—with their progressive series of bind-offs—are more difficult to shape, to seam, or to pick up and knit against. But a round neck is one of two places (the shirttail is the other) where I think we really do need to offer a curve.

And before drafting, I will acknowledge that I know the round neck could be made easier to pick up and knit from if it were shaped with short rows and live stitches (rather than binding off). But if I don't bind off for this curve, no matter what I do, I get holes when I finish it. On the other hand, when I pick up and knit from a bound-off edge as described on page 153, I get the neatest possible neck edging. So while I love to make life easier, this is not a place where I think we can.

round neck

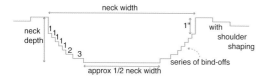

Measurements You Have

You know (from the work of the previous chapter) your garment's finished length and the #stitches remaining in the front as you approach the neck.

And if you are working shoulder shaping, you already have the number of rows and the series of stitches to be bound off (steps 3 and 5, page 62).

Measurements You Need

You still need your neck dimensions—your front neck depth and your neck width.

For the round neck, we need to refer to the rule of 10 (page 66). But my standard round neck—which is slightly larger than the rule suggests—is the following.

- neck width = 7½″ (19cm)
- front neck depth = 3″ (7.5cm)

You might call this a flat round neck, because it's wider and shallower than it needs to be. But in my experience, a 6″ × 4″ (15cm × 10cm) round neck makes the opening look small and makes your neck look larger.

I'd also call mine a flat round neck because I choose to put half its stitches into the base of the neck (as you'll see in the following calculations). If your neck is wider than this standard, you could put more than half its stitches into its base.

You'll also notice that I ask you to work some rows unshaped (usually 1″ [2.5cm]) at the end of your neck's shaping. This makes room for shoulder shaping (so you don't have to do two things at once) and softens the upper corners (making it a friendlier space for the neck band to circumnavigate).

Round Neck
Calculations

#stitches/inch (2.5cm) = _____
#rows/inch (2.5cm) = _____
front/back finished length = _____ inches (cm)
#stitches remaining in front = _____
neck width = _____ inches (cm)
front neck depth = _____ inches (cm)
(if applicable) #rows for shoulder shaping (step 3, page 62) = _____
(if applicable) shoulder-shaping bind-off series (step 5, page 62) = _____

1. neck width × #stitches/inch (2.5cm) = #stitches in neck _____ (This should be odd or even, whichever matches the #stitches in front/back.)
2. #stitches in neck ÷ 2 = #stitches in base of neck _____ (If #stitches in the neck is even, make this even: if odd, make this odd. You may increase this number if your neck is wider than standard.)
3. (#stitches in neck – #stitches in base of neck) ÷ 2 = #stitches in curve at each side of neck _____
4. #rows/inch (2.5cm) × front neck depth = #rows in neck depth _____ (Make this an even number.)

5. *With shoulder shaping:* #rows in neck depth – #rows for shoulder shaping or #rows in 1″ (2.5cm)— whichever is greater = #rows for curve _____ (Make this an even number.)
With no shoulder shaping: #rows in neck depth – #rows in 1″ (2.5cm) = #rows for curve _____ (Make this an even number.)
6. #rows for curve ÷ 2 = #opportunities to bind off stitches at each side of the neck _____
7. Write a series of numbers, beginning with 3 or 2, following with one or more 2s, and ending with some 1s (4–6) that, when added together, equal #stitches for curve at each side of neck (step 3). *At the same time,* the number of numbers in the series must be the same as the #opportunities to bind off stitches at each side of the neck (step 6). (With 10 stitches and 7 opportunities, your series might be 3, 2, 1, 1, 1, 1, 1.)
_____
8. finished length – front neck depth = length to front neck _____ inches (cm)
9. (#stitches remaining in front before neck shaping – #stitches in base of neck) ÷ 2 = #stitches from side of garment to base of neck _____

Pattern

note Depending on your style or neck depth, you might be working armhole shaping *at the same time* as neck shaping.
• Work to neck (step 8). End after working a WS row.

For Left Front
• Work a RS row over #stitches of step 9. Turn.
• Over #rows for curve (step 5), shape left front neck by binding off—at the beginnings of WS rows—stitches in series of step 7. (Work RS rows even.) After neck shaping is complete, #stitches in left shoulder remain.
• *With no shoulder shaping:* Work straight to finished length. End after working a WS row. On the next RS row, bind off remaining stitches (for your shoulder).

• *With shoulder shaping:* Work shoulder shaping over #rows for shoulder shaping—0 stitches remain.*

For Right Front
• Return to remaining stitches.
• Put #stitches in base of neck (step 2) onto holder.
• Work 1 RS and 1 WS row over stitches of right front.
• Over #rows for curve (step 5), shape right front neck by binding off—at the beginnings of RS rows—stitches in series of step 7. After neck shaping is complete, #stitches in right shoulder remain.
• Finish by working from * to * above.

Chapter 4

Hem Alternatives

Straight hems were put onto the garments through the basic shapes work of chapter 2. Now we can consider alternatives: diagonal, standard shirttail, and reverse shirttail hems. If you look at the chart for which shapes combine well (page 20), you'll see my opinion about what works with what: I'll explain the combinations that I don't think work in the appropriate sections. But I do expect you to consider my opinions and then discard them whenever your vision takes you someplace I haven't imagined.

For this chapter, you need your garment's pattern from chapter 2. Then you'll introduce your alternative hem. So through all calculations that follow, it is assumed that

- you know #stitches in front/back hem
- front and back are the same width.

Diagonal

A diagonal hem can be worked into any basic style and is an attractive thing—offering no horizontal line as a clear measure of the hips.

It has one side shorter than the other—the short side in the directions that follow. And you'll see the front and back are not identical but, rather, mirror images of each other.

To produce a diagonal hem, you could cast on stitches in steps, but I prefer to bring stitches into working with short rows—which is how the following is written. And it'll be easier to do this if you aren't trying to do something else (like side shaping) at the same time. So the following

diagonal hem

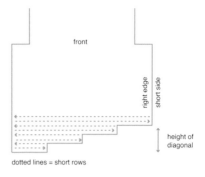

dotted lines = short rows

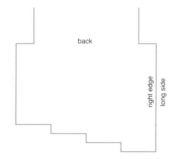

calculations and patterns assume straight sides. (If you wish to do side shaping, carry the information from this section to the next chapter: page 101 explains how to work hem and side shaping concurrently.)

Measurements You Need

You need to know the *height of the diagonal*—the difference between the short and long sides. A height of 3″ (7.5cm) is probably minimum so it doesn't look like a mistake.

See the notes at the beginning of the pattern for a discussion of the short and long side.

#stitches/inch (2.5cm) = _____
#rows/inch (2.5cm) = _____
#stitches in front/back at hem = _____
height of diagonal = _____ inches (cm)

1. #rows/inch (2.5cm) × height of diagonal = #rows in diagonal _____ (Make this an even number.)
2. #rows in diagonal ÷ 2 = #short-row opportunities (because only bringing stitches into working at one side means you only do so on alternate rows) _____

3. #stitches in hem ÷ #short-row opportunities = #stitches to bring into working at each short row _____ (Fudge #rows in diagonal to make this a whole number [for example, 5 stitches] or a half [for example, 5.5, which would mean *adding 6 stitches once, adding 5 stitches once, repeat from *].)

Pattern

notes The short side is the side that is shorter when looking at the piece with RS facing. (In the drawing, it's the right edge of the front and the left edge of the back). I know we usually refer to right and left "as worn," but in this case it's easier to refer to them as we see them in our drawings.

If you're starting with a bottom band, you probably should not cast on with smaller needles or fewer stitches because this hem needs a soft and loose band.

You will probably slip the first stitch purlwise after the turn, and you may work a wrap (which you may work or leave alone on the following row), but this pattern's short-row directions simply say "turn."

- Cast on #stitches for the hem.
- After the cast-on (or completion of the band), you may have to work 1 row over all stitches before beginning the short rows.
- If the short side is the left edge of this piece (the back, in the drawing), be ready to work a RS row, then work the next 4 steps.
- **First RS short row** Work #stitches in first short row (step 3); turn.
- **WS rows** Work in pattern.
- **All following RS short rows** Work to the "break" + #stitches in next short row; turn. (You will see the break: it's the place at which you worked your last short-row turn, and it's very visible.)
- The diagonal shape is complete when all stitches are brought into working and all rows of the diagonal (step 1) have been worked.
- If the short side is the right edge of this piece (the front in the drawing), be ready to work a WS row, then work the next 4 steps.
- **First WS short row** Work #stitches in first short row (step 3); turn.
- **RS rows** Work in pattern.
- **All following WS short rows** Work to the "break" + #stitches in the next short row; turn. (You will see the break: it's the place at which you worked your last short-row turn, and it's very visible.)
- The diagonal shape is complete when all stitches are brought into working and all rows of the diagonal (step 1) have been worked.

Standard Shirttails

A shirttail is a curve that, like the diagonal, can be worked into any basic style and is flattering—offering no horizontal that is a clear measure of the hips. Unlike the diagonal, it is usually symmetrical—with the same curve on each side of center—and I will assume so through what follows.

To understand a shirttail, it helps to understand a curve as a shape formed with a large number of stitches in its base, and the rest "worked"—perhaps in even increments, perhaps not—until all stitches are included. (I use the ambiguous term *worked* because a curve can be formed by casting on or by bringing stitches into working.) For the shirttail directions that follow, I suggest that you bring stitches into working with short rows.

But there is huge variation in curves and, therefore, shirttails. It could be shallow (lots of stitches at its base, subsequent stitches worked in large numbers), or it could be tall (not so many stitches in its base, subsequent stitches worked in smaller and smaller numbers, ending with many worked one at a time.) The two drawings at right show both possibilities. (And you might find it helpful to draw out your shape as is done in these drawings—with stair steps that express the number of stitches worked each time.)

Measurements You Need

You need to know the *height of the shirttail*—that is, the difference between its low front and short sides. This style has a broad range—from 2″ (5cm) to 6″ (15cm).

You also need the number of *stitches in its base,* approximately half the stitches of the hem for a medium–tall shirttail and more for a shallow one.

shirttails

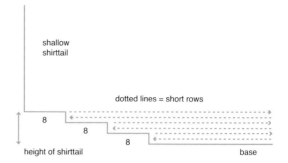

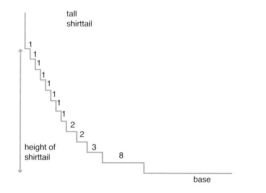

#stitches/inch (2.5cm) = _____
#rows/inch (2.5cm) = _____
#stitches in front/back at hem = _____
height of shirttail = _____ inches (cm)

1. #stitches in base of shirttail _____ (Make this odd or even, whichever matches the #stitches in hem.)
2. (#stitches in hem – #stitches in base) ÷ 2 = #stitches in each curve _____ (Make this a whole number.)
3. #rows/inch (2.5cm) × height of shirttail = #rows in shirttail _____ (Make this an even number.)
4. #rows in shirttail ÷ 2 = #short-row opportunities for stitches of each curve _____

5. Write a series of numbers that add up to #stitches in each curve (step 2) and that represent how you might bring those stitches into working _____ (No number should be larger than the one that precedes it. In the sample drawings, 8, 8, 8 is shown for the drawing on the top or 8, 3, 2, 2, 1, 1, 1, 1, 1, 1, 1, 1 is shown for the drawing on the bottom.)
6. Count how many numbers are in the list of step 5 _____ (in the samples, 3 or 12)
7. Revise the series in step 5 until the number in step 6 is the same as that in step 4. (You can change #stitches at the base or any other number.) Record your final series here. _____

Pattern

notes A shirttail does not need a band: you may just bring stitches into working from a cast-on edge. But sometimes we choose to start with a band: the best choices are garter, reverse stockinette, or rib.

If you're starting with a band, you should not use smaller needles or fewer stitches, because this shape needs a soft band to reach around its curve. If your shirttail is shallow, you may simply cast on for your band, knowing that a soft band will stretch around your shallow curve. But if your shirttail is not shallow, you will need more stitches in the band so it can stretch around your taller curve, so read Special Instructions for Bands on Taller Curves (page 82) before working your pattern. And if your band is ribbed, you need to read Additional Instructions for Ribbed Bands on Shirttails (page 83) before working your pattern.

You will probably slip the first stitch purlwise after the turn, and you may work a wrap (which you may work or leave alone on the following row), but this pattern's short-row directions simply say "turn."

- Cast on #stitches for hem.
- After the cast-on (or completion of the band), be ready to work a RS row. Cut yarn.
- With RS facing, slip #stitches in the curve (step 2), to arrive at the base.
- **First RS short row** Work #stitches in base; turn.
- **First WS short row** Work #stitches in base + first #stitches in series of step 7; turn.
- **Next RS short row** Work to the "break" + first #stitches in series of step 7; turn. (You will see the break: it's the place at which you worked your last short-row turn, and it's very visible.) Remember that every number in the series must be worked on both a RS and WS row.
- **All following short rows** Work to the "break" + next #stitches in series of step 7; turn.
- Shirttail is complete after a RS row, when all stitches are brought into working and after #rows in the shirttail (step 3) have been worked.

Special Instructions for Bands on Taller Curves

If your curve is not shallow, the band needs more stitches than the garment itself (to stretch around the curve): look at the difference between the length of the bold lines in the drawing below. For this band, three questions arise: What stitch patterns are appropriate? How many more stitches are required? Do these stitches need special treatment?

shirttail bands / #stitches

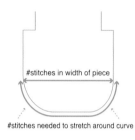

#stitches in width of piece

#stitches needed to stretch around curve

In answer to the first question, any stitch pattern you'd use for a bottom band is appropriate. A ribbed band on a shirttail is a nice choice, but it needs even more work: see Additional Instructions for Ribbed Bands on Shirttails after you work through this section.

In answer to the second question, let's recognize that the shirttail is a curve. And the best method for picking up and knitting around a curve is to pick up and knit

- 1 stitch for every stitch
- plus 1 stitch for every 2-row step (to get the extra stitches that a curve demands).

But we are working short rows, so instead of the 2-row step of a bind-off we'll have a short-row turn. So the adjusted #stitches for the band is

- #stitches in hem _____ (equivalent to 1 stitch for every stitch) + #short rows (which is the same as #rows in the height of the curve because every row is one turn) = _____.

But, can you simply cast on that number of stitches and start working? No . . . for two reasons—and now on to the answer to whether or not these stitches need special treatment.

Look at the drawings at top right. A band is perpendicular to the piece it is knit against—and that clearly is not going to work here—because the edges of

shirttails

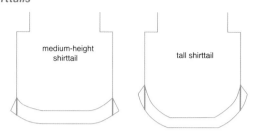

medium-height shirttail

tall shirttail

the band need to run continuously with the side seams. So by looking at the bold lines, note that the number of stitches just calculated (to fit around the curve) is the number of stitches needed at the completion of the band—not for the cast-on edge of the band, which looks like it requires somewhat fewer. Therefore, fewer stitches need to be cast on, and increases need to be made before the completion of the band.

How often do those increases need to be made?

For a medium-height shirttail (as shown at left in the drawing above), increasing at each end of every alternate row works. To increase at each end of each alternate row means you will increase 2 stitches every 2 rows, which means that the number of increases is the same as the number of rows in the band. So for a medium-tall curve, the #stitches to cast on is

- #stitches in front/back at hem + #short rows = _____ (as worked earlier)
- minus #rows in band (because we'll make the same #increases as there are rows in the band) = _____

For a tall shirttail (as shown to right in the drawing above), increasing at each end of every row works. To increase at each end of every row means you will increase 2 stitches every row, which means that the number of stitches to be increased is twice the number of rows in the band. For a tall curve, the #stitches to cast on is

- #stitches in front/back at hem + #short rows = _____ (as worked earlier)
- minus (#rows in band × 2) (because we'll make 2 increases for every row of the band) = _____

Is there anything else? Oh yes, when we finish the band, we'll have too many stitches because we will have the #stitches in the garment with the addition of the extra stitches to stretch around the curve—one extra stitch at each short-row turn. When we move from the band to the body of the garment, we need to get rid of those additional stitches. So after working the base stitches, and as we bring the stitches of the curve into working, at every short-row turn we will have one more stitch than we need so will work 2 stitches together each time. Here are some examples.

- When bringing 8 stitches into working, work 2 together, then work 7.
- When bringing 3 stitches into working, work 2 together, then work 2.
- When bringing 2 stitches into working, work 2 together, then work 1.
- When bringing 1 stitch into working, work 2 together.

note We say *work* (in *work 2 together*) because we don't know if you are on a RS or WS row or what your stitch pattern is.

Additional Instructions for Ribbed Bands on Shirttails

A ribbed band is a nice choice for a shaped piece, but it needs extra attention.

- Always have RS knits define your shape. This means that in 1x1 rib you'll start and end with one RS knit: if you're working 2x2 rib, you'll start and end with 2 RS knits. (In 1x1 rib, I seam up the center of the edge knit stitches; in 2x2 rib, I take 1 knit stitch from each side into the seam allowance.)
- If the shirttail band demands increases, maintain the integrity of these "defining" RS knit stitches (by increasing next to but never in them). Your rib will be "wrong" 2 rows out of 4, so you need to decide whether to be wrong with extra RS purl or extra RS knit stitches. Be consistent.
- When decreasing between the band and the body (to get rid of those extra stitches for the curve), always work 2 together from the rib so that the rib's RS knit stitches sit on top of the rib's RS purl stitches. (This will be clear when you have knitting in hand.)

Reverse Shirttails

This shape is less common than the previous, but I think it works in any basic style. And I've found myself combining the two shirttails with wonderful results: a shorter front (reverse shirttail) can make us look taller,

shirttails

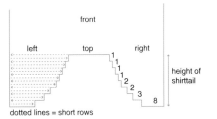

dotted lines = short rows

and the longer back (standard shirttail) can cover anything we want covered. And since this combination is the most common way for this shape to be worked, what follows is dedicated to a reverse shirttail at the front only. (The back hem could be worked straight or as a standard shirttail.) I cannot envision a reverse shirttail on the back, but if you're working one, you might make sure the short part of the back hem does not ride just above your backside—thereby framing it. My preference is a shirttail cutting across the center of it, making it look smaller.

Like the standard shirttail, this is a curve, and I prefer to work it with stitches brought into working with short rows. But this time the flat part of the curve is at its top. (It helps to draw out your shape as in the drawing above—with stair steps that express the number of stitches worked each time.) And while I have shown these stair steps with a progression of smaller numbers (8, 3, 2, 1), you could alter this order a little by ending with slightly larger numbers (8, 3, 2, 1, 2, 3). This would flatten out the top of the curve. Again, I suggest that you draw this out to see how to get the shape you want.

Measurements You Need

You need to know the *height of the reverse shirttail*—the difference between its high front and longer sides. I've made most of mine between 3″ (7.5cm) and 6″ (15cm).

You'll also need to know the number of stitches in its center top; I recommend ⅓ the stitches in the hem.

Front with Reverse Shirttail
Calculations

#stitches/inch (2.5cm) = _____
#rows/inch (2.5cm) = _____
#stitches in front/back at hem = _____
height of reverse shirttail = _____ inches (cm)

1. #stitches in flat top of reverse shirttail _____
   (Make this odd or even, whichever matches the
   #stitches in the hem.)
2. (#stitches in hem – #stitches in top of reverse shirttail)
   ÷ 2 = #stitches in each curve _____ (Make this a
   whole number.)
3. #rows/inch (2.5cm) × height of shirttail = #rows
   in reverse shirttail _____ (Make this an even
   number.)

4. #rows in shirttail ÷ 2 = #short-row opportunities for
   stitches of each curve _____
5. Write a series of numbers that add up to #stitches
   in each curve (step 2) and that represent how
   you might bring these stitches into working
   _____ (Sample drawing shows
   8, 3, 2, 2, 1, 1, 1, 1.)
6. Count how many numbers are in the list of step 5
   _____ (in the sample, 8)
7. Revise the series of step 5 until the number in step 6
   is the same as in step 4. (You can change #stitches
   at the base or any other number.) Record your final
   series here. _____

Pattern

notes You might assume that the band on the reverse
shirttail would have the same complications as the
shirttail—that a tall curve would be difficult to stretch
around and might need more stitches. But that's not
necessarily the case. The reverse shirttail mostly
expresses the inside edge of a curve, so it may not need
more stitches to stretch around the shape. If it's shallow,
you may use the same number of stitches and simply
• work from your cast-on edge
• or work from a minimal band (½″ [13mm] or less)—
  which could be worked on smaller needles.

But if your shape has a steep area (a large number
of 1-stitch-brought-into-working), you may need more
stitches over that area—one for every stitch and one for
every short-row turn. See Special Instructions for Bands
on Taller Curves, page 82. This will help you see how many
more stitches you need and how to get rid of them when
you move from the band to the body of the garment.

The right front is the right part of the garment when
looking at it with RS facing (see drawing on page 83). I
know we usually refer to right and left "as worn," but in
this instance it's easier to refer to them as we see them
in our drawings.

You will probably slip the first stitch purlwise after the
turn, and you may work a wrap (which you may work or
leave alone in the next row), but this pattern's short-row
directions only say "turn."

The following pattern assumes the same #stitches in
the band as the front/back.

• Cast on #stitches for hem.
• After the cast-on (or the completion of the band), be
  ready to work a RS row.
• **First RS short row** Work first #stitches in series of step
  7; turn.
• **WS rows** Work in pattern.
• **All following RS short rows** Work to the "break" + the
  next #stitches in the series of step 7; turn. (You will see
  the break: it's the place at which you worked your last
  short-row turn, and it's very visible.)
• Right front is complete after a RS row, when all
  stitches of one curve have been brought into working.
  Cut the yarn.
• Slip all stitches onto 1 needle, ready to work a WS row
  over the curve of the left front.
• **First WS short row** Work first #stitches in series of step
  7; turn.

- **RS rows** Work in pattern.
- **All following WS short rows** Work to the "break" + next #stitches in series of step 7; turn.
- Left front is complete after a WS row, when all stitches of one curve have been brought into working; turn.
- Work 1 RS row over stitches of left front.

- **Next WS row** Work over stitches of left front curve, then over stitches for top of curve, then over stitches of right front curve. Reverse shirttail is complete when all stitches are brought into working and #rows in step 3 have been worked.

Chapter 5

Side Shaping

Straight sides were put into the garments through the Basic Shapes work of chapter 2. Now we can consider alternatives: A-line, hourglass, and half-hourglass shaping. Again, if you look at the chart for which shapes combine well (page 20), you'll see my opinion about what works with what. I'll explain why some combinations may not work in the sections addressing them, but that is not to suggest that you won't discover alternate possibilities.

Through the calculations of this chapter, here's what we assume.

- Front and back are the same width.
- Front and back are the same length where they meet at their side seams. (If not, work separate calculations for each one whenever length is part of the equation.)
- The hem is straight. (If you're working a shaped hem, see the last section in this chapter, page 101.)
- Side shaping ends at the armhole (so circumference at bust = circumference at armhole).
- The neck does not begin until after side shaping—which ends at the armhole. (A very deep V-neck could begin before the armhole. If so, you'll work to neck depth—not armhole depth—then continue with side shaping *at the same time* as neck shaping. This might be a complication to avoid.)

A-Line

A-lines are wider at the hem than the bust, and this makes them universally attractive. (Since our hips are supposed to be bigger anyway, doesn't it make sense to shape this way? The narrowing also brings the eye in as it travels from hem to bust—all good stuff!) This shape is a simple alternative to straight sides that I hope you'll try—because it is not difficult.

While usually knit in more fitted styles (set-in sleeve or close-fitting raglan with bust + standard ease or less), an A-line can be added to the sides of a less-shaped garment—a modified drop shoulder—because it has a defined armhole at which this shaping would end. And this is best done if its armhole depth is toward its

shallower possibilities. (Can you envision why an A-line knit to a deep armhole is not a common choice? Or why A-line shaping wouldn't be appropriate for a drop shoulder?)

Shaping an A-Line at the Sides Only

The simplest way to shape an A-line is to decrease at the sides while working from hem to bust. But if we simply do that, the sides of the garment may droop. However, if the garment is long (that is, it has lots of rows between those decreases) and/or there aren't huge differences in the number of stitches between the hem and the bust, the droop is minimal. In addition, if the stitch pattern is complex, we might just let 'er droop (because the solutions for a droopy hem that appear in the next section won't apply). So we'll first work through the simple version, with shaping at the sides only, before offering alternatives to disguise a droopy hem.

Measurements You Need

You need to know your *garment's finished length*, your armhole depth, and your shoulder-shaping depth (if working shoulder shaping). These were all discussed in chapters 2 and 3.

You need to know your *garment's circumferences* at bust (which, for this shape, is usually bust + standard ease or less) and at hem (which can vary tremendously). I would suggest that a minimum hem circumference might be bust circumference + 6″ (15cm), but it could be much greater. From these circumferences you'll work out your front/back widths at hem and bust.

A-line / droopy hems

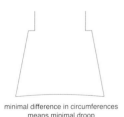

minimal difference in circumferences means minimal droop

greater difference in circumferences means a droopy hem

While these hems will look straight when knit, this drawing shows how they will look when worn.

A-line / shaping at sides only

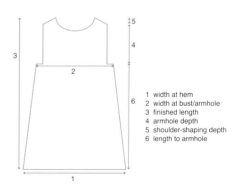

1 width at hem
2 width at bust/armhole
3 finished length
4 armhole depth
5 shoulder-shaping depth
6 length to armhole

A-Line Shaping at Sides Only
Calculations

#stitches/inch (2.5cm) = _____
#rows/inch (2.5cm) = _____
your girth at bust + ease = circumference at bust = _____ inches (cm)
circumference at hem = _____ inches (cm)
front/back finished length = _____ inches (cm)
height of bottom band (if you have one) = _____ inches (cm)
armhole depth = _____ inches (cm)
shoulder-shaping depth = _____ inches (cm)

1. (#stitches/inch [2.5cm] × circumference at hem) ÷ 2 = #stitches in front/back at hem _____
2. Do you need to fudge for a stitch pattern repeat?
3. Do you need to add selvedge stitches?
4. revised #stitches in front/back at hem = _____
5. (#stitches/inch [2.5cm] × circumference at bust) ÷ 2 = #stitches in front/back at bust _____

6. Do you need to fudge for a full stitch pattern repeat?
7. Do you need to add selvedge stitches?
8. revised #stitches in front/back at bust = _____ (This should be even or odd, whichever matches the #stitches in hem [step 4].)
9. (#stitches at hem – #stitches at bust) ÷ 2 = #stitches to be decreased at each side _____
10. finished length – height of bottom band – armhole depth – shoulder-shaping depth = length for decreases _____ inches (cm)
11. #rows/inch (2.5cm) × length for decreases = #rows for decreases _____ (Make this a whole number.)
12. #rows for decreases ÷ #stitches to be decreased at each side (step 9) = 1 stitch should be decreased at each side every _____ rows (Fudge as needed by dropping down to nearest even number.)

Pattern

note If you have a bottom band, it is assumed that the #stitches in the bottom band is the same as the #stitches in the front/back width.

- Cast on #stitches in step 4.
- After cast-on (or completion of bottom band), work #rows of step 12. End after working a WS row.

- **Decrease row (RS)** Work selvedge, decrease, work to the last 3 stitches, decrease, work selvedge.
- Repeat decrease row as often as calculated in step 12 until #stitches in step 8 remain.
- Work even to length of step 10 above cast-on or bottom band. End after working a WS row.
- Finish garment with work of chapters 2 and 3.

Solutions for a Droopy Hem

If the number of stitches to be decreased is large and the number of rows between decreases is few, the hem will droop. To minimize this, choose one of the following options.

- Decrease at the sides only, but disguise the droopy hem by shaping it—with a diagonal hem or with shirttails on both front and back or with a shirttail on the back and a reverse shirttail on the front. (If you do any of these, read Side Shaping at the Same Time As Hem Shaping, page 101).
- Work shaping by changing stitch patterns and/or needle sizes. (This requires lots of swatching and has limitless possibilities so it's not covered here.)
- Work shaping by decreasing in more than two places. (Decreasing in four places is the classic solution and offered in the following section.)

Shaping an A-Line in Four Places

Decreasing for an A-line shape in four places is a classic style that will produce a straight hem, but it does demand a stitch pattern that will accommodate decreases in the middle of rows. (If this is not your situation, consider the other solutions.)

Measurements You Need

You need to know your garment's finished length, your armhole depth, and your shoulder-shaping depth (if working shoulder shaping).

As with the shaping in two places, you need to know your *garment's circumferences* at bust (which for this shape is usually bust + standard ease or less) and at hem (which could certainly be greater than the minimum 6″ [15cm] established in the previous sample). From these circumferences you'll work out your front/back widths at hem and bust.

In addition, you need to know where to put those extra decreases—the ones that aren't at the side seams. Unless you have a stitch pattern that dictates otherwise, I'd suggest they should be in line with your *bust width*—like vertical darts. So measure yourself between breasts.

A-line / shaping in four places

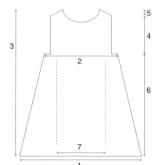

1 width at hem
2 width at bust/armhole
3 finished length
4 armhole depth
5 shoulder-shaping depth
6 length to armhole
7 distance between
  center decreases

A-Line Shaping in Four Places
Calculations

Go to Calculations for A-Line Shaping at Sides Only (page 89). Use all those measurements plus the following one.

measurement between breasts = _____ inches (cm).

Work steps 1–8 of Calculations for A-Line Shaping at Sides Only—then continue with the following 6 steps.

9. (#stitches in front/back at hem – #stitches in front/back at bust) ÷ 4 = #stitches to be decreased in 4 places _____ (This needs to be a whole number, so fudge as needed.)

10. finished length – height of bottom band – armhole depth – shoulder-shaping depth = length for decreases _____ inches (cm)

11. #rows/inch (2.5cm) × length for decreases = #rows for decreases _____ (Make this a whole number.)

12. #rows for decreases ÷ #stitches to be decreased in 4 places (step 9) = 1 stitch should be decreased at each side and on each side of center panel every _____ rows (Fudge as needed by dropping down to the nearest even number.)

13. #stitches/inch (2.5cm) × measurement between breasts = #stitches in center panel _____ (Make this a whole number—even or odd—the same as steps 4 and 8.)

14. (#stitches in hem – #stitches in center panel) ÷ 2 = #stitches between side edge and center panel at hem _____

Pattern

note If you have a bottom band, it is assumed that the #stitches in the bottom band is the same as the #stitches in the front/back width.

- Cast on #stitches of step 4.
- After cast-on (or completion of bottom band), and before the first decrease, work one row as follows: work #stitches between side edge and center panel (step 14); place marker; work #stitches in center panel (step 13); place marker; work to end.
- Continue to #rows of step 12 above cast-on or bottom band. End after working a WS row.

- **Decrease row (RS)** Work selvedge, decrease, work to 2 stitches before marker, decrease; work stitches of center panel and to next marker, decrease, work to the last 3 stitches, decrease, work selvedge.
- Repeat decrease row as often as calculated in step 12 until #stitches in step 8 remain.
- Work even to length of step 10 above cast-on or bottom band. End after working a WS row.
- Finish garment with work of chapters 2 and 3.

Hourglass

The hourglass is the archetypical female shape—wider at the hips and bust than at the waist. Some of us still have our youthful hourglasses intact; others have a more mature version. But whatever your shape, a sweater with hourglass shaping looks good on almost everyone and can be worn with almost anything, so we should all find ways to draft, knit, and wear it.

You could make a big sweater into an hourglass by simply belting it: so any style, knit to any ease, could potentially be "hourglassed." But if you are high-waisted or large-busted, you'd never belt a big sweater, and you'd still like the option of the hourglass shape in a big sweater. So what about a big sweater with some sort of pull-in at the waist? (This probably would not be a drop shoulder, but it could be a modified drop shoulder or a loose-fitting raglan.) Could this be done?

The good news is that this can be done very easily and at the completion of the garment. How? With a front pleat (see page 164). You don't draft the shape in: you try it on and pull the garment to an hourglass shape after it's knit! You'll decide if you want the pleat, how big to make it, and how to decorate it.

But most hourglass garments have the shape knit into them, and these are usually knit in fitted styles (the set-in sleeve or close-fitting raglan with bust + standard ease or less). An hourglass can be added to the sides of a less-shaped garment—a modified drop shoulder—because it has a defined armhole at which this shaping would end. But this is best done if its armhole depth is toward the shallower possibilities.

Somehow I don't envision an hourglass knit into the larger and less-fitted drop shoulder.

Measurements You Need

You need to know your garment's *finished length*, and the following paragraphs explain how this length influences the garment's circumference at the hem.

Other length measurements you need are armhole depth and shoulder-shaping depth (if you're working shoulder shaping).

The other length measurement you need is your *waist length*. The garment's waist length is measured from the tallest part of the shoulder seam down to where the garment has been decreased to its waist circumference. And you'll notice in the drawing at right

that after these decreases the waist area is worked even, without shaping, for 2″ (5cm) or more, before it begins to increase for the bust. (See pages 25–26 for a further discussion of waist length).

For the hourglass, we need to know three girth measurements:

- circumference at hem
- circumference at bust
- circumference at waist.

As usual, we will use these to work out our front/back widths at hem, waist, and bust.

For the *garment's circumferences* at hem and circumference at bust, your girth + standard ease is commonly used. But while it's easy to know your bust measurement, is the circumference at hem always a function of your hip measurement? Here is where finished length comes into play.

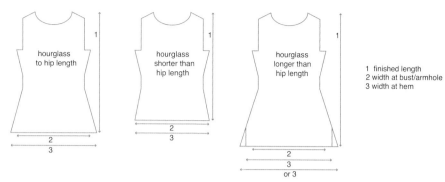

1 finished length
2 width at bust/armhole
3 width at hem

If your garment's finished length ends at the widest part of your hips, you need your hip girth (which is usually larger than your bust), and you will add ease (probably standard ease or less) to that. But if the garment's finished length falls shorter than your hips, you should be able to make the garment the same circumference at the hem as at the bust. And if your garment's finished length falls longer than your hips, you have two choices.

- Knit straight up from the hem to where you want side shaping to begin (a true hourglass shape).
- Make the hem wider below the hips and make the shaping continuous from hem to waist—like an extended A-line. (This will mean a hem circumference larger than your hips + standard ease.)

But what about that third measurement—the *garment's circumference at waist*? Even though our bodies are supposed to have an 8″ (20.5cm) differential between waist and bust, and a 10″ (25.5cm) differential between waist and hips, this shape is beautifully accomplished with only half that differential shaped into the garment. This is good news for those of us without our youthful hourglasses intact, and it means the following.

- Waist circumference needs to be only 4″ (10cm) narrower than bust circumference.
- Waist circumference needs to be only 5″ (12.5cm) narrower than hip circumference (if the garment falls to the widest part of your hips or longer).

If you don't have this much differential between your hips and waist, you can still create this style by making your garment's circumference larger than it needs to be at your hips, then narrowing in to give yourself a waist.

Hourglass Shaping with Waistband Only

Before working through a Classic Hourglass (which follows), there is a simple execution of this shape to explore—just "knitting in" the shape by working a waistband area in a stitch pattern that gets a tighter gauge than the stitch pattern of the garment (perhaps ribbing), which might also be worked on smaller needles than the rest of the garment.

Measurements You Need

You need all the measurements discussed on the previous page: finished length, armhole depth, shoulder-shaping depth (if you're working shoulder shaping), waist length, plus height of waist area worked even.

hourglass / waistband only

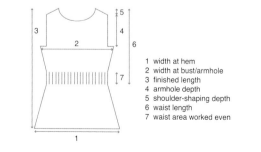

1 width at hem
2 width at bust/armhole
3 finished length
4 armhole depth
5 shoulder-shaping depth
6 waist length
7 waist area worked even

We don't need a *waist circumference*, because we know this work will draw the garment in by at least the 4–5″ (10–12.5cm) we want. (If it narrows more than that, we can steam-press or block it wider.)

And for *circumference at hem and bust*, apply one of the following:

- *If your garment starts at the widest part of the hips,* your hem's circumference will be larger than your bust circumference: work all steps that follow.
- *If your garment is shorter than hip length,* your hem's circumference may be the same as your bust circumference: work as below but without inserting your girth measurement at hips, without calculating steps 5–8, and without the decrease row of the pattern.

• .... •

Hourglass Shaping with Waistband Only

Calculations

#stitches/inch (2.5cm) = _____
#rows/inch (2.5cm) = _____
your girth at bust + ease = circumference at bust _____ inches (cm)
your girth at hips + ease = circumference at hem _____ inches (cm)
waist length = _____ inches (cm)
length of waist area worked even = _____ inches (cm) (usually 2″ [5cm] or more)
front/back finished length = _____ inches (cm)
armhole depth = _____ inches (cm)
shoulder-shaping depth = _____ inches (cm)

1. (#stitches/inch [2.5cm] × circumference at hem) ÷ 2 = #stitches in front/back hem _____
2. Do you need to fudge for a stitch pattern repeat?
3. Do you need to add selvedge stitches?
4. revised #stitches in front/back at hem = _____
5. (#stitches/inch [2.5cm] × circumference at bust) ÷ 2 = #stitches in front/back at bust_____
6. Do you need to fudge for a stitch pattern repeat?
7. Do you need to add selvedge stitches?
8. revised #stitches in front/back at bust = _____ (This can be even or odd, whichever matches the #stitches in step 4.)
9. finished length – waist length = length to waist _____ inches (cm)
10. finished length – armhole depth – shoulder-shaping depth = length to armhole _____ inches (cm)

Pattern

note If you have a bottom band, it is assumed that the #stitches in the bottom band is the same as the #stitches in the front/back width.

- Cast on #stitches in step 4.
- After cast-on (or completion of bottom band), work stitch pattern to length of step 9. End after working a WS row.
- Change to smaller needles, and work tighter stitch pattern to height of waist area worked even.
- **Decrease row** Decrease evenly across row to #stitches in step 8.
- Return to larger needles. Work even in stitch pattern to length of step 10 above cast-on or bottom band. End after working a WS row.
- Finish garment pattern with work of chapters 2 and 3.

• .... •

Classic Hourglass

A classic hourglass has decreases from hem to waist, increases from waist to bust, and is usually shaped in four places—at the sides and through the center. If your stitch pattern will not accommodate shaping in the middle of rows, or if you want a diagonal or reverse shirttail hem (that would make decreasing in four places a bit of a nightmare), you may shape only at the sides but twice as often as the following calculations suggest. (For example, if the following calculations say to decrease in four places every 12 rows, you'll decrease only at the sides but every 6 rows.)

By the way, it is perfectly appropriate to decrease at the sides only. Bordered Lace (shown on page 96) was worked this way because of its stitch pattern.

Measurements You Need

You need all the measurements discussed on pages 92–93: finished length, armhole depth, shoulder-shaping depth (if you're working shoulder shaping), waist length, height of waist area worked even, circumference at hem and/or circumference at bust, and circumference at waist.

In addition, you need to know where to put those extra decreases—the ones that aren't at the side seams. Unless you have a stitch pattern that dictates otherwise, I'd suggest they should be in line with your *bust width*—like vertical darts. So measure yourself between breasts.

hourglass / classic

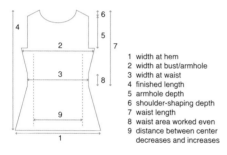

1 width at hem
2 width at bust/armhole
3 width at waist
4 finished length
5 armhole depth
6 shoulder-shaping depth
7 waist length
8 waist area worked even
9 distance between center decreases and increases

Classic Hourglass (Shaping in Four Places)
Calculations

#stitches/inch (2.5cm) = _____
#rows/inch (2.5cm) = _____
your girth at bust + ease = circumference at bust _____ inches (cm)
your girth at hips + ease = circumference at hem _____ inches (cm). If your garment falls above the widest part of your hips, you don't need this measurement: circumference at hem can be the same circumference at bust.)
circumference at waist (usually 4″ [10cm] less than circumference at bust) = _____ inches (cm)
measurement between breasts = _____ inches (cm)
waist length = _____ inches (cm)
length of waist area worked even = _____ inches (cm) (usually 2″ [5cm] or more)
front/back finished length = _____ inches (cm)
height of bottom band (if you have one) = _____ inches (cm)
armhole depth = _____ inches (cm)
shoulder-shaping depth = _____ inches (cm)

Hem to Waist

1. (#stitches/inch [2.5cm] × circumference at hem) ÷ 2 = #stitches in front/back at hem _____
2. Do you need to fudge for a stitch pattern repeat?
3. Do you need to add selvedge stitches?
4. revised #stitches in front/back at hem = _____
5. (#stitches/inch [2.5cm] × circumference at waist) ÷ 2 = #stitches in front/back at waist _____
6. Do you need to add selvedge stitches?
7. revised #stitches in front/back at waist = _____ (We don't bother with a stitch pattern repeat here, but make this odd or even—the same as #stitches in step 4.)
8. (#stitches in hem – #stitches at waist) ÷ 4 = #stitches to be decreased in 4 places _____ (This needs to be a whole number, so fudge as needed.)
9. finished length – waist length – height of bottom band = length for decreases _____ inches (cm)
10. #rows/inch (2.5cm) × length for decreases = #rows for decreases _____ (Make this a whole number.)

11. #rows for decreases ÷ #stitches to be decreased (step 8) = 1 stitch should be decreased at each side and on each side of center panel every _____ rows from hem to waist (Fudge as needed by dropping down to the nearest even number.)

Waist to Armhole

12. (#stitches/inch [2.5cm] × circumference at bust) ÷ 2 = #stitches in front/back at bust _____
13. Do you need to fudge for a stitch repeat?
14. Do you need to add selvedge stitches?
15. revised #stitches at bust = _____ (This may be even or odd, but it needs to be the same choice as step 4.)
16. (#stitches at bust – #stitches at waist [step 7]) ÷ 4 = #stitches to be increased in 4 places _____ (This needs to be a whole number, so fudge as needed.)
17. Waist length – height of waist area worked even – armhole depth – shoulder-shaping depth = length from top of waist to armhole _____ inches (cm)
18. #rows/inch (2.5cm) × length from top of waist to armhole = #rows for increases _____ (Make this a whole number.)
19. #rows for increases ÷ #stitches to be increased (step 16) = 1 stitch should be increased at each side and on each side of center panel every _____ rows from waist to armhole (Fudge as needed by dropping down to nearest even number.)

Center Panel

20. #stitches/inch (2.5cm) × measurement between breasts = #stitches in center panel _____ (Make this a whole number and even or odd, whichever matches the #stitches in step 4.)
21. (#stitches in hem – #stitches in center panel) ÷ 2 = #stitches between side edge and center panel at hem _____

Length

22. finished length – armhole depth – shoulder-shaping depth = length to armhole _____ inches (cm)

Pattern

note If you have a bottom band, it is assumed that the #stitches in the bottom band is the same as the #stitches in the front/back width.

- Cast on #stitches in step 4.
- Above cast-on (or completion of bottom band), and before the first decrease, work 1 row as follows: work #stitches between side edge and center panel (step 21); place marker; work #stitches in center panel (step 20); place marker; work to end.
- Continue to #rows of step 11 above cast-on or bottom band. End after working a WS row.
- **Decrease row (RS)** Work selvedge, decrease, work to 2 stitches before marker, decrease; work stitches of center panel and to next marker, decrease, work to the last 3 stitches, decrease, work selvedge.

- Repeat decrease row as often as calculated in step 11 until #stitches in step 7 remain.
- Work even to end of waist area. End after working a WS row.
- **Increase row (RS)** Work selvedge, increase 1 in next stitch, work to stitch before marker, increase 1 in next stitch, work stitches of center panel and to marker, increase 1 in next stitch, work to the last 2 stitches, increase 1 in next stitch, work selvedge.
- Repeat increases as often as calculated in step 19 to #stitches in step 15.
- Work even to length of step 22 above cast-on or bottom band. End after working a WS row.
- Finish garment pattern with work of chapters 2 and 3.

Half-Hourglass

The half-hourglass is the top half of the hourglass—a narrower hem widening to the bust. And like the hourglass, it is successfully worked in a fitted style (a set-in sleeve or raglan). But a looser version (not as tight to the body) could also be worked in a less-fitted style (a modified drop shoulder). It's probably not appropriate for a drop shoulder.

Measurements You Need

You need to know your garment's *finished length*—which can vary according to how tightly the garment fits: if making a looser version of this shape, finished length might be to the balance point; if making a tighter version, finished length would probably be to the waist. Can you see why you might not make this shape longer, falling onto the hips?

In addition, you need your armhole depth and shoulder-shaping depth (if you're working shoulder shaping).

You need both your *circumferences* at hem and bust (and, as usual, front/back widths will be worked

from these circumferences). Whatever your garment's style, this shape does not need to hug tight to the body, so a differential of 4–5″ (10–12.5cm) between the circumferences of the hem and bust is sufficient to show the shape. (If you made a pullover with more of a differential, you might need a zipper to get it on!)

Because this differential is not very large, and because the hem sits close to the body, we don't worry about a droopy hem: increasing at the sides only is fine.

half-hourglass

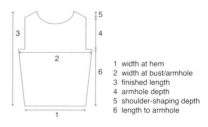

1 width at hem
2 width at bust/armhole
3 finished length
4 armhole depth
5 shoulder-shaping depth
6 length to armhole

Half-Hourglass Shaping
Calculations

#stitches/inch (2.5cm) = _____
#rows/inch (2.5cm) = _____
your girth at bust + ease = circumference at bust =
_____ inches (cm)
circumference at hem = _____ inches (cm)
(This is usually circumference at bust – 4–5″ [10–12.5cm]
or less.)
front/back finished length = _____ inches (cm)
height of bottom band (if you have one) = _____
inches (cm)
armhole depth = _____ inches (cm)
shoulder-shaping depth = _____ inches (cm)

1. (#stitches/inch [2.5cm] × circumference at hem) ÷ 2 =
   #stitches in front/back at hem _____
2. Do you need to fudge for a stitch pattern repeat?
3. Do you need to add selvedge stitches?
4. revised #stitches in front/back at hem = _____

5. (#stitches/inch [2.5cm] × circumference at bust) ÷ 2 =
   #stitches in front/back at bust _____
6. Do you want to end with a full stitch pattern repeat?
7. Do you need to add selvedge stitches?
8. revised #stitches in front/back at bust = _____
   (This may be even or odd, but it must be the same
   choice as step 4).
9. (#stitches at hem – #stitches at bust) ÷ 2 = #stitches
   to be increased at each side _____
10. finished length – height of bottom band – armhole
    depth – shoulder-shaping depth = length to armhole
    for increases _____ inches (cm)
11. #rows/inch (2.5cm) × length for increases = #rows for
    increases _____ (Make this a whole number.)
12. #rows for increases ÷ #stitches to be increased at
    each side (step 9) = 1 stitch should be increased at
    each side every _____ rows (Fudge as needed
    by dropping down to nearest even number.)

Pattern

note If you have a bottom band, it is assumed that
the #stitches in the bottom band is the same as the
#stitches in the front/back width.

- Cast on #stitches in step 4.
- After cast-on (or completion of bottom band), work
  #rows of step 12. End after working a WS row.
- **Increase row (RS)** Work selvedge, increase 1 in next
  stitch, work to the last 2 stitches, increase 1 in next
  stitch, work selvedge.

- Repeat increase row as often as calculated in step 12
  until #stitches in step 8 remain.
- Work even to length of step 10 above cast-on or
  bottom band. End after working a WS row.
- Finish garment pattern with work of chapters 2 and 3.

Side Shaping at the Same Time as Hem Shaping

It's not difficult to combine these shapes, although it's always made easier if you are not doing more than two things at once. For this reason, I would advise working diagonal or reverse shirttail hems along with an A-line or hourglass if it is shaped at the sides only.

Side Shaping with Diagonal Hem

For this, you will have a short side and a long side. And you will have fewer rows for side shaping on the short side.

- If you're shaping an A-line or the lower part of an hourglass at the same time as a diagonal hem, the short side is missing some decreases you would have made over the height of that side, so you need to "replace" those decreases by casting on fewer stitches than for a straight hem.
- If you're shaping a half-hourglass at the same time as a diagonal hem, the short side is missing some increases you would have made over the height of that side, so you need to "replace" those increases by casting on more stitches than for a straight hem.

The calculations for a diagonal hem plus side shaping are in the following three steps. These steps should be added to the end of your calculations for side shaping.

1. Enter finished length as measured along the long side.
2. #rows/inch (2.5cm) × height of diagonal = #rows for diagonal _____
3. *Working A-line or hourglass* #rows for diagonal ÷ how often decreases for A-line or hourglass shaping are made = #decreases you did not work on the short side of the diagonal _____ This is the same as how many fewer stitches you should cast on for your hem than if it were straight. (This needs to be a whole number, so fudge as needed.)
3. *Working half-hourglass* #rows for diagonal ÷ how often increases for half-hourglass shaping are made = #increases you did not work on the short side of the diagonal _____ This is the same as how many more stitches you should cast on for your hem than if it were straight. (This needs to be a whole number, so fudge as needed.)

Side Shaping with Standard Shirttail

This one is easy. Finish your hem shape, and then start your side shaping. They are, in fact, independent of each other.

Side Shaping with Reverse Shirttail

You will need to work hem shaping *at the same time* as side shaping. One way to simplify this would be to not start side shaping until after the hem shaping is completed.

side shaping + hem shaping

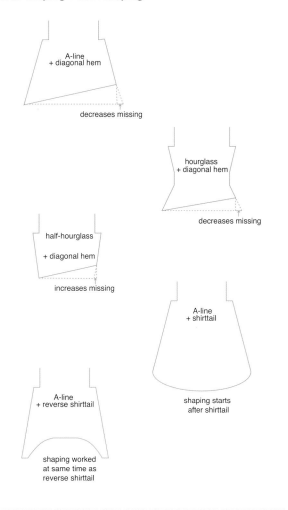

A-line + diagonal hem

decreases missing

hourglass + diagonal hem

decreases missing

half-hourglass + diagonal hem

increases missing

A-line + shirttail

shaping starts after shirttail

A-line + reverse shirttail

shaping worked at same time as reverse shirttail

Chapter 6

Sleeve Alternatives

The drafting of a standard sleeve—full-length, narrow at the cuff, appropriately fitted at the armhole—is included in the basic shapes of chapter 2. In this chapter are modifications to the sleeve—starting with no sleeve at all and ending with the sleeve that becomes the saddle-shoulder. The choices in this chapter will add facility to your drafting and versatility to your wardrobe.

Sleeveless

Any basic shape can be sleeveless. And there are many advantages to sleeveless garments: you don't have to knit the sleeves (duh!), they are appropriate for most indoor situations, you can change their style by what you wear underneath, . . . and you probably have other good reasons.

Measurements You Need

A sleeveless garment can be just the front and back of a garment without sleeves . . . except that some of our measurements need to be reconsidered. Will the garment have an armhole band, and how wide will it be? What do you plan to wear the garment with?

Without an Armhole Band

If your garment is knit in a stitch pattern that lies flat, the armhole edge will lie flat; if your garment is knit in a stitch pattern that rolls under, the armhole edge will roll under. Both of these will look finished without a band.

So without an armhole band, you may simply knit the front and back as drafted in chapter 2. You may just use your calculations and pattern from chapter 2, and we don't need additional instructions here. (The right edges of the drawings below show how your sleeveless garment will look if you make a front and back—from chapter 2—and don't add an armhole band.)

But before doing so, there are two things to reconsider:
- armhole depth
- shoulder shaping for the drop shoulder.

Your armhole depth needs to be appropriate for whatever you wish to wear under it: deep enough to accommodate a deep-armholed blouse or shallow enough to wear with no top underneath. For the drop shoulder, this armhole depth is determined by how high you sew the side seams: but for all other shapes, you might work to a revised armhole depth.

And if you make a sleeveless drop shoulder without shoulder shaping, it will have wings at the shoulder—where the shoulder seam does not lie flat on your shoulder. To solve that problem, work shoulder shaping over the last 2″ (5cm) of the garment's length (page 62).

With an Armhole Band

For any sleeveless garment, you need to reconsider armhole depth, because the garment needs to be deep enough to accommodate a deep-armholed blouse or shallow enough to wear with no top underneath. But when we add an armhole band, we see that—for the set-in sleeve and raglan—the width of the armhole band fills in some of our armhole depth: see the armhole bands at left in the drawing. (Note that the width of the band has no effect on the armhole depth of the drop or modified drop shoulder.)

In addition to filling in armhole depth for the set-in sleeve and raglan, you'll notice that the armhole band fills some of the shoulder width for three of these shapes. To allow for this, we do two things:
- increase the armhole bind-off
- draft the shoulder width narrower

You can see both of these in the armhole bands at left in the drawings, and these are both part of the following calculations.

sleeveless shapes

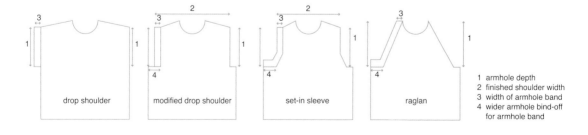

drop shoulder

modified drop shoulder

set-in sleeve

raglan

1 armhole depth
2 finished shoulder width
3 width of armhole band
4 wider armhole bind-off
for armhole band

Sleeveless with Armhole Bands
Calculations and Pattern

Work the calculations and pattern for your front and back as specified in chapter 2 but with the following changes.

- For the drop shoulder, work the front and back as specified but with shoulder shaping over the last 2″ (5cm) of the garment.
- For the set-in sleeve or raglan, determine your armhole depth but add the width of the band to that depth. (For example, if you want a 10″ [25.5cm] deep armhole, and your armhole band is 1″ [2.5cm] wide, then you must make your armhole depth 11″ [28cm].)
- For the modified drop shoulder, set-in sleeve, or raglan, for which you have a bind-off at the armhole, add the width of the band to that initial bind-off. (For example, at 5 stitches/inch [2.5cm], and a band width of 1″ [2.5cm], bind off 5 stitches more than the pattern suggests at the armhole.)
- For the set-in sleeve or modified drop shoulder, determine the shoulder width you want but subtract twice the width of the band from that width: you will shape the front/back to this narrower shoulder width, so after you add the bands you'll have the shoulder width you want. (For example, if you want a shoulder width of 16″ [40.5cm], and your armhole band is 1″ [2.5cm] wide, then you must make your front/back shoulder width 14″ [35.5m].)

Shorter-Than-Full-Length Sleeves

To change the length of the sleeve requires minimal changes to your pattern.

Measurements You Need

When you work shorter-than-full-length sleeves, your sleeve length (page 26) changes. So does the length of your sleeve to the armhole plus perhaps your lower sleeve width.

For the lower sleeve width of a full-length sleeve, I advised wrapping a cast-on edge around your fist to find the #stitches that allowed your hand to pass through. You used this #stitches to determine the narrowest possible lower sleeve width or #stitches for a cuff. It made the sleeve fit well to the wrist and allowed the sleeve to be pushed up the arm and stay there.

So if you want a three-quarter-length sleeve, this #stitches will still be appropriate for the start of your sleeve because there is usually little difference between the circumference of your fist and your arm at three-quarter sleeve length. If you have no cuff, this is your lower sleeve width; if you have a cuff, your cuff will have this #stitches. (If you want a fuller lower sleeve width, you will increase stitches after your cuff.)

If you want a shorter sleeve, wrap a cast-on edge around your arm where you want the sleeve to start and with the degree of tightness you want: this will be the fewest #stitches to cast on for your lower sleeve width or cuff. (If you want a fuller lower sleeve width above the cuff, you can increase stitches after the cuff.)

For your new sleeve length, measure as for sleeve length (page 26), stopping where you want your sleeve to start. Your length of sleeve to armhole will be part of the following calculations.

shorter-than-full-length sleeves

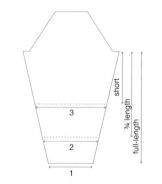

1 lower sleeve width / full-length
2 lower sleeve width / ¾ sleeve
3 lower sleeve width / short sleeve

Shorter-Than-Full-Length Sleeves
Calculations and Pattern

Work the calculations and pattern for your sleeve as specified in chapter 2, with the following changes.

- Above chapter 2's calculations, insert your new sleeve length—which will be shorter than your sleeve length as measured in chapter 1.
  If you're making a ¾-length sleeve, no other changes are necessary.
  If you're making anything shorter than a ¾-length sleeve, "#stitches to allow the hand to pass through" becomes "#stitches for arm." Then make the following changes to your calculations.
- *With no cuff:* Replace step 4 in drop shoulder or modified drop shoulder, step 5 in set-in sleeve, or step 7 in the raglan with "#stitches for arm."
- *With a cuff:* Work step 4 in drop shoulder or modified drop shoulder, step 5 in set-in sleeve, or step 7 in the raglan as written.

Gathered Sleeves

A gathered sleeve always has a cuff and then a substantial increase of stitches between the cuff and the lower sleeve. The lower sleeve width would be greater than anything in chapter 2's calculations—possibly as large as the upper sleeve width.

Measurements You Need

For what follows, I assume full-length sleeves. If you're working both gathered and short sleeves, combine this section with the previous.

Since the gathered sleeve always has a tight cuff, you will find the #stitches to cast on for the cuff in the usual manner (by wrapping a cast-on edge around your fist and counting stitches). You then need to determine how much wider you want your lower sleeve to be than the cuff from which it arises. Wrap a tape measure loosely around your arm, to the circumference you want for your lower sleeve width.

To produce the gathering, you'll be working lots of increases between the cuff and the lower sleeve. And this gathering will need extra length, so you should add an inch (2.5cm) to your sleeve length.

gathered sleeve

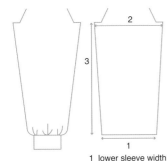

1 lower sleeve width
2 upper sleeve width
3 length to armhole

Gathered Sleeves
Calculations and Pattern

Work the calculations and pattern for your sleeve as specified in chapter 2, with the following changes.

• Above chapter 2's calculations, insert your new sleeve length—which will be longer than your sleeve length as measured in chapter 1 (to accommodate the gathering).

• In all sleeves, ignore the "without a cuff" step.

Bell Sleeves

Similar to an hourglass garment, the bell sleeve starts wider than usual (at the lower sleeve), narrows toward its center (at the elbow), is worked even for a while (perhaps 2″ [5cm]), then widens toward its end (at the upper sleeve). And if it has an edging, the edging does not draw it in.

A bell sleeve is usually made to full-length, so your sleeve length and the length of sleeve to the armhole will not change from chapter 2. (I assume a full-length sleeve in what follows, but if you choose to make a shorter sleeve, adjust your sleeve length as needed.)

The upper sleeve width has already been established in chapter 2 and should not be changed. As noted at the beginning of the following calculations, you will bring that information with you from chapter 2.

Measurements You Need

For this style, you need the following:
- lower sleeve width (determined by wrapping a tape measure around your wrist to establish the fit you want for lower sleeve or by measuring an existing garment)
- width at elbow (determined by wrapping a tape measure around your elbow to establish the fit you want for the sleeve at that point or by measuring an existing garment)
- height of area worked even at elbow (perhaps 2″ [5cm])
- length from lower sleeve to elbow (by measuring yourself or an existing garment).

bell sleeve

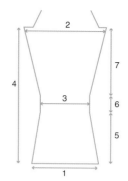

1 lower sleeve width
2 upper sleeve width
3 width at elbow
4 length to armhole
5 length to elbow
6 area worked even at elbow
7 length from elbow to armhole

Bell Sleeves
Calculations

Work through the sleeve calculations of chapter 2 to find your length of sleeve to armhole and #stitches in upper sleeve.

Ignore your lower sleeve width and the calculations that take you from lower sleeve to upper sleeve width.

Enter length of sleeve to armhole and #stitches in upper sleeve below.

#stitches/inch (2.5cm) = _____
#rows/inch (2.5cm) = _____
length of sleeve (to armhole) = _____ inches (cm)
length (from start of sleeve) to elbow = _____ inches (cm)
lower sleeve width = _____ inches (cm)
elbow width = _____ inches (cm)
height of area worked even at elbow = _____ inches (cm)
height of cuff (which could be 0) = _____ inches (cm)
#stitches in upper sleeve width = _____

1. circumference at lower sleeve × #stitches/inch (2.5cm) = #stitches in lower sleeve _____
2. Do you need to fudge for a stitch pattern repeat?
3. Do you need selvedge stitches?
4. revised #stitches in lower sleeve = _____ (Make this even or odd, whichever matches #stitches in upper sleeve width.)

5. circumference at elbow × #stitches/inch (2.5cm) = #stitches at elbow _____
6. (#stitches in lower sleeve – #stitches at elbow) ÷ 2 = #stitches to be decreased at each side of sleeve between lower sleeve and elbow _____
7. length to elbow – height of cuff = length between cuff and elbow _____ inches (cm)
8. length between cuff and elbow × #rows/inch (2.5cm) = #rows to elbow _____
9. #rows to elbow ÷ #stitches to be decreased (step 6) = 1 stitch should be decreased at each side every _____ rows (Fudge to make this a whole number, preferably even.)
10. length of sleeve to armhole – height of area worked even at elbow – length to elbow = length from top of elbow to armhole _____ inches (cm)
11. length from elbow to armhole × #rows/inch (2.5cm) = #rows for increases between elbow and armhole _____
12. (#stitches in upper sleeve – stitches at elbow [step 5]) ÷ 2 = stitches to be increased at each side between elbow and armhole _____
13. #rows for increases (step 11) ÷ #stitches to be increased (step 12) = 1 stitch should be increased at each side every _____ rows (Fudge or round down to a whole number, preferably even.)

Pattern

note I assume the cuff has the same number of stitches over the same size needles as the rest of the sleeve.

• Cast on #stitches for lower sleeve (step 4).
• After edging (if there is one), work to elbow, *at the same time* decreasing as often as determined in step 9. End decreases at #stitches in step 5.
• Work even to end of elbow area.
• Work to armhole, *at the same time* increasing as often as determined in step 13. End increases with #stitches in upper sleeve.
• Continue with sleeve pattern as specified in chapter 2.

Puffed Sleeves (in Set-in Sleeve Style)

The puffed sleeve gives height and width at the shoulders, so if you have narrow or sloping shoulders, you'll like this style. Having said that, this is one sleeve shape that regularly comes into—and goes out of—style. If it is currently out of fashion in your world, but you want its advantages, make a small puffed sleeve. If it is currently in fashion, do as you will!

A puffed sleeve only works in a style with a seam that defines the shoulders (out of which the puff can rise), and the set-in sleeve is the obvious choice.

The gathering that creates the puff usually happens across what we would call the final sleeve cap—not along the whole sleeve cap's length. So what needs to be bigger is only the part of the sleeve that would seam into the final sleeve cap, with 5–6″ (12.5–15cm) centered over the shoulder seam. For the puff, we will want more than the usual 5–6″ (12.5–15cm) final sleeve cap width that we will gather and seam over that 5–6″ (12.5–15cm) area. How much more can it be? That's up to you. It just has to be enough that it doesn't look like a bad seaming job. A discussion of this measurement follows.

puffed sleeve

set-in sleeve

puffed sleeve assembly

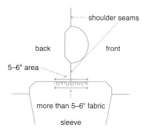

shoulder seams

back   front

5–6" area

more than 5–6" fabric

sleeve

Measurements You Need

A puff in a set-in sleeve means that instead of decreasing the upper sleeve down to a final sleeve cap width of 5–6″ (12.5–15cm), you could create a minimal puff by decreasing down to a final sleeve cap width of 8″ (20.5cm) or a maximum puff by not decreasing at all—by working straight up after the armhole bind-offs. To work through your calculations, you need to establish this final sleeve cap width (those stitches that seam across the shoulder seam) as something greater than the standard 5–6″ (12.5–15cm) and then use it in step 14 of the following calculations.

puffed sleeve in set-in sleeve

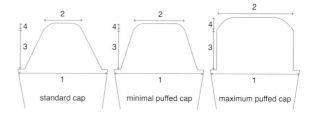

standard cap   minimal puffed cap   maximum puffed cap

1 upper sleeve width (the same for all)
2 final cap width
  (shown as 6" for a standard sleeve cap,
   8" for minimal puff,
   12" for a maximum puff)
3 cap height (the same for all)
4 extra rows for curve at top

In addition, a minimal puff requires no extra rows, while a large puff should have more rows at the end of the cap (which is taken care of in the pattern that follows).

An important feature to understand is that the upper sleeve width is a function of armhole depth—which does not change with this style—so this width is established in the calculations of chapter 2 and should not be changed. As noted at the beginning of the following calculations, you will bring that information with you from chapter 2.

Puffed Sleeves in Set-in Sleeve Calculations

Work calculations for the set-in sleeve as specified on page 49, using the standard final sleeve cap width of 5–6″ (12.5–15cm) for those calculations. (You need those calculations, because they give you the appropriate #stitches for your upper sleeve width.) Then, after step 13 of chapter 2, work as follows.

14. desired final sleeve cap width = _____ inches (cm) (instead of your standard 5–6″ [12.5–15cm])
15. desired final sleeve cap width × #stitches/inch (2.5cm) = desired #stitches in sleeve cap _____ (Make this even or odd, the same as the #stitches in upper sleeve.)
   For a maximum puff: #stitches in step 15 is the same as the sleeve after the armhole bind-offs, so you are done.

For a minimal puff: work the following 3 steps.
16. #stitches in upper sleeve – #stitches in both underarm bind-offs – #stitches in sleeve cap = #stitches to be decreased before sleeve cap

   _____
17. #rows for sleeve cap = _____ (Enter #rows in step 2, page 49.)
18. #stitches to be decreased (step 16) ÷ #rows in sleeve cap (step 17) = _____ Go to chart of Ratios for Decreasing (page 218) to find the number closest to your result. This will tell you how to decrease between the underarm and the final sleeve cap width.

Pattern

Work the first 4 bullets of the pattern on page 49, then work as follows (after the armhole bind offs).

- Decrease as often as indicated in step 18, ending with #stitches in step 15. (If you are working a maximum puff, there will be no decreases: you will simply work #rows of step 17 even.)

For a Maximum Puff
- Finish the final sleeve cap by binding off 2 stitches at the beginning of the next 4–8 rows, then binding off 4 stitches at the beginning of the next 4–8 rows. (Choose whichever range seems appropriate to your number of stitches.)
- Bind off remaining stitches.

For a Minimal Puff
- Finish the sleeve pattern as written (page 49).

For All Puffs
- Sew sleeve into armhole in 2 parts—starting separately at each underarm and sewing the cap to the sleeve to within 2½–3″ (6.5–7.5cm) of the shoulder seam. Then gather and sew the remaining fabric of the sleeve cap, centered over the shoulder seam.

Cap Sleeves

I prefer cap sleeves in garments with seams that define the shoulders—the modified drop shoulder or the set-in sleeve. And since my cap sleeves are not technically sleeves (which encircle the arm and meet at the underarm) but are, rather, little bits added to the top of the armhole only, I treat them as a partial armhole band (picked up and knit out from the armhole edge) over which I will decrease or work short rows to achieve the shape of the cap. (And, yes, this could be considered part of finishing rather than drafting, but it seems appropriately placed here.)

Measurements You Need

Because it does not encircle the entire armhole, you need to know where on the armhole you plan to start and end the cap—probably two-thirds of the way down the armhole from the shoulder seam). This determines the width of the cap at its base.

You then need to know the width of the cap at its finish—maybe half the width of its base.

You then need to know the height of the cap, maybe 2½–3″ (6.5–7.5cm).

This work requires that you know your pick-up-and-knit rate: how many stitches against how many rows is it appropriate for you to pick up and knit stitches along your armhole edge to achieve the number of stitches that will become your cap sleeve? This is worked out in step 1.

cap sleeve assembly

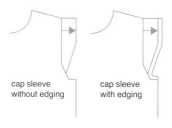

cap sleeve
without edging

cap sleeve
with edging

arrow indicates direction of knitting

cap sleeve

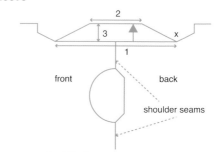

front

back

shoulder seams

1 width of cap at base
2 width of cap at finish
3 height of cap
x beginning of pick-up-and-knit for cap

arrow indicates direction of knitting

Cap Sleeves
Calculations

#stitches/inch (2.5cm) = _____
#rows/inch (2.5cm) = _____
width of cap at base = _____ inches (cm)
width of cap at finish = _____ inches (cm)
height of cap = _____ inches (cm)

1. *If cap sleeve is the same stitch pattern as the garment itself,* #stitches/inch (2.5cm) ÷ #rows/inch (2.5cm) = rate of pick up and knit _____.
   See the chart on page 219 to find the rate closest to your result = _____ stitches / _____ rows.
   If your cap sleeve is a different stitch pattern from the garment itself, read about different pick-up-and-knit rates (page 147), then enter rate of pick up and knit _____ stitches / _____ rows.
2. width of cap at base × #stitches/inch (2.5cm) = #stitches in cap at base _____
3. width of cap at finish × stitches/inch (2.5cm) = #stitches in cap at finish _____ (Make this even or odd, the same as #stitches in step 2.)

4. #stitches in cap at base – #stitches in cap at finish = stitches to be decreased or left behind (with short rows) through height of cap _____
5. height of cap × #rows/inch (2.5cm) = #rows in cap _____ (Make this an even number.)
6. #rows in step 5 includes the pick-up-and-knit row, and it should include a final row (that takes you back to the RS), so subtract 2 rows = #actual rows in cap _____
7. #stitches to be reduced (step 4) ÷ #rows in cap = #stitches to be decreased or left behind (with short rows) _____. (Fudge to make this a whole number.)
   If the result is 1, decrease 1 stitch at each end of each RS row.
   If the result is 2 or more, work short rows, leaving this number of stitches behind every row.
   If the result is a half (1.5), work short rows, leaving the number of stitches on either side of the half (1 and 2) behind at alternate pairs of short rows.

Pattern

note You will probably slip the first stitch after the turn purlwise, and you may work a wrap (which you work or leave alone on the next row), but this pattern's short-row directions only say "turn."

- After sewing the shoulder seam, and with RS facing, mark a place on your armhole opening that is half the width of the cap below the shoulder seam: see X in the drawing.
- Beginning at this place, pick up and knit around the armhole at the rate established in step 1 until you have #stitches of step 2 on needle, centered over your shoulder seam; turn.

If You're Decreasing
- Work 1 WS row (and all following WS rows) even.
- **RS decrease rows** Work selvedge, decrease, work to the last 3 stitches, decrease, work selvedge.

- End with #stitches in step 3.
- If you're working an edging, cut yarn. Otherwise, bind off.

If You're Working Short Rows
- Work 1 WS row over #stitches in step 2 – #stitches in step 7; turn.
- Continue to work short rows, leaving #stitches in step 7 behind each time until #stitches in step 3 remain. Cut yarn.
- If not working an edging, bind off all stitches.

Finishing with an Edging
- Pick up and knit for the edging—beginning and ending at the underarm and working over the stitches of the cap—to finish the entire armhole edge and cap-sleeve edge (as shown in the drawing).

Saddle Shoulder

A saddle is a piece—a yoke—that runs continuously up from the sleeves across the shoulders, and ends with the neck. It is a wonderful shape with multiple advantages, including the following:

- It gives the garment an attractive, wide shoulder. This is particularly nice for the drop shoulder (which has no shoulder definition) and for anyone with narrow shoulders.
- You don't need to, but you can reduce the upper sleeve width for those styles—drop and modified drop shoulder—that normally require a wide upper sleeve. In fact, they can be made the same size as a standard set-in sleeve (the style that allows for the smallest upper sleeve). And the smaller this is, the slimmer we look.
- It provides a frame to the front and back. This is particularly nice if the front and back are quite complex (in color and texture) and the saddle is worked in a simpler stitch pattern.
- Neck (and sleeve) shaping all occur in the saddle. This means that the front and back—which could be more complex—have no neck shaping and are identical.

All this makes the style worth mastering. But it is complex, so I've limited its discussion to a round neck in a drop shoulder, a modified drop shoulder, and a set-in sleeve. These are the easiest shapes to master and the most appropriate. (Other neck shapes don't fit as well, and the raglan has many added calculations.)

Measurements You Need

This shape is an adaptation of the sleeve; hence its positioning in this chapter. The sleeve itself—from start to armhole—does not change. But because the saddle

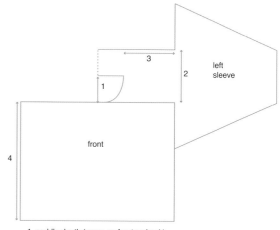

1 saddle depth (same on front as back)
2 saddle width (twice saddle depth)
3 saddle length (from top of sleeve to start of neck)
4 front/back length

includes the neck, there are changes to the garment's front and back length of the garment. In addition, we need to determine the saddle's measurements. So for this style we need measurements for

- depth of the saddle
- width of the saddle
- length of the saddle to start of neck
- front/back finished length.

First, how deep should that saddle be? (And by *depth* I mean the saddle as you see it from the front of the garment: for the saddle's width, read what follows.) For this, what we need to know is that the saddle depth should be as deep as the neck. (And how simple is that?!)

saddle shoulder / all styles

arrow indicates direction of knitting

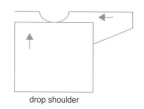

drop shoulder

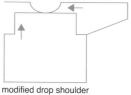

modified drop shoulder

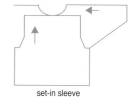

set-in sleeve

saddle shoulder / saddle depth + neck depths

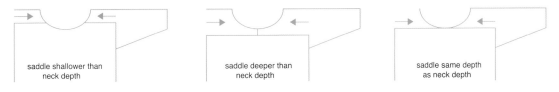

saddle shallower than neck depth | saddle deeper than neck depth | saddle same depth as neck depth

If the saddle is shallower than neck depth, then some of the front body piece would have to be shaped for the neck—and meet up with the saddle's neck shaping (which seems an unnecessary complication). If the saddle is deeper than neck depth, then the saddle extends across the center front of the garment. This would produce a center front seam (which seems an unpretty choice).

But if the *saddle depth* is the same as neck depth, then all neck shaping occurs in the saddle, and the saddle would disappear to nothing at the center front. This seems like the right choice.

Saddle width—the piece that extends up from the sleeves—will then be twice the depth of the neck. The fronts will disappear to nothing after front neck shaping. The back will have a little back neck shaping, and then what remains will be worked straight to center back.

Here is what saddle width means as we knit the sleeves.

- For the drop or modified drop shoulder, the sleeve will be worked as specified in chapter 2, but at its end everything but this saddle width will be bound off over the next 2 rows. The saddle is then worked from these stitches.
- For the set-in sleeve—which usually ends with a final sleeve cap of something close to 6″ (15cm)—this final sleeve cap simply becomes the saddle width. The saddle is then worked from these stitches.

The other measurement we need is *saddle length to neck*. How long do we knit this piece before working the neck? For that, we need to know the width of the front/back at its top edge (where the saddle is sewn to it).

- For the drop shoulder, it's just the width of the garment.
- For the modified drop shoulder or set-in-sleeve, it's the width of the garment at the shoulders.

With that information, we do the following:

saddle shoulder / saddle width

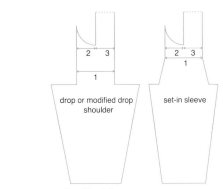

drop or modified drop shoulder | set-in sleeve

1 saddle width
2 front saddle depth   dotted line = center back
3 back saddle depth

- divide the width of the garment (at its top edge) by 2, then subtract half the width of the neck.

This is the saddle length to neck. After the saddle is worked to this length, it's time to shape the neck.

But it's important to remember that the neck is part of the saddle. So while we can work the front and back as specified in chapter 2, the front/back finished length has to be shorter—because it doesn't include the neck.

Drop Shoulder

- You will make the front and back to finished length minus saddle depth. At that length, you will bind off all stitches.

Modified Drop Shoulder and Set-in Sleeve

- You will make the front and back to finished length minus saddle depth. At that length, you may bind off all stitches (as shown in the drawing).
- But if you want shoulder shaping, you will make the front and back to finished length minus saddle depth and minus shoulder-shaping depth. At that point, you will shape the shoulders as calculated in chapter 3. (You won't be working neck shaping at the same time, so you will simply bind off the stitches for the shoulders. The stitches that remain after shoulder shaping are your neck width, and you'll just bind them off all at once.)

saddle shoulder / saddle length to neck

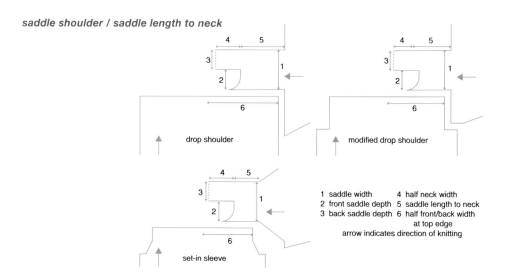

1 saddle width 4 half neck width
2 front saddle depth 5 saddle length to neck
3 back saddle depth 6 half front/back width
at top edge
arrow indicates direction of knitting

saddle shoulder / modified drop shoulder + set-in sleeve

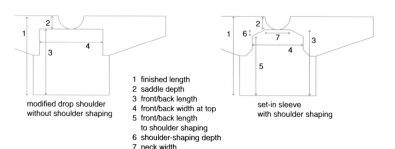

modified drop shoulder
without shoulder shaping

set-in sleeve
with shoulder shaping

1 finished length
2 saddle depth
3 front/back length
4 front/back width at top
5 front/back length
to shoulder shaping
6 shoulder-shaping depth
7 neck width

saddle shoulder / drop shoulder

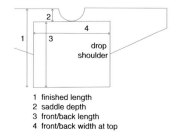

1 finished length
2 saddle depth
3 front/back length
4 front/back width at top

The Round Neck

This section isn't about measurements so much as execution: how is the round neck worked into the saddle?

As established earlier, the saddle is worked straight until it's time to shape the neck, and at that point, the piece will be divided into a front and back. Both will have neck shaping executed as if working side to side. So how does that happen?

For the front round neck, it helps to reexamine how a round neck is shaped working bottom up.

- Half the neck's stitches were put onto a holder (or bound off) at the base of the neck.
- Some larger number of stitches were bound off (maybe 3 stitches once).
- Some smaller number of stitches were bound off (usually 2 stitches, one or more times).
- 1 stitch was bound off some number of times (usually 4–6 times).
- To finish, 1″ (2.5cm) was worked straight.

So, once we split the saddle, the first thing we do is produce that inch straight—which is accomplished by binding off 1″ (2.5cm) of stitches. Then we shape the curve, working the same as we did when working up from the bottom—bind off 3 stitches once, 2 stitches one or more times, and then 1 stitch at a time until 2 stitches remain. Why do we stop at 2? Because 1 stitch will be taken into for the front/back seam, and 1 stitch will be the selvedge for the neck band.

You might ask—and it's a good question—what happened to the flat center at the base of the round neck? In this shape, the round neck will stop short of center when seamed, leaving some number of inches of the garment front without any saddle attached. This is the center of the round neck.

For the back neck, we will work a little back neck shaping—by binding off 1 or 2 stitches once, then 1 stitch once or twice. (You'll bind off 4 for a fine yarn and only 2 for a heavy yarn.) Then we'll work the remaining stitches straight to center back. At that point, we'll put those stitches onto a holder, waiting to join them to the other saddle at center back.

---

saddle shoulder / front and back with round neck shaping

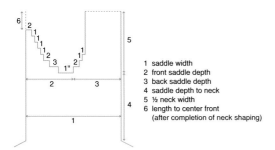

1 saddle width
2 front saddle depth
3 back saddle depth
4 saddle depth to neck
5 ½ neck width
6 length to center front
    (after completion of neck shaping)

round neck

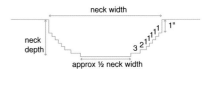

Saddle with Round Neck
Calculations

note Work front and back and sleeves as specified in chapter 2 but with changes as discussed in the previous section.

#stitches/inch (2.5cm) = _____
#rows/inch (2.5cm) = _____
front/back width at the end (front/back width for drop shoulder, shoulder width for set-in sleeve or modified drop shoulder) = _____ inches (cm)
neck depth = _____ inches (cm) (usually 3″ [7.5cm], but it could be shallower)
neck width = _____ inches (cm) (usually 7–8″ [18–20.5cm])
for drop or modified drop shoulder #stitches at the end of sleeve = _____
for set-in sleeve #stitches in final sleeve cap =
_____ (5–6″ [12.5–15cm] + 2 selvedge stitches)
(This becomes #stitches in saddle.)

For Drop or Modified Drop Shoulder

a. saddle width × #stitches/inch (2.5cm) = #stitches in saddle _____
b. Do you need to fudge for a stitch pattern repeat?
c. Do you need to add 2 stitches for selvedges?
d. revised #stitches in saddle = _____ (Make this even or odd, the same choice as the #stitches at the end of sleeve.)
e. (#stitches at the end of sleeve – #stitches in saddle) ÷ 2 = #stitches to bind off at each edge of sleeve before saddle _____

For All Styles

1. (width of front/back at end – width of neck) ÷ 2 = length of saddle to work before neck split _____ inches (cm)
2. #stitches in saddle ÷ 2 = #stitches in front saddle _____ and #stitches in back saddle _____ (If the #stitches in the saddle is odd, make the larger number the front saddle.)
3. #stitches in back saddle (step 2) – 2 or 4 stitches = #stitches in back saddle after back neck shaping _____
4. #stitches/inch (2.5cm) = #stitches for first bind-off at front neck _____ (Make this a whole number.)
5. #stitches in front saddle – #stitches for first bind-off (step 4) = #stitches remaining to shape neck _____
6. Write a series of numbers, beginning with 3 or 2, followed with one or more 2's, followed with a number of 1's (3–5), and ending with a 2, for the series of bind-offs for neck shaping _____ (For example, with 11 stitches, the series might be 3, 2, 1, 1, 1, 1, 2.)
7. Write a pattern for the stitches to be bound off for back neck shaping _____ (It would be 2, 1, 1 for a fine yarn and 1, 1 for a heavy yarn.)

Pattern

For Drop or Modified Drop Shoulder

• At the end of the sleeve, bind off #stitches in step *e* at the beginning of the next 2 rows—#stitches in step *d* remain.

For a Set-in Sleeve

• At the final sleeve cap, #stitches in saddle width remain.

For All Styles

• Work saddle to length of step 1. End after working a WS row for the right sleeve and after a RS row for the left sleeve.

Right Sleeve

• **First RS row** Work #stitches in front neck (step 2). Turn—leaving #stitches for back neck behind.

- **First WS row** Bind off #stitches in step 4, work to end.
- Work all following RS rows even.
- **Following WS rows** Bind off at neck edge as series in step 6—2 stitches remain.
- **Next WS row** Bind off 2 stitches.
- Return to #stitches for back neck, RS facing.
- **Following RS rows** Bind off for back neck shaping as series in step 7.
- Work all following WS rows even.
- Continue with #stitches in step 3 to half the width of the neck. Put stitches on holder, leaving some tail. (The reason for this tail is explained in the assembly section to follow.)

Left Sleeve
- **First WS row** Work #stitches in front neck (step 2). Turn, leaving #stitches for back neck behind.
- **Next RS row** Bind off #stitches in step 4, work to end.
- Work all following WS rows even.
- **Following RS rows** Bind off at neck edge as series of step 6—2 stitches remain.
- **Next RS row** Bind off 2 stitches.
- Return to #stitches for back neck, WS facing.
- **Following WS rows** Bind off for back neck shaping as series in step 7.
- Work all following RS rows even.
- Continue with #stitches in step 3 to half the width of the neck. Put stitches on a holder, leaving some tail.

Assembling the Saddle

The easiest way to seam this piece is to start where the right sleeve corner meets the back corner (marked by an X on the drawing). The rows of the back saddle are sewn to the bound-off stitches of the back, ending at center back.

You are seaming stitches against rows, so you'll need to find the ratio between the two.
- Count #rows in the back saddle, from the corner (marked by X) to the center back.
- Determine #stitches in the half-back width.
- *Divide the smaller number by the larger (to find your ratio).
- Go to the chart of Ratios for Seaming (page 219), find the closest number to your ratio, then seam the stitches against rows as directed there.*

Across the back, both saddles should meet at the center. If they don't, subtract or add rows from the stitches on hold (that's why we left extra yarn!). Then at the center back, graft the saddle pieces together—avoiding two heavy bind-off edges running along your sensitive spine. If you do not like your grafting, or your stitch patterns don't line up, pull your grafting line tight—for a seam with no seam allowance.

For the drop or modified drop shoulder, a stitches-to-rows seam is worked to continue this assembly, joining the sides of the back to the sleeve bind-off edges. (You may have the same stitches-to-rows ratio, but it never hurts to check by working from * to *, above.) For the set-in sleeve, a row-to-row relationship makes the remaining seaming fairly straightforward.

Sew the front saddles to the front of the garment as for the back. Your front saddle will end 1½–2″ (4–5cm) from center front.

saddle shoulder / assembly

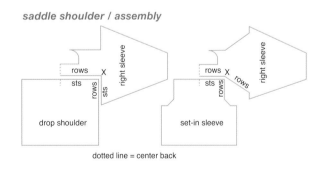

dotted line = center back

Chapter 7

Cardigans

•···•

I'm a big fan of the cardigan. It is a highly versatile garment whose front opening makes us look slimmer. Turning pullovers into cardigans is not difficult. Sometimes it can be as simple as cutting the front in two; sometimes it involves more work. But it's never a difficulty that I find myself avoiding, given its advantages.

The one time it can be challenging, however, is within a complex stitch pattern. Sometimes it's a puzzle to solve—how to get the right number of stitches for both the pattern repeat and the width when the front is divided into two and if a band might be added. One answer is not to worry about the stitch pattern being a full repeat. Another may be to add side panels of other, more "reasonable" stitch patterns. And another may be to make the garment all in one piece—without side seams below the armhole. Whatever complications you deal with, the versatility of the cardigan will overrule them!

Through what follows, I chose to simplify by assuming the following:

- selvedge stitches but no stitch pattern repeat
- a cardigan that is worked in three pieces: back, left front, right front
- a straight hem.

Once you master this, you'll be able to challenge these assumptions.

Since a pullover is easier, here's how I recommend working a cardigan.

- Photocopy your schematic from chapter 2, then draw a line for the cardigan opening: this will help you visualize what you are doing and follow the instructions that speak of the two fronts as mirror images.
- Write the pattern for the back first, making numbers of stitches for body width, shoulder width, and neck width all even numbers. This makes it easier to divide in two and to turn the back into two fronts.
- Make your neck width narrower than the standards of chapter 3 (page 66). See measurements you need on the next page, to address this.

Cardigan Styles

There are only two issues in turning a pullover into a cardigan—#stitches in each front plus changes that might need to be made to the neck.

And there is one style—the saddle shoulder—that doesn't involve the neck. Once you have the #stitches for each front, you are done, because neck shaping happens in the saddle and doesn't involve the fronts.

To determine the #stitches for each front, you need to choose one of the following styles.

- Do you want no front overlap? (If you add front bands, they will be minimal.)
- Do you want front bands that overlap? How wide are those front bands?
- Do you want the fabric of each front to overlap? How wide is that overlap? (You may still add front bands, but I assume they are minimal.)

All these choices influence the number of stitches for each front and its neck. The following calculations and patterns are organized based on your answers to these questions.

Measurements You Need: All Styles

The only measurements that need revisiting are your *neck dimensions*. Since a cardigan does not have to go over the head, its neck width does not need to be as wide as that of a pullover. In fact, a wide cardigan neck may be uncomfortable, always tending to slide off the shoulders. If your neck band is a standard 1″ (2.5cm) or less, you may make your neck width 1–2″ (2.5–5cm) narrower than for a pullover but your neck depth need not change. If your neck band is wider, change your neck width and depth accordingly.

And now, based on your answer to those three questions, go to one of the following sections.

Cardigan with No Front Overlap

The easiest cardigan to make is one in which you just divide the back of a pullover in half to produce two fronts. If the stitch pattern of the garment lies flat, no front band is required: the pieces will meet at center and may be left open. Or they may be finished with a minimal band (like reverse stockinette), which could be left alone or house a zipper or have clasps added.

cardigan styles

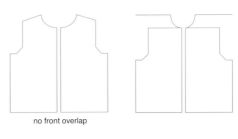

no front overlap

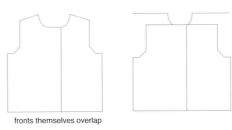

front bands overlap

fronts themselves overlap

left column shows 3 cardigan styles in set-in sleeve but applies to all basic shapes
right column shows 3 cardigan styles in set-in sleeve but applies to all saddle shapes

cardigans / no front overlap

no front bands   minimal front bands
1 right front width (half front width)

Cardigan with No Front Overlap
Calculations

note Through what follows, it is assumed you have the pattern for the back and that it has 2 selvedge stitches.

#stitches in back width = _____
#stitches in back neck width = _____
front neck depth = _____ inches (could be 0)

1. #stitches in back width – 2 selvedge stitches = _____ stitches
2. #stitches in step 1 ÷ 2 = #stitches in each front width without selvedges _____
3. #stitches in step 2 + 2 selvedge stitches = #stitches in each front with selvedge stitches _____
4. #stitches in back neck width + 2 selvedge stitches = _____
5. finished length – neck depth = length to front neck _____ inches (cm)

For a Straight Neck
6. #stitches in step 4 ÷ 2 = #stitches for each front neck

_____

For a Square Neck
6. #stitches in step 4 ÷ 2 = #stitches to be bound off at each front neck _____

For a V-Neck
6. #stitches in step 4 ÷ 2 = #stitches to be shaped at each side of neck _____. Enter this #stitches to step 3, page 72, then continue with steps 4–6 there.

For a Round Neck
6. Enter #stitches in step 4 to step 1, page 75, continue with steps 2–7 there, then work the following step.
7. #stitches in step 2 (page 75) ÷ 2 = #stitches for initial bind off at each front neck _____

Pattern

- If there is no bottom band, cast on #stitches for one front (step 3).
- If you're starting with a bottom band, you may cast on fewer stitches and with smaller needles (page 145). You may need to change to larger needles and increase stitches at the end of the band. End with #stitches in one front (step 3).
- You have the pattern for the back. Use this pattern to work each front as a mirror image of the other through armhole and shoulder shaping.
- *At the same time,* work front neck shaping as follows. (Note that no shoulder shaping is included in what follows. Work this as for the back.)

For a Straight Neck
- Work to finished length: #stitches in step 6 remain for neck. Bind off, or add an edging.

For a Square Neck
- Work to length of step 5.
- Bind off #stitches in step 6 at each front neck, then work neck edge straight to finished length.

For a V-Neck
- Work to length of step 5.
- Work neck decreases as calculated in step 6, page 72, while working to finished length.

For a Round Neck
- Work to length of step 5.
- Bind off #stitches in step 7 (above), then continue to bind off for neck shape as calculated in step 7, page 75, while working to finished length.

Cardigan with Overlapping Front Bands

In the next cardigan option, front bands (1″ [2.5cm] wide or wider) are added. They will overlap when the garment is closed and will probably be home to buttons and buttonholes.

Measurements You Need

In this case, the overlapping bands add width to the front. The extra width when the garment is closed is the same as the width of one band. So if we simply make each front half the width of the back with a 1″ (2.5cm) front band, the closed-front width will be 1″ (2.5cm) wider than the back. This difference is usually something the body can absorb. But since this extra width sits at center front—as part of the neck—the front neck opening might not appreciate being 1″ (2.5cm) wider.

But if we remember that we made the neck opening narrower for a cardigan, we might be okay with this. For example, if the garment's round-neck width were calculated as 6″ (15cm), the back neck will be 6″ (15cm), and the closed front (with a 1″ [2.5cm] band) would be 7″ (18cm). That might work for you. If so, then work your calculations and pattern as for the previous section—cardigans with no front overlap—because you are not making an allowance for your front overlap.

But sometimes we are not okay with this, especially if the front band is wider than 1″ (2.5cm). In this case, we need to recalculate the neck—with an allowance for the *width of the front band.*

As you can see in the drawing below, the finished neck width has an allowance for the width of the front band: the part of each front into which shaping is worked is less than half the finished neck width. This

cardigans / minimal front band overlap

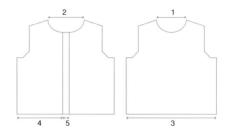

1 back neck width
2 front neck width (wider than back by width of front band)
3 back width
4 right front width (half back width)
5 width of front band

allowance is done through the following calculations and pattern.

In theory, your front band could be any width—even as wide as the neck itself. But in round necks, a front band wider than the flat base of the neck means shaping the curve into the upper corner of the front band, and I find this an unnecessary complication. So my maximum width of front band for the round neck is never greater than half the neck width—what I would have put into its flat, center base.

Neck depth does not have to change. As you can see in the drawing below, overlapping fronts cover some of the V-neck's depth, but so did our V-neck band (and you were warned about the depth of this coverage in the V-neck's section). So if your bands are wide, you'll need to make your V-neck deeper.

cardigans / front band overlap

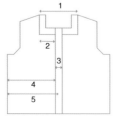 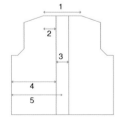 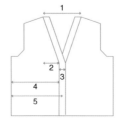 

1 finished neck width
2 neck width at right front (into which neck shaping is worked)
3 width of front band
4 width of right front (without band)
5 half front width

Cardigan with Overlapping Front Bands
Calculations

note Through what follows, it is assumed you have the pattern for the back and that it has 2 selvedge stitches.

#stitches in back width = _____
#stitches in back neck width = _____
front neck depth = _____ inches (cm) (could be 0)
front-band width = _____ inches (cm)

1. #stitches in back width – 2 selvedge stitches =
_____

2. #stitches in step 1 ÷ 2 = #stitches in each front width without selvedge stitches _____

3. #stitches in step 2 + 2 selvedge stitches = #stitches in each front with selvedge stitches (without allowance for front band) _____

4. #stitches in back neck width + 2 selvedge stitches =
_____

5. (width of front band × #stitches/inch [2.5cm]) ÷ 2 = #stitches to allow for front band width at each front _____ (Fudge to make this a whole number.)

6. finished length – neck depth = length to front neck _____ inches (cm)

For a Straight Neck

7. (#stitches in step 4 ÷ 2) – #stitches in step 5 = #stitches for each front neck _____

For a Square Neck

7. (#stitches in step 4 ÷ 2) – #stitches in step 5 = #stitches to be bound off at each front neck
_____

For a V-Neck

7. (#stitches in step 4 ÷ 2) – #stitches in step 5 = #stitches to be shaped at each side of neck _____. Enter this #stitches to step 3, page 72, then continue with steps 4–6 there.

For a Round Neck

7. Enter #stitches in step 4 to step 1, page 75, continue with steps 2–7 there, then work the following step.

8. (#stitches in step 2 [page 75] ÷ 2) – #stitches in step 5 (above) = #stitches for initial bind off at each front neck _____

Pattern

- If there is no bottom band, cast on #stitches for one front (step 3).
- If you're starting with a bottom band, you may cast on fewer stitches and with smaller needles (page 145). You may need to change to larger needles and increase stitches at the end of the band. End with #stitches in one front (step 3).
- You have the pattern for the back. Use this pattern to work each front as a mirror image of the other through armhole and shoulder shaping.
- *At the same time,* work front neck shaping as follows. (Note that no shoulder shaping is included in what follows. Work this as for the back.)

For a Straight Neck

- Work to finished length: #stitches in step 7 remain for each front neck. Bind off, or add an edging.

For a Square Neck

- Work to length of step 6.
- Bind off #stitches in step 7 at each front neck, then work the neck edge straight to finished length.

For a V-Neck

- Work to length of step 6.
- Work neck decreases as calculated in step 6, page 72, while working to finished length.

For a Round Neck

- Work to length of step 6.
- Bind off #stitches in step 8, then continue to bind off for neck shape as calculated in step 7, page 75, while working to finished length.

Cardigan with Overlapping Front Pieces

Finally, you could make a cardigan with a large overlap that is part of the garment front itself: think double-breasted. These fronts are each wider than half the back, and buttonholes will probably be worked into the right front. Front bands may be applied, but I assume them to be minimal (so they do not affect the following calculations).

Measurements You Need

The *width of the overlap*—which you need in the calculations below—is the amount you want both fronts to cover each other.

Neck depth does not have to change. As you can see in the drawing, overlapping fronts cover some of the V-neck's depth, but so did our V-neck band (and you were warned about the depth of this coverage in the V-neck's section).

cardigans / fronts themselves overlap

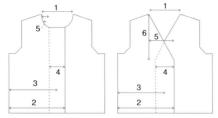

1 finished neck width
2 width of each front with overlap
3 width to center front
4 width of overlap
5 neck width at right front
   (into which neck shaping is worked)
6 neck depth (V-neck only)

note Through what follows, it is assumed you have the pattern for the back and that it has 2 selvedge stitches.

#stitches in back width = _____

#stitches in back neck width = _____

front neck depth = _____ inches (cm) (could be 0)

width of front overlap = _____ inches (cm)

1. #stitches in back width – 2 selvedge stitches = _____
2. #stitches in step 1 ÷ 2 = #stitches in each front width without selvedge stitches _____
3. #stitches in step 2 + 2 selvedge stitches = #stitches in each front with selvedge stitches (without allowance for front overlap) _____
4. #stitches in back neck width + 2 selvedge stitches = _____ (Make this an even number.)
5. (width of front overlap × #stitches/inch [2.5cm]) ÷ 2 = #stitches to add to each front _____ (Fudge to make this a whole number.)
6. finished length – neck depth = length to front neck _____ inches (cm)

For a Straight Neck
7. (#stitches in step 4 ÷ 2) + #stitches in step 5 = #stitches for each front neck _____

For a Square Neck
7. (#stitches in step 4 ÷ 2) + #stitches in step 5 = #stitches to be bound off at each front neck _____

For a V-Neck
7. (#stitches in step 4 ÷ 2) + #stitches in step 5 = #stitches to be shaped at each side of neck _____. Enter #stitches from step 7 to step 3, page 72, then continue with steps 4–6 there.

For a Round Neck
7. Enter #stitches in step 4 to step 1, page 75, continue with steps 2–7 there, then work the following step.
8. (#stitches in step 2 [page 75] ÷ 2) + #stitches in step 5 = #stitches for initial bind-off at each front neck _____

Pattern

- If there is no bottom band, cast on #stitches for one front (step 3).
- If you're starting with a bottom band, you may cast on fewer stitches and with smaller needles (page 145). You may need to change to larger needles and increase stitches at the end of the band. End with #stitches in one front (step 3).
- You have the pattern for the back. Use this pattern to work each front as a mirror image of the other through armhole and shoulder shaping.
- *At the same time,* work front neck shaping as follows. (Note that no shoulder shaping is included in what follows. Work this as for the back.)
- Working the left front first to determine where you'd like buttons. Make buttonholes, to match, while working the right front.

For a Straight Neck
- Work to finished length: #stitches in step 7 remains for each front neck. Bind off, or add an edging.

For a Square Neck
- Work to length of step 6.
- Bind off #stitches in step 7 at each front neck, then work neck edge straight to finished length.

For a V-Neck
- Work to length of step 6.
- Work neck decreases as calculated in step 6, page 72, while working to finished length.

For a Round Neck
- Work to length of step 6.
- Bind off #stitches in step 8, then continue to bind off for neck shape as calculated in step 7, page 75, while working to finished length.

Chapter 8

Fabrics, Finishes, and Fixes

This chapter deals with the material that supports your pattern drafting: the stitch patterns we choose (important features that need to be understood through design, drafting, and finishing), the large topic of bands (those bits that start or complete our pieces), and then the maneuvers we use when things don't turn out quite as expected. I think you need to know all this stuff because it will help you make informed decisions, avoid surprises, reinvent disappointments, and understand your work.

What is not included in this chapter—because it would have taken too much space—is a discussion of all the maneuvers every knitter should have in her arsenal: particular cast-ons, decreases, increases, bind-offs, buttonholes, and seams. Instructions for these are available in many knitting manuals, but a list of what I see as our Essential Skills appears in the appendix (page 212).

Common Stitch Patterns

Individual stitch patterns have ways of behaving that we may know but have taken for granted. When drafting our own patterns, however, these different behaviors need to be understood. What follows is a discussion of our common stitch patterns as they behave when used for the garment itself. A separate discussion follows for their use as selvedge stitches, as hems, as cuffs, or as front, neck, and armhole bands.

For the samples, I used a needle size that gave me an appropriate fabric. What is important is not the actual needle size I used; rather, you are meant to notice that sometimes a different-size needle was used when I thought it appropriate for the fabric.

And while you might get the same number of stitches as me, or the yarn label, or a pattern, you may not get the same number of rows, nor should you expect to. This is where our gauges most often differ.

Stockinette Stitch (st st)

Right-side knit, wrong-side purl—this is our most common stitch pattern. (It is also the stitch pattern against which standard gauge is measured.)

- It rolls at the edges (so we usually add seams and edgings to hold it flat).
- It rolls to the back at the sides (which makes mattress stitch side seams invisible), but it does require a selvedge stitch (that will be taken into the seam).
- It rolls to the front at the bottom and top (so it may require a stitch pattern at the hem to hold it flat and is the main reason we struggle with shoulder seams).
- It will never give a square gauge: for example, you would never get 19 stitches and 19 rows over 4″ (10cm).

Stockinette stitch (RS knit, WS purl)
on size 6 (4mm) needles, 19 stitches and 27 rows = 4″ (10cm) after steam-pressing

Reverse stockinette stitch (RS purl, WS knit)
on size 6 (4mm) needles, 19 stitches and 27 rows = 4″ (10cm) after steam-pressing

Reverse Stockinette Stitch (RSS)

This lengthy name refers to the wrong side of stockinette (RS purl and WS knit).

- Like stockinette, it rolls at the edges (so we usually add seams and edgings to hold it flat).
- It rolls to the front at the sides (which makes mattress stitch side seams difficult). When appropriate, I have counteracted this roll—and produced tidier side seams—by adding two stockinette stitches to the sides of all pieces: one of these stitches goes into the side seam; the other frames the seam.
- It rolls to the back at the bottom and top (which means it may not require another stitch pattern at the hem and which makes shoulder seams invisible).
- It can be wonderful as the right side of a variegated yarn—with increased color integration.
- It shares the last feature of stockinette stitch.

stockinette stitch

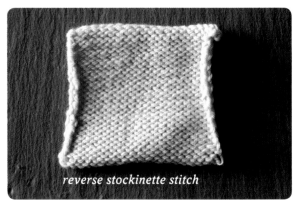

reverse stockinette stitch

Garter Stitch

Usually the first stitch pattern we learn, it's accomplished by knitting all stitches of every row.

- Because it lies flat, and doesn't look bad at the edges, it doesn't need an edging and can be seamed without selvedge stitches or a seam allowance.
- It gives a square gauge: 2 rows = 1 ridge, and the number of stitches per inch (2.5cm) is usually the same as the number of ridges. This is wonderful for multidirectional knitting.
- One could understand garter as 1 row stockinette followed by 1 row reverse stockinette. And then it makes sense to say that the RSS rows come forward and the stockinette rows recede.
- This "stacking" produces a dense fabric, so we usually use one size larger needles than for stockinette.
- Even when knit on larger needles, it may get fewer stitches and will certainly get more rows than stockinette.
- It can be used in unexpected places—as an alternative to reverse stockinette in a rib or cable pattern. The garter rib shows the former.

Garter stitch (knit all stitches, all rows)
on size 7 (4.5mm) needles, 17 stitches and 34 rows (17 ridges) = 4″ (10cm)

garter stitch

Rib

Classic rib is the regular use of RS knit stitches with WS purl stitches.

- In classic rib, the stitch pattern is maintained with all RS knits (stockinette stitches) lined up vertically beside RS purls (reverse stockinette stitches). (In other words, what is knit on a RS row is purled on a WS row, and vice versa.) What is a stockinette stitch remains a stockinette stitch for the duration.
- Although it lies flat, the more stockinette stitches it has at the sides, the more it will behave like stockinette—rolling to the back at its sides.
- The stockinette stitches will come forward; the reverse stockinette stitches will recede (which is the opposite of garter). Because of this, it gets many more stitches to the inch (2.5cm) than stockinette (which is—again—the opposite of garter). But it will get a similar row gauge to stockinette.
- It is usually expressed as so many knit stitches x so many purl stitches as worked on RS rows. (In other words, 2x1 rib is k2, p1 on RS rows and k1, p2 on WS rows.)

2x2 rib (over a multiple of 4 + 2 stitches and 2 rows)
Row 1 *K2, p2; repeat from * to the last 2 stitches, k2.
Row 2 *P2, k2; repeat from * to the last 2 stitches, p2.
on size 7 (4.5mm) needles, 30 stitches and 25 rows = 4″ (10cm) before steam-pressing, 22 stitches and 25 rows = 4″ (10cm) after steam-pressing

2x2 rib

- When used as an edging, we often use two sizes smaller needles than for stockinette. But when used as a fabric, we often use one size larger needles (because of its denseness). And then we steam-press our swatch—to flatten out its denseness before measuring gauge.

- Even when we use larger needles, we will get many more stitches per inch (2.5cm) than for stockinette.
- There are many ways to express rib other than classically—with garter instead of "purls," for a flatter-lying fabric as shown in garter rib. And we could even work RS knit stitches as twisted stitches (see cable rib, page 139).

Garter rib (over a multiple of 6 + 3 stitches and 2 rows)
Row 1 Knit.
Row 2 *K3, p3; repeat from * to the last 3 stitches, k3.
on size 7 (4.5mm) needles, 18 stitches and 26 rows = 4″ (10cm) after steam-pressing

garter rib

Knit and Purl Combinations

These are a large group of stitch patterns with combinations of knit and purl that aren't as simple as garter or rib but provide texture and also solve problems.

- The most common knit and purl combination is seed (sometimes called moss) stitch: k1, p1 on all rows but offset, unlike rib.
- Seed stitch lies as flat as garter—so it does not require an edging and can be seamed without selvedge stitches or a seam allowance.
- While it does not match exactly, seed stitch usually gets a gauge closer to stockinette than garter or rib does, so it works well in combination with stockinette or reverse stockinette. If you want to knit a textured shape—a square, a triangle, a heart—on a stockinette fabric, this is your best choice. Neither garter nor rib works as well.

- Because knit and purl combinations are often dense, we usually use one size larger needles than for stockinette.
- There are many knit and purl combinations other than seed stitch: two examples are shown here. It's difficult to generalize about their gauges. (The more they are like stockinette, the more like stockinette they will behave; the more like rib, the more like rib they will behave).

Seed stitch (over a multiple of 2 + 1 stitches)
All rows *K1, p1; repeat from * to the last stitch, k1.
on size 7 (4.5mm) needles, 18 stitches and 32 rows = 4″ (10cm) after steam-pressing

seed stitch

Tumbling blocks (over a multiple of 10 stitches and 20 rows)
on size 7 (4.5mm) needles, 18 stitches and 28 rows = 4″ (10cm) after steam-pressing
(Chart is on page 174.)

tumbling blocks stitch

Easy over-under (over a multiple of 8 stitches and 8 rows)
on size 7 (4.5mm) needles, 18 stitches and 27 rows = 4″ (10cm) after steam-pressing
(Chart is on page 211.)

easy over-under stitch

Lace

Many knitters use lace for accessories but fear using it for garments. Perhaps understanding what follows, and choosing easier lace patterns, can change this trend. (Or you could knit the garment on page 183, in which the lace is not shaped.)

- Even though it is technically stockinette (RS knit, WS purl), it may get a different number of stitches and rows over 4″ (10cm) than stockinette.
- Even though it is technically stockinette, it usually lies flatter after blocking. In a garment, it may not need lower edgings, but it will need selvedge stitches and side seams.
- Because we like to exaggerate its openness, we might use one or more sizes larger needles than for stockinette.
- Lace is accomplished by yarn-overs paired with decreases (although some lace patterns have occasional unequal pairings, so the #stitches in a row may temporarily change).
- Easier lace patterns have WS rows that are purled.
- Easier lace patterns have fewer stitches and rows in their repeats.
- If you are new to lace, try the following: a lifeline (sewing a thread through every stitch of each row 1—so if you need to rip back you can stop there) and/or regular steam-pressing (to set your stitches and make your fabric easier to "read.")

- Every yarn-over has a decrease that balances it. The larger the stitch pattern repeat, the further the yarn-over is from its decrease.
- Stitch patterns with a wide repeat and a lot of double decreases will produce a scalloped lower edge: the scalloped lace is an example. This can curl upwards if the cast-on is not loose enough to accommodate the scallops.
- Shaping lace requires an understanding of the yarn-over and decrease relationship; that is, which decrease pairs with which increase. (If we shape by decreasing a stitch at an edge—and lose a yarn-over—we must not do its decrease; if we shape by decreasing a stitch at an edge—and lose a decrease—we must not do its yarn-over. If we shape by increasing a stitch—and can insert a new yarn-over—we must not do so unless we also have enough stitches to do its decrease; if we shape by increasing a stitch—and can insert a new decrease—we must not do so unless we also have enough stitches to do its yarn-over.
- I find it easier to sort out the previous bullet if I work my decreases or increases on WS (straight purl) rows. Then I'm not trying to decrease or increase while also working the stitch pattern.
- Through shaping, stitches will occur at the edges that cannot be worked in lace. These are best worked in stockinette. (The larger the stitch repeat, the larger these stockinette areas will be—until the pattern attains its full repeat again.)
- When drafting, you might want to work your shaping so that—once done—you are back to a full stitch repeat. (For example, we usually begin our hem with a full stitch repeat, but we might want our shoulder width to be a full stitch repeat as well.)

Simple lace (over a multiple of 6 + 3 stitches and 8 rows)

on size 6 (4mm) needles, 18½ stitches and 30 rows =
4″ (10cm) after steam-pressing
(Chart is on page 198.)

simple lace stitch

Scalloped lace (over a multiple of 12 + 15 stitches and 10 rows)

on size 7 (4.5mm) needles, 18 stitches and 29 rows =
4″ (10cm) after steam-pressing.
(A similar lace pattern is charted on page 186.)

scalloped lace stitch

Slip Stitches

These are wonderful stitch patterns with a lot of possibilities—for both texture and color.

- Even though RS rows may be knit and WS rows may be purled, the slipping of stitches can change both the stitch and row gauges to something very different from stockinette.
- Because slip stitches add density, we usually use at least one size larger needles than for stockinette.

- Even though RS rows are knit and WS rows are purled, these stitch patterns usually lie flatter than stockinette. But while garments may not need lower edgings, these stitch patterns still need selvedge stitches and side seams.
- Sometimes the yarn is moved, and if the yarn is to be moved, the stitch pattern must tell us. But it doesn't have to tell us to take it back to where it belongs for the next stitch. (In other words, a pattern might read *yf sl 1, k1:* the yarn is brought forward for the slip—and the pattern says so—but it is then taken back for the knit—and the pattern doesn't need to say so because the yarn is always at the back when we knit.)
- Patterns don't always tell us to slip purlwise (p-wise), but for most slip-stitch patterns we will (to orient the stitch appropriately for the following row).
- Sometimes these stitch patterns can be worked in one color or two: half-linen stitch is an example. But some of these stitch patterns are only meant to be worked in two colors, and the houndstooth sample is one of these.
- For many of these stitch patterns, the wrong side is as wonderful as the right side. The half-linen is an example.

Half-linen (over a multiple of 2 stitches and 4 rows)

Row 1 *K1, yf sl 1; repeat from * to last 2 stitches, k2.
Rows 2 and 4 Purl.
Row 3 K1, *k1, yf sl 1; repeat from * to last stitch, k1.
On size 7 (4.5mm) needles, 19 stitches
and 32 rows = 4″ (10cm) after steam-pressing

RS half-linen stitch

WS half-linen stitch

Garter slip (over a multiple of 4 + 3 stitches and 12 rows)

All RS rows Knit.

Rows 2, 4, 6 (WS) *K3, yf sl 1; repeat from * to the last 3 stitches, k3.

Rows 8, 10, 12 (WS) K1, *yf sl 1, k3; repeat from * to the last 2 stitches, yf sl 1, k1.

on size 7 (4.5mm) needles, 18 stitches and 32 rows = 4″ (10cm)

garter slip stitch

Houndstooth (over a multiple of 3 + 2 stitches and 4 rows)

Row 1 (MC) K1, *k2, sl 1; repeat from * to the last stitch, k1.

Row 2 (MC) Purl.

Row 3 (CC) K1, *sl 1, k2; repeat from * to the last stitch, k1.

Row 4 (CC) Purl.

on size 7 (4.5mm) needles, 19 stitches and 28 rows = 4″ (10cm) after steam-pressing

2-color half-linen

on size 7 (4.5mm) needles, 19 stitches and 32 rows = 4″ (10cm) after steam-pressing

Use half-linen stitch pattern but work rows 1–2 in MC and rows 3–4 in CC.

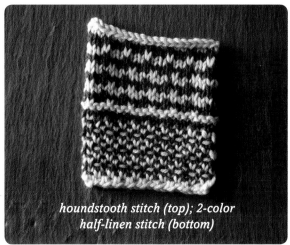

houndstooth stitch (top); 2-color half-linen stitch (bottom)

Cables and Twisted Stitches

Cables and twisted stitches are a textural expression that knitting does better than any other craft—and you can quote me on that!

- Because these stitch patterns may be dense, we usually use at least one size larger needles than for stockinette.
- Cables are usually worked in stockinette on a bed of RSS (although a bed of garter is a lovely alternative).
- One kind of cable could be called braids: they don't move over the background but cross over themselves. (See 9-stitch braid).
- Another kind of cable could be called traveling cables: the stitches "travel" over their background and may or may not cross over themselves. (See traveling cable.)

- Many cables are combinations of braids and traveling stitches, but it is the braids that most tighten gauge and distort their start and finish. To compensate for this, I do the following: only cast on half to two-thirds of the stitches the braid "wants." (For 9-stitch braid, cast on 5 instead of 9, then knit 1 row over these 5 stitches.) On the row before the first cross, increase to the number of stitches needed. (Purl the first stitch but then purl increase in each of the next 4 stitches: 5 stitches = 9 stitches.) Keep the full number of stitches for the duration of the cable until the row after the last cross, then decrease in the opposite manner. (After the final cross, purl-2-together 4 times, then purl 1: 9 stitches = 5 stitches.)
- Twisted stitches are also called crossed stitches—and can look much like cables, but are simpler. They only move one stitch at a time, which means not moving stitches from the left needle. Instead, we work the second stitch on the left needle before working the first stitch on the left needle as usual (see twisted-cable rib).

9-stitch braid (over 9 stitches and 8 rows, on a bed of RSS)

Pattern that follows is for cable only.

Row 1 Slip 3 stitches to cable needle (cn), hold to back, k3 from left needle, k3 from cn, k3.

All WS rows P9.

Rows 3, 7 K9.

Row 5 K3, slip 3 stitches to cn and hold to front, k3 from left needle, k3 from cn.

on size 7 (4.5mm) needles, width of 9-stitch cable = 1½″ (4cm) after steam-pressing

Traveling cable (over a multiple of 16 + 4 stitches)

Row 1 P2, *slip next 2 stitches onto cable needle and hold at front, p1 from left needle, k2 from cable needle (cross-2-left), p3, k2, p8; p2.

Row 2 K2, *p4, k4, p2, k3, p2, k1; k2.

Row 3 P2, *p1, cross-2-left, p2, k2, p3, slip next stitch onto cable needle and hold at back, k2 from left needle, p1 from cable needle (cross-2-right), k2; p2.

Row 4 K2, *p2, k1, p2, k3, p2, k2, p2, k2; k2

Row 5 P2, *p2, cross-2-left, p1, k2, p2, cross-2-right, p1, k2; p2.

Row 6 K2, *p2, k2, p2, k2, p2, k1, p2, k3; k2.

Row 7 P2, *p3, cross-2-left, k2, p1, cross-2-right, p2, k2; p2.

Row 8 K2, *p2, k3, p2, k1, p4, k4; k2

Row 9 P2, *p8, cross-2-right, p3, k2; p2

Row 10 K2, *p2, k4, p2, k8; k2

Row 11 P2, *p8, cross-2-left, p3, k2; p2

Row 12 K2, *p2, k3, p2, k1, p4, k4; k2

Row 13 P2, *p3, cross-2-right, k2, p1, cross-2-left, p2, k2; p2.

Row 14 K2, *p2, k2, p2, k2, p2, k1, p2, k3; k2.

Row 15 P2, *p2, cross-2-right, p1, k2, p2, cross-2-left, p1, k2; p2.

Row 16 K2, *p2, k1, p2, k3, p2, k2, p2, k2; k2.

Row 17 P2, *p1, cross-2-right, p2, k2, p3, cross-2-right, k2; p2.

Row 18 K2, *P4, k4, p2, k3, p2, k1; k2

Row 19 P2, *cross-2-right, p3, k2, p8; p2

9-stitch braid

traveling cable stitch

twisted-cable rib stitch

Row 20 K2, *k8, p2, k4, p2; k2.
on size 7 (4.5mm) needles, 24 stitches and 28 rows =
4″ (10cm) after steam-pressing

Twisted-cable rib (over a multiple of 10 + 2 stitches and 8 rows)

Row 1 *K2, p2, k4, p2; repeat from * to last 2 stitches, k2.
All WS rows P2, *k2, p4, k2, p2; repeat from *.
Row 3 *K2, p2, k2, knit into second stitch on left needle, then knit into first stitch on left needle, p2; repeat from * to last 2 stitches, k2.
Row 5 *K2, p2, k1, knit into second stitch on left needle, then knit into first stitch on left needle, k1, p2; repeat from * to last 2 stitches, k2.
Row 7 *K2, p2, knit into second stitch on left needle, then knit into first stitch on left needle, k2, p2; repeat from * to last 2 stitches, k2.
on size 6 (4mm) needles, 22 stitches and 26 rows =
4″ (10cm) after steam-pressing

Bobbles

Bobbles are little or big bumps and another textural expression in knitting.

- Classic bobbles are produced by knitting in the front and back of a stitch to produce 3 or 4 stitches out of 1. The stitches of the bobble can then be worked in stockinette or RSS. After 3 rows (turning the work each time), they are decreased back down to 1 stitch. (Unless you know how to knit-back-backward, you may find this tedious.)
- I prefer a no-turn bobble, worked as follows: using the knit cast-on, cast 3 stitches onto the left needle (making 4 stitches out of 1 and without turning your work); purl these 4 stitches (from the left needle onto the right); call the one closest to the tip of the right needle the first stitch, then pass the second over the first, the third over the first, then the fourth over the first—1 stitch remains, and no turning!
- If we don't slip the stitch of a bobble on its WS row (purlwise), we'll get droopy bobbles. (This applies to both the classic bobble and the "no-turn" bobble.)

Bobbles

Four samples shown on a bed of stockinette and on size 6 [4mm] needles)
Lower right, classic 4-stitch bobble in reverse stockinette
Lower left, classic 4-stitch bobble in stockinette
Upper right, no-turn bobble
Upper left, no-turn bobble not slipped on following WS row (It doesn't hold as tightly into the fabric, which would be more obvious if gravity were working on it!)

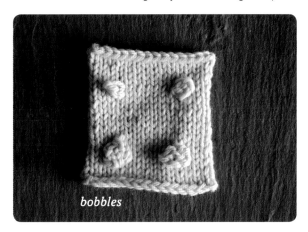

bobbles

Fairisle

Sometimes called *Fair Isle*, sometimes *fairisle*, sometimes *two-color stranded*, none is inclusive enough of this tradition. Sometimes it has more than two colors, sometimes it is woven (rather than stranded), and it doesn't always have the tightly prescribed motifs of the Shetland Islands. Here I've called it *fairisle* (which is a machine-knitting term) for lack of an alternative and to not infringe upon the trademarked Fair Isle (only to be used when referring to the particular work of those islands).

- Traditional Fair Isle is always stranded—with the color not in use simply carried behind for less than an inch (2.5cm).But if the stranded color is carried for an inch (2.5cm) or more, we want to trap its long "float" by weaving it across the back—that is, by knitting the working color under the carried color for 1 stitch, then over the carried color for 1 stitch. (Sometimes this is done once in the middle of a small motif, sometimes it is done constantly across a large motif, and sometimes it is done for an entire garment. Swatch to see what works for your color pattern.)

- Even though fairisle is usually worked in stockinette, it often gets a gauge close to square, especially if it's stranded (rather than woven).
- Because the fabric is dense, I prefer to use two sizes larger needles for fairisle than I would for one-color knitting in the same yarn.
- If you're combining plain stockinette with areas in fairisle, using two sizes larger needles for the fairisle areas will give close to the same stitch gauge over both stitch patterns. You will not achieve the same row gauge: there will be more rows/inch (2.5cm) in the single-color work.
- Because the gauge becomes close to square, you may use regular (not knitter's) graph paper.

Inspired by Escher (over a multiple of 6 stitches and 10 rows)
on size 8 (5mm) needles, 18 stitches and 22 rows = 4″ (10cm) after steam-pressing
(Chart is on page 193.)

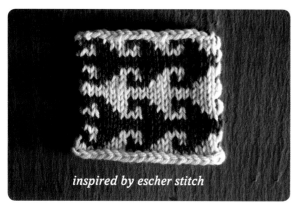

inspired by escher stitch

Intarsia

Intarsia (sometimes called *picture knitting*) is a color technique in which a separate bit or ball of yarn is used for each area of color. It's an advanced form of knitting that many of us find tedious because it requires us to stop and regularly check a chart. Here are its most important features.

- The colors must be crossed at the color change; otherwise, we will get holes.
- The cross is best described as *old* (the yarn we have just finished using) over *new* (the yarn we will use next).

- Sometimes this cross is already done by virtue of where the color change happens. (In other words, if the old color has already been knit over and is past where the new color hangs, all we need to do is bring up the new. This may make absolutely no sense unless you have knitting in hand and can see it happening.)
- Sometimes we don't want to use a separate ball of yarn: we want to carry the main color behind to where it will be used next. But the main color cannot simply be carried behind a motif; doing so would yield puffy, unsecured areas. We must weave it across (*knitting under the carried color for 1 stitch, then knitting over the carried color for 1 stitch, repeat from *). And when we do this, the main color will peek through.
- Sometimes we don't want to knit in all details: we use duplicate stitch (as shown in the sample and as discussed in the following section).
- Intarsia is usually done in stockinette, which does not have a square gauge. So because we are attempting to draw something, this work requires knitter's graph paper (which has stitches wider than rows are tall). This will allow our motif to be proportionally accurate.

Intarsia + duplicate stitch
Yellow and gray are knit in; white is worked after in duplicate stitch; see below.
on size 6 (4mm) needles, 19 stitches and 28 rows = 4″ (10cm) after steam-pressing

intarsia + duplicate stitch

- If you print out some knitter's graph paper, do not print the lines in black: print in a light color so you can see what you're drawing.
- If you're copying something from a square chart (a needlepoint motif), do the following: make a photocopy of the original chart; highlight every third row; when knitting, everything highlighted must be a repeated row (in other words, worked twice vertically). This will stretch it taller and to an appropriate proportion.

Duplicate Stitch

Duplicate stitch is embroidery that is added after and "duplicates" the knit stitch. It's an essential skill for knitters because it can be used to

- repair a hole
- add details too small to be knit in (as shown in the sample)
- put a third (or fourth) color into fairisle work
- work a motif too busy or too delicate to be knit in
- replace a color: this maneuver is part of the "rescue" discussion, page 160.

If you're using it for a motif from a nonknitting source, see the final bullet under Intarsia for when your motif comes from square graph paper.

Selvedge Stitches

Here's my definition of selvedge stitches: stitches that may be added to the edges of a piece, that may be turned into a seam allowance, and that may be treated differently from the rest of the knitting. (Whew! Quite a mouthful!) They're obviously complex little things that require a practical clarification after such an open-ended definition.

In my classes, I've seen much confusion (and bad choices) surrounding selvedge stitches. Do we need them? When do we add them? Do patterns include them? Is slip stitch always the best choice? Because you are drafting your own patterns here and asked in every garment piece if you want to add them, they demand a discussion.

Adding Selvedge Stitches

Do we always add selvedge stitches? No, not if the stitch pattern

- lies flat at its side edges
- and we like the look of those edges left alone
- and we are not seaming or adding bands to the sides

or we are seaming or adding bands but don't mind doing so from the existing, flat-lying edge.

All this can happen with garter or seed stitch (or stitch patterns that behave like them). As long as this list seems, this is not our most common knitting environment.

When do we add selvedge stitches? When the stitch pattern

- doesn't lie flat at its side edges
- and we are seaming or adding bands to the sides in a way that turns an edge stitch to the wrong side
- or we aren't seaming or adding bands but don't like the look of the stitch pattern at the edges.

All of this most often happens with stockinette (or stitch patterns that behave like it). This is actually knitting's most common environment: so, yes, we usually want selvedge stitches at each edge of our knit pieces.

Treating Selvedge Stitches

By "treating" I mean in what stitch pattern are these selvedge stitches worked? Here are our choices:

- slip stitch (slip, purlwise, the first stitch of every row)
- garter (knit the first and last stitch of every row)
- stockinette (knit the first and last stitch of every RS row, purl the first and last stitch of every WS row)

In addition, there is the following general "rule": maintain the integrity of selvedge stitches. This means not disrupting them for increases or decreases. If we leave them alone (and increase or decrease inside them), we'll have tidy edges and lovely seams.

Slip Stitch

When I ask which selvedge students prefer, this is the usual answer. I am very surprised by this, because this lovely thing is the one I would choose to use least often.

- She's pretty, but she makes the stockinette stitch next to her look unattractive. (We all know that stockinette stitches are ugly at the edges: the slip stitch doesn't alleviate this, she just transfers the ugliness to the stitch next door. If I could characterize her, she's the tall, good-looking one who likes to stand next to someone less attractive. Not nice!)
- She is pretty but tall and airy, so she leaves holes—in stockinette seams and around a round neck if you "slip the first stitch of the row at every neck edge bind-off." (The final bullet is an exception.)

- She will occur every second row, which means not enough spaces to pick up and knit against for any gauge that does not offer a 2-to-1 relationship of rows-to-stitches (which most do not).
- With all of this said, she's an excellent choice for the edges of a garter piece. If you are leaving the edge alone, her prettiness is welcome: if you are picking up and knitting against her, garter's 2-to-1 relationship makes her work.
- She is the perfect selvedge for any edge that will not be seamed or picked up and knit against. (So if you are shaping a round neck that will not have any additional finishing, slip the first stitch at each edge bind-off to achieve a pretty, finished neck edge.)

Slip-stitch selvedge on stockinette

The right edge of the stockinette swatch has a barely visible slip-stitch selvedge: note that the edge is pulled tight and the stitch next to the selvedge is distorted (It looks fat!). The left edge has a stockinette selvedge, and the stitch next to the selvedge is not distorted.

Slip-stitch selvedge on garter

The right edge of the garter swatch has a slip-stitch selvedge and is quite lovely.

Garter selvedge on garter

The left edge of the garter swatch has garter at its edge: the final stitch is not as pretty as all the others, but it does lie flat and would be easy to seam or pick up and knit from it.

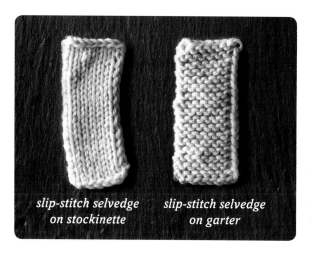

slip-stitch selvedge on stockinette | slip-stitch selvedge on garter

Garter

Oddly enough, the second most popular selvedge is this one—which I also find surprising because she doesn't behave much better than the slip stitch.

- She's pretty (short and stocky and still attractive), but stubborn! She wants to lie flat (as you can see on the left edge of the garter piece in the sample) and fights against being turned into a seam allowance. This is problematic when used as a selvedge on stockinette, because this will make the seams difficult to execute and bulky.
- She occurs every second row as a neat and tight little knot (as you can see on the left edge of the garter piece in the sample). At the edge of a stockinette piece, this is difficult to pick up and knit against.
- With all this said, she's well-behaved in a garter garment. She'll produce pretty and flat seams (and no seam allowances), and she'll produce bumps along the edge (perfectly spaced and easy to pick up from).

Stockinette

- This is often the least popular choice, 'cause she's not pretty. But she is ever so well-behaved! (Yes, she's unattractive—with her one long stitch followed by one short, knotty stitch. But here's a case where the unattractive one has the better personality!)
- She naturally rolls her unattractive self to the wrong side, so she produces beautiful side seams.
- She does not distort the stitch next door: the left edge of the stockinette swatch in the sample shows this.
- She offers lots of spaces for picking up and knitting a band.
- She is the best choice along all edges of pieces worked in stockinette or any similar stitch pattern, whose edge is to be seamed or picked up and knit against.

Bands and Their Stitch Patterns

Bands (sometimes called edgings) are garment features that sometimes start the garments, are sometimes knit along with the garment pieces, and are sometimes added later. They include bottom bands, cuffs, cardigan front bands, neck bands, and armhole edgings.

What follows is a discussion of stitch pattern choices and how they behave. To avoid repetition, all the issues of numbers of stitches, needle sizes, and techniques of picking up and knitting are discussed in the specific sections dedicated to a particular band (bottom, cuff, neck, etc.).

Rib (Single Layer or Folded)

What we love about rib is its elasticity. So it's a wonderful choice for bands that need to hold curves or hug a shape: neck bands, armholes, cuffs, and bottom bands that grab. And speaking of hugging, the taller the rib, the more it will hug.

Because its primary characteristic is elasticity, we wonder about rib for front bands—where elasticity is not required or even appropriate. But rib worked to only an inch (2.5cm) won't hug much and will produce a flat-lying front band.

That it lies flat is the other reason we love rib for bands. And it can be used for wide, flat front bands, whose elasticity can be eliminated with steam-pressing.

Sometimes we want a rib band with more body, so we double it and fold it over.

- Pick up and knit (casting on an extra stitch at any edge that needs to be closed), then work the rib to an inch (2.5cm) or so.

Rib and doubled rib edgings

A simple rib is shown along the lower edge and the right-side edge.
A doubled rib band is shown along the left-side edge (with the bottom edge of the band sewn closed and the top edge left open).

- Work a reverse stockinette row (as a fold line).
- Work in rib until the band just reaches the selvedge (when folded over).
- Bind off in pattern.
- Finish by sewing the bound-off row to the selvedge and by sewing the extra edge stitches under (to close the open edges).

Reverse Stockinette

My favorite band is reverse stockinette. I should probably be embarrassed by how often I use it, but I make no apologies. Why do I love it?

- It's easy (2–5 rows of RS purl and WS knit).
- It's a quick alternative to applied I-cord (which I find tedious).
- It has no particular "character" so it doesn't demand attention and fits anywhere.
- It takes a curve surprisingly well, but also works wonderfully on straight edges.
- You generally don't have to sew it down (but you may choose to if it has buttonhole treatments).
- The fact that it rolls to the wrong side makes it a perfect choice to sew down over a cut edge (of fairisle that has been cut) or tails (of a striped garment with tails that can be cut, knotted, and tucked under the band).

I am sure I could go on, but I won't. But I will add that I have had success working continuous bands—up the

Reverse stockinette edgings

A reverse stockinette band is shown along the lower edge.
A second reverse stockinette band is shown along the right side edge, which turns the top corner and continues along the top edge.

rib and doubled rib edgings

reverse stockinette edgings

right front, then around the neck, and then back down the left front, all in one row—by simply working front and neck bands as usual but with a (k1, yo, k1) on the pick-up-and-knit row at each corner (where neck meets front). Can't say that works with any other edging!

Stockinette

You might wonder why stockinette is a separate topic from reverse stockinette. But you probably know by now that the answer is the roll. Reverse stockinette rolls under; stockinette rolls up. And while that's fine for a tall funnel or turtleneck, where reverse stockinette doesn't work, I don't really see the point in a small stockinette neck or front band that rolls up to the right side: reverse stockinette is ever so much neater. But a tall stockinette band forced flat is a beautiful thing—the perfect choice when you want the smoothest possible band or one in which you might introduce colorwork. How do we force a stockinette band flat? By doubling it.

If it is a hem that starts a garment piece, work as follows:

- Cast on with a smooth waste yarn and a provisional cast-on: the crochet cast-on is a good choice.
- Work stockinette (for the back side of the hem) to desired height.
- Work 1 row of reverse stockinette (for the turn of the hem).
- Work stockinette (for the front of the hem) until the front is the same height as the back.
- Remove the waste yarn, and put the stitches that are revealed onto a small, spare needle.
- **Next row** Work-2-together, over the stitches of both needles, to join the front of the hem to the back. (You will have 1 fewer stitch on the back side of the hem, so somewhere in the row work 1 stitch from the front needle alone.)

If it is a front band that finishes a garment piece, work as follows:

- Pick up and knit (casting on an extra stitch at any edge that needs to be closed), then work stockinette to desired length (for the front side of the band).
- Work 1 row of reverse stockinette (for the fold line of the band).
- Work stockinette until the back side of the band just reaches the selvedge (when folded) before binding off.

- Finish by sewing the bound-off row to the selvedge and by sewing the extra edge stitches under (to close the open edges).

RS of stockinette hem and front band

A stockinette hem is shown along the lower edge. A stockinette band is shown along the right side edge (with the bottom edge of the band sewn closed and the top edge left open).

WS of stockinette hem and front band

Most of the stockinette hem is attached, but some was left unattached and with the provisional cast-on still visible.

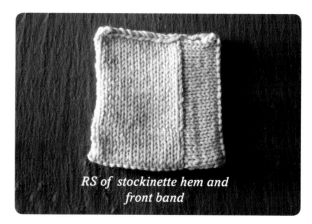

RS of stockinette hem and front band

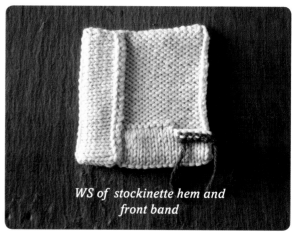

WS of stockinette hem and front band

Garter

Lovely, simple, but much-maligned garter stitch! It's fabulous for front bands because it lies flat and never needs to be doubled. But while a garter band of only a few rows would take a curve, it doesn't take a curve well if knit to an inch (2.5cm) or more. So I'd understand a preference for reverse stockinette.

Garter stitch edging

A garter stitch band is shown on the lower edge and the right side edge.

Moss stitch edging

A moss stitch band is shown on the left side edge.

garter stitch and moss stitch edgings

Moss

I'm not much of a fan of this stitch pattern for an edging: it's too flimsy for my liking. Ribbing doubles into itself, as does garter; reverse stockinette rolls back onto itself; stockinette is always worked to two layers. Moss stitch just lies there—flat and thin and pretty, but wimpy.

The only way it would take a curve is if it were only worked for a few rows, and this stitch pattern needs at least an inch (2.5cm) to reveal its loveliness. So because it doesn't take a curve, it is too limiting for me.

Starting Bands—Bottom Bands and Cuffs

Before discussing these, I want to address why they are here and not in the pattern drafting chapters, since they are usually knit along with our garments. The main reason is that we have many choices (whether or not to even have a bottom band or cuff and what stitch pattern to use), and I wanted to write the drafting instructions without the complication of those choices.

Your Choice of Stitch Patterns

Since much of our knitting rolls up at the bottom, we often choose to hold it down with a band in a stitch pattern that lies flat or that rolls under. Your common choices (rib, reverse stockinette, stockinette, garter, and moss) were all discussed in the previous section.

But sometimes even these will be affected by the powerful upward roll of the garment's stitch pattern. If your bottom bands flip up, treat them as follows: wet or wash them, then pin them to something that will hold them flat (either a carpet or other garment pieces rolling the opposite way—front pinned to back, for example), then let them dry.

If you want a tall bottom band, a stockinette hem or rib are the usual choices. But do note that the taller you work your rib, the narrower it gets. If you truly want a tall band, you must work it to the height you want when it is stretched to the width you want.

Needle Sizes and Numbers of Stitches

It is extremely rare for me not to work a bottom band or cuff on two sizes smaller needles—whatever its stitch pattern. It is also rare for me not to work a bottom band on 10 percent fewer stitches than the garment piece itself—whatever the stitch pattern of the bottom band. So you may realize from this that I don't do swatches in the stitch patterns of my bands. I just know that it's appropriate to use 10 percent fewer stitches and smaller needles.

I can't explain why, but if we do both these things—fewer stitches and smaller needles—the garment hangs straight: if we don't, the bottom band flares wider than the garment. If you want a bottom band that hugs the body, you may need even fewer stitches and smaller needles.

A special note about cuffs. I don't address the measurement for a cuff because I want a cuff that fits you. Whatever its stitch pattern, for a cuff that fits do the following: wrap a cast-on edge from the garment around your fist; count this number of stitches; this will give you the minimum number of stitches for a cuff that will fit your wrist and that will stay on your arm if the sleeve is pushed up to three-quarter length. (This is addressed in all the sleeve patterns of chapters 2 and 6.)

For both bottom bands and cuffs, you might need to increase stitches for the garment body or sleeve. To simplify, do the following:

- End the band with a RS row.
- Purl, and work increases in, the next WS row (staying on smaller needles).

This accomplishes two things.

- You purl instead of struggling to incorporate increases into a stitch pattern.
- When done, you are ready to work row 1 of the garment's stitch pattern, complete with the correct number of stitches.

The only time you wouldn't do this is if the stitch pattern of the band were running contiguously into the stitch pattern of the garment.

Finishing Bands—Armhole, Front, and Neck Bands (Including Collars and Hoods)

I had a very clever student who once said, "It doesn't matter how much money you spend on yarn, or how much time you spend knitting, it's what you do in the last two hours that makes all the difference."

She's not entirely right, because picking the right style, working the right size to the right length, and wearing the garment with the right thing (all discussed in chapter 1) matter very much. But she is mostly right, because we can ruin all that good work with bad finishing.

Finishing comes in two parts: seaming (as mentioned in the Essential Skills list in the Appendix) and bands added at the garment's completion. And while seaming is very important, nowhere does finishing matter quite as much as with our armhole, front, and neck bands— holding the pieces to shape at the edges, often front and center in our garments.

Finishing Principles

There are a few things to be said up front that apply to all bands discussed in the following sections.

- I am not a fan of front bands knit along with the garment or knit separately (to length) and sewn down. I don't think these hold their shape well or offer the options I want. So all that follows is dedicated to front bands picked up and knit out from an edge.
- With rare exceptions, I recommend working these bands on two sizes smaller needles. (This gives firmness at the edges that helps your garment hold its shape. And the proportions that follow assume smaller needles.)
- All of what follows also assumes that you use the same yarn for the bands as for the garment.
- To *pick up and knit* means to insert your needle through an edge (usually 1 stitch from the edge), wrap the needle with yarn, and draw through a stitch. We usually work from right to left and will have one RS row of knitting on the needle when we're done.
- Our usual method is to pick up and knit 1 stitch from this edge: this turns 1 stitch into the "seam allowance," which means that our garment piece needs a selvedge stitch.
- If you encounter a hole when you're picking up and knitting, pick up and knit in the tight spot next to the hole, never in the hole itself.
- Despite all the specific pick-up-and-knit instructions that follow, if you need to pick up and knit an extra stitch to close a space, do so.
- If your band's stitch pattern requires a particular multiple of stitches, don't try to achieve it while picking up and knitting. Count stitches after your pick-up-and-knit row, figure out what you need to increase or decrease, and do so evenly across the next row.
- For any of the finishing bands that follow, if you find that you have too many stitches, you can tighten the bind-off row to draw the band in (page 159).

Armhole Bands

Remembering that I shape armholes with diagonals, to achieve the right number of stitches for an armhole band I recommend picking up and knitting

- 1 stitch in every bound-off stitch (at the underarm)
- 3 stitches for every 4 rows along the row edge (whether diagonal or straight) if your band is rib, garter, or reverse stockinette and your garment is stockinette
- 2 stitches for every 3 rows along the row edge (whether diagonal or straight) if your band is stockinette and your garment is stockinette

- 1 stitch for every 2 rows along the row edge (whether diagonal or straight) if your band is garter and your garment is garter.

Armhole band

A partial armhole band—rib against a stockinette fabric.

armhole band

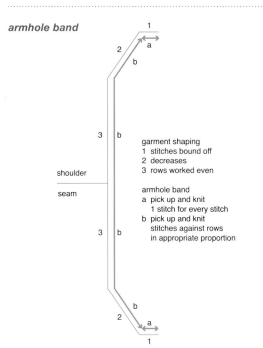

armhole band

1

2

a

b

3

b

shoulder

seam

3

b

b

2

a

1

garment shaping
1 stitches bound off
2 decreases
3 rows worked even

armhole band
a pick up and knit
      1 stitch for every stitch
b pick up and knit
      stitches against rows
      in appropriate proportion

Front Bands

I find it frustrating when instructions say "pick up and knit 137 stitches along the right front edge . . . evenly." Not only are they not helpful, they are wrong. If you shorten or lengthen your garment (as you should, and as suggested in chapter 1), then you need to pick up and knit the right number of stitches for your length. If you pick up and knit too many stitches, your front band will be too long (and you'll have what is fondly referred to as *dread frontal droop*). And if you pick up and knit too few stitches, your front band will be too short (and will flip open unless it's held closed with buttons). Each of these results is to be avoided!

Here are the proportions that work for me when picking up and knitting for a front band along a straight-row edge. (These proportions are based on my stitch-to-row gauge, and if your row gauge is very different, it will matter here.)

- 5 stitches for every 6 rows if the band is a single-layer rib and the garment is stockinette.
- 3 stitches for every 4 rows if the band is a folded rib and the garment is stockinette.
- 3 stitches for every 4 rows if the band is reverse stockinette and the garment is stockinette.
- 3 stitches for every 4 rows if the band is garter and the garment is stockinette.
- 3 stitches for every 4 rows if the band is moss and the garment is stockinette.
- 3 stitches for every 5 rows if the band is stockinette and the garment is stockinette.
- 1 stitch for every 2 rows if the band is garter and the garment is garter.

One exception to this is if you are planning to add a zipper, where a reverse stockinette band is a good choice. But if your experience is like mine, you can produce a perfect band that waffles and stretches once you sew in the rigid zipper. What I have found works is the following: find the proportion that should work with the band. See chart on page 219 and find that proportion numerically, find two proportions lower (that is, to two bullets higher on the list), then pick up and knit in this proportion instead. You will have picked up and knit too few stitches, and your band will look too tight until it is stretched out by the rigid zipper.

Continuous Front Band + Round Neck

Some band stitch patterns will allow you to pick up and knit for your front band then turn the corner and continue with the round neck band. To do so, work the front band as specified, work a (k1, yo, k1) at each corner (working the yo's to twist them on the following row), then continue with the round neck band as described on page 153.

Continuous Front Band + V-Neck

Most definitely, you can pick up and knit below the V and then continue through the V shaping. But we need to do so in such a way as to not get a pull at the point of the V and to have enough stitches along the diagonal.

V-neck cardigan band

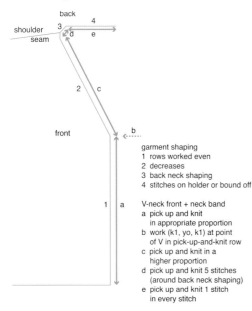

garment shaping
1 rows worked even
2 decreases
3 back neck shaping
4 stitches on holder or bound off

V-neck front + neck band
a pick up and knit
  in appropriate proportion
b work (k1, yo, k1) at point
  of V in pick-up-and-knit row
c pick up and knit in a
  higher proportion
d pick up and knit 5 stitches
  (around back neck shaping)
e pick up and knit 1 stitch
  in every stitch

- Choose a proportion for your straight-row edge based on the suggestions on page 147.
- At the point of the V, work a (k1, yo, k1) in the pick-up-and-knit row. (Twist the yarn over on the following row.)
- On the diagonal-row edge, you will need a higher proportion than on the straight-row edge, or your band will have too few stitches. (There's Pythagorean theorem at work again!) I suggest

adding 2 to each number of the lower proportion. (For example, if you're picking up and knitting 3 stitches for every 4 rows on the straight, pick up and knit 5 stitches for every 6 rows on the diagonal.)
- At the back neck, pick up and knit 5 stitches in the back neck's shaping and then 1 stitch for every stitch (on a holder or bound off) across the back neck.

I prefer to work a V-neck cardigan band in two parts—starting with the button band. This allows me to use that band to plan the placement of my buttonholes. This means that if the button band is the left front, it starts at center back. And this will also mean a small seam at the bands' center back neck.

Neck Bands (Plus Collars and Hoods)

Perhaps the most frustrating instructions are those that say "pick up and knit 101 stitches around the neck edge . . . evenly." It's one of the hardest things we have to do, and this is all the help we get? And if we are drafting our own patterns, we won't even have this to rely on!

What follows is how I recommend working the neck bands (plus collars and hoods) for all the neck shapes in this book. (It bears repeating here that this is part of a garment's finishing: the neck's shape happens in the drafting: the bands, collars, and hoods are added to finished pieces.)

Through what follows, I don't state a preference for working neck bands in the round (on a circular needle) or flat (on a circular or straight needles and with a seam at a shoulder). The only neck band that demands a circular needle is a collar with a front split. For this, you'll work back and forth—with a front split—but on a circular needle.

Straight (Boat) Neck

The straight neck is an unshaped neck edge left with live stitches. It doesn't require a band, so you may just bind off. Or you may work a small band onto those live stitches (in any stitch pattern) before binding off.

Funnel Neck

The funnel neck (not to be confused with the turtleneck, which is a tall, round neck band) is also an unshaped neck edge left with live stitches. It doesn't require a band, so you may bind off after working your collar's height. Or you may finish the collar in any stitch pattern before binding off.

Square Neck

A square neck has stitches left on a holder or bound off with straight row edges (up its sides) plus back neck shaping. For its band, pick up and knit

- 1 stitch for every stitch (whether bound off or on a holder)
- 3 stitches for every 4 rows along straight-row edges
- 5 stitches at back neck shaping.

These instructions assume a stockinette garment. If the garment has a denser row gauge than stockinette, pick up and knit in a lower proportion along the straight-row edges.

If your neck band is minimal, you will bind off soon. If your neck edge has more depth, you'll need to miter at the corners of the front neck (as shown in the sample). Through what follows, I assume a rib neck band, which is what shows off these miters best.

- Pick up and knit as above, being sure to have a stitch right at each corner of the square. Always make this corner stitch a RS knit (and WS purl) stitch.
- Decrease on either side of this stitch every RS row—including the bind-off row.
- When you decrease, your rib will be "wrong" until decreasing makes it "right" again. I prefer to be "wrong" with an extra knit stitch—meaning that there will be 3 purls at the corner of the next WS row.

square neck band

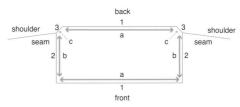

garment shaping	square neck band
1 stitches on holder or bound off	a pick up and knit 1 stitch in every stitch
2 rows worked even	b pick up and knit 3 stitches for every 4 rows
3 back neck shaping	c pick up and knit 5 stitches (around back neck shaping)

Square neck band with miter

A partial square neck band—rib against a stockinette fabric—with a miter at the corner.

square neck band with miter

V-Neck

A V-neck has stitches left on a holder or bound off (at the base of the V and across the back), plus diagonals (for front and back neck shaping), plus a straight edge (at the end of the front's V-neck shaping). For its band, pick up and knit

- 1 stitch for every stitch (whether bound-off or on a holder)
- 4 stitches for every 5 rows along diagonals
- 3 stitches for every 4 rows along any straight-row edges
- 5 stitches in each corner of back neck shaping.

These instructions assume a stockinette garment. If the garment has a denser row gauge than stockinette, pick up and knit in a lower proportion along the diagonal edge.

V-neck bands are usually worked in rib, although the same choices are available as for the round neck (garter, stockinette, reverse stockinette). I think the reason rib is the traditional choice is that it is crisper, especially when mitering is required for the bottom of the V. (If you don't miter the V, you'll get a soft and messy bottom!) Here's how to miter a ribbed V-neck band.

- Pick up and knit as above, being sure to have 1 or 2 stitch(es) at the base of the V.
- Always make the stitch(es) at the base RS knit (and WS purl).
- Decrease on either side of this (or these) stitch(es) every RS row or every row if your V is steep—and this includes the bind-off row.
- When you decrease, your rib will be "wrong" until decreasing makes it "right" again. I prefer to be "wrong" with an extra knit stitch—meaning that there will be 3 purls at the corner of the next WS row.

V-neck band

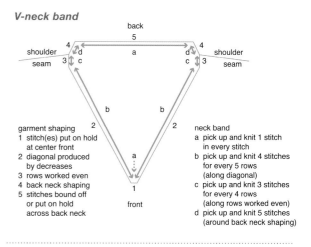

garment shaping
1 stitch(es) put on hold at center front
2 diagonal produced by decreases
3 rows worked even
4 back neck shaping
5 stitches bound off or put on hold across back neck

neck band
a pick up and knit 1 stitch in every stitch
b pick up and knit 4 stitches for every 5 rows (along diagonal)
c pick up and knit 3 stitches for every 4 rows (along rows worked even)
d pick up and knit 5 stitches (around back neck shaping)

V-neck band with miter

A small V-neck (shaped by decreasing on each side each fourth row), with a rib band and a miter at its center (which has decreases each side of center every RS row).

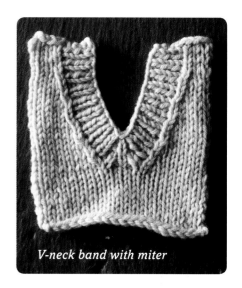

V-neck band with miter

V-Neck with Shawl Collar

The term *shawl collar* has an interesting history, and knowing where the name came from can help you understand how it is constructed. It came from the "collar" that was formed when the long straight edge of a shawl was wrapped around the neck. Because there was no neck shaping, the straight edge rolled over—producing the "shawl" collar.

While this collar happens naturally in a shawl, to produce this collar in a V-neck, we need to "fill in" the V shape. (In the drawing, I show this "area to be filled" and I show it ending at the center of the neck. If you want your shawl larger, this area could be larger.)

We fill in this area by working short rows, leaving stitches behind until we have filled the shape. The drawing only shows one front (which makes it easier to visualize) and does not show the back (because it is not part of the shaping).

A shawl collar is best worked in a reversible stitch pattern (like rib or garter). And because I like a soft shawl collar, I'll use the same size needles as the garment—larger than I normally would for a rib or garter band. Larger needles might mean picking up and knitting only 3 stitches for every 4 rows (instead of the higher proportion usually dedicated to the diagonal of the V-neck).

Measurements You Need

For this shape, you'll need your neck width and depth, just as for a usual V-neck. But one difference between this and the usual V-neck pullover is that this one will have a "flat bottom"—the width of the V-neck at its base. This width, whether you are making a pullover or a cardigan, is the width (or depth) of the band before starting the shawl portion.

Another measurement you'll need for the following calculations is the #rows/inch (2.5cm) of the band. To get this information, just pick up and knit the neck or front band as usual, and then continue to the depth you want before the shawl collar part of the band. At that point, you can stop, measure your band's row gauge, and continue with the work on the next page.

But one final measurement to know is that you will stop your shawl collar shaping 2″ (5cm) before the shoulder seam, and this is written into the following calculations.

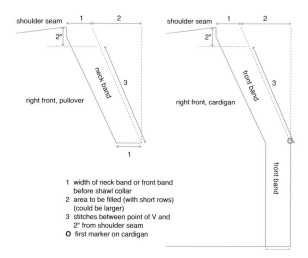

shawl collar from V-neck

1 width of neck band or front band before shawl collar
2 area to be filled (with short rows) (could be larger)
3 stitches between point of V and 2″ from shoulder seam
O first marker on cardigan

Shawl Collar
Calculations

neck width = _____ inches (cm)
#rows/inch (2.5cm) in neck or front band stitch pattern = _____

note These calculations cannot be worked until you have picked up and knit and then worked the band to its depth before the shawl collar. See pages 150–51.

For a Pullover

1. #stitches in band from base of neck to 2″ (5cm) from shoulder seam = _____

For a Cardigan

1. #stitches in band from start of V-neck shaping to 2″ (5cm) from shoulder seam = _____

2. neck width ÷ 2 = _____ inches (cm) (This is the minimal width for the shawl portion of the collar; you can make this wider.)
3. #inches (#cm) in step 2 × #rows/inch (2.5cm) in band stitch pattern = #rows for shawl collar _____
4. #rows for shawl collar ÷ 2 = #opportunities to leave stitches behind at each side of the collar _____
5. #stitches in step 1 ÷ #opportunities (step 4) = #stitches to leave behind each time at each side of collar _____ (Fudge to make this a whole number.) If the result is half (3.5), leave the number of stitches on either side of the half (3 and 4) behind at alternate pairs of short rows.

Pattern

note You will probably slip the first stitch purlwise after the turn, and you may work a wrap which you can work or leave alone on the next row, but this pattern's short-row directions only say "turn."

For a Pullover

- End neck band after working a WS row.
- Work 1 RS row until #stitches in step 5 remain on the left needle; turn.
- Work 1 WS row until #stitches in step 5 remain on the left needle; turn.

For a Cardigan

- End front band after working a RS row.
- **Next WS row** Work row, placing markers as follows: 1 at the beginning of V-neck shaping on the left front (#2), one at the beginning of V-neck shaping on the right front (#1).
- Work 1 RS row to #stitches in step 5 before marker #2; turn.
- Work 1 WS row to #stitches in step 5 before marker #1; turn.

For All Styles

- *Work 1 RS row to #stitches in step 5 before previous short row; turn.
- Work 1 WS row to #stitches in step 5 before previous short row; turn.
- Repeat from * until all required stitches have been left behind and all required rows have been worked, ending after a WS short row. Remove markers in cardigan.
- Cut yarn. Slip to beginning of RS row (at base of V or beginning of front band), and bind off all stitches.
- *optional* To close holes at turns, and to make sure the bind-off row isn't too tight, work an increase in each turn space while binding off.

For a Pullover

- Sew the front edge of the shawl collar to the base of the V, then sew the back edge behind.

round neck band

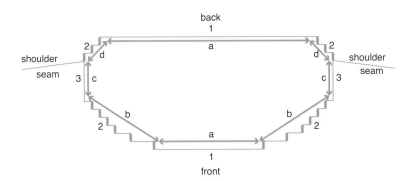

garment shaping
1 stitches bound off or on a holder
2 shaping with bound-off stitches
   (bold verticals show stair steps
   between bound-off stitches)
3 rows worked even
neck band
a pick up and knit 1 stitch
   in every stitch
b pick up and knit 1 stitch
   in every bound-off stitch and
   1 stitch in every stair step
c pick up and knit 3 stitches
   for every 4 rows
   (along rows worked even)
d pick up and knit 5 stitches
   (around back neck shaping)

Round Neck

This is our most challenging neck band, because we are picking up and knitting around a curve. And that curve throws everything at us: some live stitches (at the base of the front and across most of the back), some bound-off stitches (at the front's base for a cardigan and to produce the front curves and back neck shaping), and some straight-row edges (to finish the fronts).

And yes, you may have noticed that I bind off for the curves—instead of leaving live stitches. While I might put large numbers of stitches on a holder at the front and back base of a round neck (especially for a pullover), I would not recommend leaving live stitches (and working short rows) for the curves. In my experience, short rows and live stitches leave holes: bound-off edges give a "facing" that holds the neck to shape (and which is not visible on the front of the work after you pick up and knit).

But those bound-off stitches do make the neck band more difficult to execute than live stitches would. Here is a method for picking up and knitting around a round neck that absorbs them. It's simple and intuitive, and gives you the perfect number of stitches every time.

For the right number of stitches that evenly fill the round neck, pick up and knit

- 1 stitch for every stitch (whether on a holder or bound-off)
- 1 stitch in the tight spot (not the big hole) of every stair step (between the bound-off stitches of the curve)
- 3 stitches for every 4 rows of any straight row edges

- 5 stitches in each corner of back neck shaping (which you will get if you follow the previous 2 bullets).

These instructions assume a garment knit in stockinette. If the garment has a denser row gauge than stockinette, pick up and knit as specified, but you may need to decrease stitches by 10–15 percent on your next row.

After the pick-up-and-knit row, you may change to a variety of stitch patterns: ribbing, garter, reverse stockinette, stockinette. (I don't recommend moss, because it doesn't hold a curve well.)

Round neck

A partial round neck, shaped by binding off 6, then 3, then 2 stitches, then 1 stitch 4 times, finished with 8 rows even.

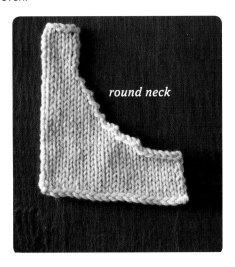

round neck

Round neck band

The same round neck as the previous photo, finished with a reverse stockinette band.

round neck band

Turtleneck (Mock or Full)

A turtleneck is a round neck band (picked up and knit as specified above) worked tall. It is usually ribbed (although I've done many in stockinette). How tall should it be? If it's too short to fold over, it's a mock turtleneck. If it's tall enough to fold over, you might want to work the folded-over part on larger needles—so it will fold easily and not be too tight.

Round Neck with Collar

A collar is usually worked from a round neck, and that is assumed through what follows.

- Using a circular needle, begin and end at center front (which—for a cardigan—will be at the center of each front band or at the garment's center front with overlapping front pieces).
- Pick up and knit as for the round neck, above. (Remember, this is done on smaller needles.)

You now have choices: do you want a collar stand? when (if ever) do you want the collar to fold over? when do you want the collar to split?

- If you want a collar stand (a portion of the collar that stands straight before folding over), work an inch (2.5cm) on smaller needles.
- If you want the collar to continue to stand up, keep using smaller needles and decrease stitches—probably 20 percent—as you work the collar to its height.
- If you want the collar to fold over, change to larger needles at the fold.

For a pullover, when you want the collar to split, turn at center front to work back and forth.

And finally, you might want to deal with the shape of the collar. To have the collar sit straight at the front (and not spread too wide), increase 1 stitch at each front edge every RS row. (See the 2x2 rib collar.)

A collar is usually done in a stitch pattern that lies flat and is reversible: rib or garter are the usual choices, but stockinette (doubled and sewn down) also works.

2x2 rib collar (underside)

The underside of this collar shows 4 rows on smaller needles before changing to larger needles.

2x2 rib collar (underside)

2x2 rib collar

This same collar, folded over, shows an increase in the third stitch of every RS row (to keep the collar's edge straight at front).

2x2 rib collar

Round Neck in Saddle Shoulder

The difference between the usual round neck and the round neck in a saddle shoulder is the direction of knitting: the saddle means a neck worked side to side. Does this change the methodology for picking up and knitting? Not at all. However, you might appreciate the following differences:

- The small straight-row edges that finish the traditional round neck are now a number of bound-off stitches (so you will pick up and knit 1 stitch in each of these).
- The live stitches usually found at the base of the front neck are now a large number of bound-off stitches at the end of the front piece (so you will pick up and knit 1 stitch in each of these).
- The live stitches usually found at the back neck are now long row edges along the back of the saddle (so you will pick up and knit 3 stitches for every 4 rows or in a proportion that works for your garment's stitch pattern).
- The curve is the same despite the direction of knitting, so you will pick up and knit 1 stitch in every bound-off stitch and 1 stitch in every stair step.

round neck band in saddle shoulder

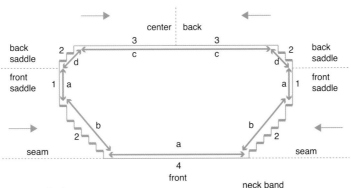

garment shaping
1 stitches bound off
2 shaping with bound-off stitches (bold horizontals show stair steps between bound-off stitches)
3 rows worked even
4 bound-off edge of garment front

arrow = direction of knitting

neck band
a pick up and knit 1 stitch in every bound-off stitch
b pick up and knit 1 stitch in every bound-off stitch and 1 stitch in every stair step
c pick up and knit 3 stitches for every 4 rows
d pick up and knit 5 stitches

Hoods

A hood is easily worked as an extension of a round neck band.

- Pick up and knit for your round neck band—as directed on page 154.
- Work perhaps 1″ (2.5cm) on smaller needles.
- Change to larger needles and increase stitches by 10 to 20 percent across the back neck in the next row.
- Work until the hood is the desired height. (Too tall is more comfortable than too short).
- Fold the hood in half, and graft live stitches together (joining the two sides of the hood from front to crown).
- If needed, add a band to the front of the hood (which could be continuous from the front band, if this is part of a cardigan).

hood

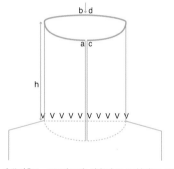

dotted line = round neck, picked up and knit as usual
V = stitches increased across back neck
h = height of hood
arrow = center back hood
bold line = live stitches to be grafted together
(attaching point a to point c, point b to point d, and all stitches between)

When Things Don't Turn Out as Expected

You aren't following a pattern—good for you! Things may not work out the way you planned: perfectly to be expected in this landscape. You may feel twinges of discouragement: let 'em pass, because there are solutions for much of what you will encounter. I offer some, you'll develop your own, and at the end of the process you'll be a more confident, optimistic, and accomplished knitter.

Much of the work that follows is more easily accomplished if you don't proceed too far before realizing you need to do some rescue work. So read the first steps in each section: they tell how, early in your knitting, you can determine if you'll need the help offered in that section.

If Your Garment Is Not Working to the Width You Want

Sometimes stitch patterns behave differently between a small swatch and a large piece. Maybe gravity had a field day, maybe you got into the rhythm of your work and it relaxed, maybe you had wine with dinner. The good news is that there are fixes.

Modified Drop Shoulder, Set-in Sleeve, and Raglan

After you've knit for a while, you may have a suspicion that your piece is not getting the width you wanted. Here's how to rescue all that knitting.

- Stop knitting this piece before the armhole.
- Put the stitches onto a thread, and steam-press or wash and dry.
- Measure its width.
- If the piece is too wide, call it the front. Bind off whatever you need at the armhole to bring the piece down to the width you wanted after your pattern's armhole bind-off but before any armhole decreases.
- If the piece is too narrow, call it the back. Bind off whatever you need at the armhole to bring the piece down to the width you wanted after your pattern's armhole bind-off but before any armhole decreases. (For the back, this could be 0.)
- Cast on for the alternate piece, casting on more or fewer than the piece you just worked—whatever it takes so that when both are added together you get the circumference you wanted at your garment's hem. Bind off at this piece's armhole to bring it down to the same width after your pattern's armhole bind-off but before any armhole decreases. (Again, for the back, this could be 0.)
- With this rescue, you will have the circumference you want below the armhole, you did not change your armhole shaping (other than the bind-off), you did not change the neck, and the only odd thing you'll have is side seams slightly skewed to the back.
- Recalculate your new gauge, and then work your sleeves to this gauge.

modified drop shoulder rescue

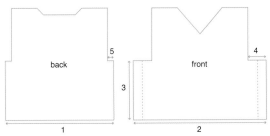

1 back width
2 front width
   (2 + 1 = the circumference you wanted)
3 length to armhole
4 stitches bound off at each front armhole
5 stitches bound off at each back armhole
Dotted lines show side edge of front after seaming

set-in sleeve rescue

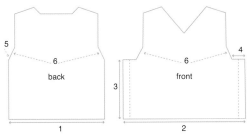

1 back width
2 front width
   (2 + 1 = the circumference you wanted)
3 length to armhole
4 stitches bound off at each front armhole
5 stitches bound off at each back armhole (could be 0)
6 armhole decreases
Dotted lines show side edge of front after seaming

raglan rescue

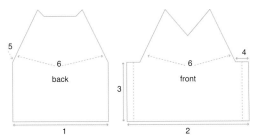

1 back width
2 front width
   (2 + 1 = the circumference you wanted)
3 length to armhole
4 stitches bound off at each front armhole
5 stitches bound off at each back armhole (could be 0)
6 armhole deceases
Dotted lines show side edge of front after seaming

Drop Shoulder

The rescue of a drop shoulder turns it into a kind of modified drop shoulder.

- While there is no defined armhole on a drop shoulder, there is a theoretical armhole: finished length – ½ upper sleeve width = length to armhole _____ inches (cm). Stop knitting this piece sometime before this length.
- Put the stitches onto a thread, and steam-press or wash and dry.
- Measure its width.
- If the piece is too wide, call it the front. *Work to the garment's armhole, then bind off the number of inches that it is too wide at each armhole (For example, if the front is 2″ [5cm] too wide, bind off 2″ [5cm] at each armhole.)* Record how many stitches remain, and continue on this number of stitches to finished length and with neck shaping. For the back, cast on the number of stitches that remained after the front's armhole bind-off, and work this number of stitches straight to finished length and with neck shaping.
- If the piece is too narrow, call it the back. Work straight to finished length and with neck shaping. Determine how much too narrow it is, multiply this number of inches (cm) by 2, then for the front cast on the number of stitches for the back plus the number of stitches just calculated. (For example, if the back is 2″ [5cm] too narrow, cast on the back's #stitches + 4″ [10cm] for the front.) Complete the front by working from * to above.
- With this rescue, you will have the circumference you want below the armhole, and the only odd thing you'll have is side seams slightly skewed to the back.
- Finished length – length to armhole = armhole depth _____ inches (cm). Recalculate your new gauge, and then work your sleeves to this gauge. Your upper sleeve width must not exceed armhole depth × 2. You will also need to make your sleeves longer than you planned—by half the width of each front's armhole bind-off.

drop shoulder rescue

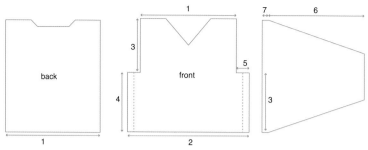

1 back width
2 front width
  (2 + 1 = the circumference you wanted)
3 armhole depth (same as ½ upper sleeve width)
4 length to armhole
5 stitches bound off at each front armhole
6 original sleeve length
7 extra length added to sleeve (which will be half the width of 5)
Dotted lines show side edge of front after seaming

If Your Garment Is Not Working to the Length You Want

What follows assumes you have finished the garment. But if your garment is too long or too short, you can save yourself lots of work by sorting this out before you've sewn the side seams or added front bands to a cardigan.

- Sew the shoulder seams.
- Add the neck band (if you have one).
- Sew in the sleeves (if you have any).
- Steam-press or wash and dry your partially assembled garment.
- Try it on to see if it needs adjustment.

If Your Garment Is Too Long

- Determine how much too long it is = _____ inches (cm) too long. Mark this spot on the front and back, above the bottom band (if it has one) or above the cast-on edge (if it has no bottom band).
- Cut 1 thread at that spot.
- Gently unpick, from side to side, the row of knitting you have cut.
- After the extra length (plus the edging, if you have one) falls off, stitches will present. Put them onto a needle and either bind them off or knit a new edging down before binding off.

To shorten

This swatch is partially unpicked and shows open stitches (along the top of the opening) ready to be finished.

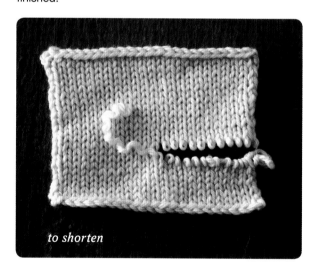

to shorten

If Your Garment Is Too Short and You Have Only Used One Color and One Stitch Across the Row

- Determine how much too short it is = _____ inches (cm) too short.
- Cut 1 thread above the bottom band (if it has one) or above the cast-on edge (if it has no bottom band).

- Gently unpick, from side to side, the row of knitting you have cut.
- After the cast-on edge or bottom band has fallen off, stitches will present. You will see 1 fewer stitch than you had for your garment plus what look like half-stitches at each edge.
- Put all stitches on a needle, including the 2 half-stitches.
- Knit new length down, then bind off (if you have no bottom band) or knit a new band down from these stitches before binding off.
- Be careful to make your side seams contiguous through these extra half-stitches: seam allowances below the new length will each have ½ extra stitch than the seam allowances above the new length.

If you have used more than 1 color or 1 stitch (knit + purl) across the row, you cannot continue your garment's stitch pattern to knit the new length down—because you will be ½ stitch "off." But you can choose some other stitch pattern to work the new length down. (See point 1 in Helpful Design Principles, page 161.)

To lengthen, part 1
This swatch is partially unpicked above band: open stitches are ready to be worked down.

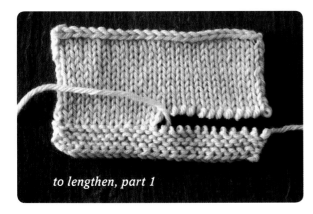

to lengthen, part 1

To lengthen, part 2
The previous swatch's stitches have been undone, all the way to the edge, and the garter stitch edging has fallen off. The right edge of the swatch now has new length worked down: note the extra stitch at its side edge.

to lengthen, part 2

Reusing Yarn After Ripping
Sometimes you have to rip the entire garment, but ripping should be your last resort. (Better to have tried one of the previous solutions.) Having said that, sometimes you really must rip and redo a section, and I'll confess that it's rare that I don't find myself ripping out part of a piece that's not quite right.

After ripping, your yarn may be kinky. Here's the quickest way to straighten it.
- As you rip, wind the yarn into a skein. (I wind loosely between my hand and elbow. This makes a skein that is smaller than a commercial skein.)
- Tie the skein off (in two or more places).
- If the yarn can be safely steam-pressed, do so to remove much of its kinkiness.
- If it cannot be steam-pressed, wash it to remove its kinks, then let it dry.
- Wind it into a ball, and reuse it.

Yarn that has been treated this way may react differently than yarn that has never been knit. The solution is to treat any unknit yarn the same way.

Bands That Have Too Many Stitches: Tightening the Bind-Off Row

Sometimes we pick up and knit too many stitches in a neck band, or a front band, or an armhole band—all bands that end with a bind-off row. But I would much prefer to have too many stitches, rather than too few, because I can always employ my favorite technique: tightening the bind-off row. This technique rescues a floppy band and produces one with a tight and secure bound-off edge that holds it to shape.

- Start at the beginning of the bind-off row (opposite the tail).
- See the bind-off row as a series of interconnected chains.
- Insert a knitting needle or tapestry needle under the front thread of the first bound-off stitch (chain); tug excess yarn toward you.
- Insert the tool under the back thread of the same bound-off stitch; tug excess yarn toward the back.
- *Insert the tool under the front thread of the next bound-off stitch; tug excess yarn toward you.
- Insert the tool under the back thread of the next bound-off stitch; tug excess yarn toward the back.
- Repeat from * until you reach the end of the bind-off row.
- If you have not sewn in the tail, pull out the last stitch to absorb the long loop into the tail.
- If you have sewn in the tail, cut at the center of the long loop you will have created, and sew in its tails.

This is a technique you may employ many years after the garment is completed. But if you think you may use it, you must be careful not to split your yarn while binding off. And it's better to do it twice rather than overdoing it once (because it cannot easily be undone).

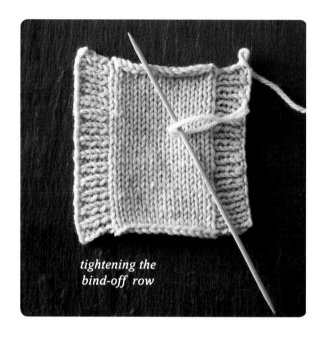

tightening the bind-off row

Tightening the bind-off row

On the left, the swatch shows an edging that clearly has too many stitches; on the right, you can see a mostly tightened bind-off (showing the long loop that will be absorbed into the tail).

If You've Used a Contrast Color That You'd Like to Replace

This technique is helpful when a little of something—whether fairisle or intarsia—has been knit in the wrong color. You can use duplicate stitch to replace the offending color with a new color.

- With the new color, duplicate-stitch over row 1 of the stitches you wish to replace.
- *From the wrong side, cut out the wrong-colored stitches.
- Be sure to "hook" the yarn of the replacement color at the edges (following the course of the offending color), then duplicate-stitch over the next row of stitches you wish to replace.
- Repeat from *.

Fixing the Fit

I've started doing this, and I must say that it is more fun and more creative than simply ripping and knitting something smaller. It involves pulling the garment in to narrow it, with some sort of addition after the garment is knit. (The Three-Bow Pullover in chapter 9 is an example of this.) But you could just as easily need side panels to make your garment wider. Can you imagine straight sides turned into an A-line with the addition of knit pieces? (See page 89.) But read Helpful Design Principles (page 161) first.

To Pull the Garment In

To narrow your garment, you can pleat its front or back. But pleats often need some sort of closure: ties or buttons: page 165 offers an example. Buttons don't require anything but themselves, but ties may require adding pieces as follows.

1. Try the garment on. Decide how much you want to pull it in. Mark the top and bottom spots of both the right and left edges of your pleat.
2. Find the spot that represents the top of the pleat's left edge. (Right and left are "as looking at the garment with RS facing.")
3. With RS facing, slip a needle through an edge of a stitch at this spot.
4. Slip the needle through successive edges of this stitch along a straight vertical below this stitch—to the bottom of the pleat—working in a proportion that works with the stitch pattern of the piece you are adding. (For example, 3 stitches for every 4 rows.)
5. Add yarn, and begin with a RS knit row. (If your stitches are twisted, knit through the back of them.) Continue knitting until you've created the piece you want.
6. From the bottom stitch of the piece just knit, work across to find the stitch that represents the bottom of the pleat's right edge.
7. With RS facing, slip a needle through an edge of a stitch at this spot.
8. Slip the needle through successive edges of this stitch along a straight vertical above this stitch—to the top of your pleat—working in the same proportion as the previous piece.
9. Repeat step 5.

adding pieces to pull a garment narrower

Adding pieces to pull a garment narrower

The sample shows the four corners of a pleat.
On the left edge, the photo shows a needle threaded through a vertical line of stitches, 3 stitches for every 4 rows—18 stitches over 23 rows.
On the right edge, the photo shows a reverse stockinette band knit from the same 18 stitches. These would be pulled together to form—and highlight—your pleat.

Helpful Design Principles

There are two major principles that I rely on routinely, and for both of them I am grateful to my friend Lee Andersen.

1. Once is a mistake (because you've just created a focal point), twice is a problem (because it could look like "headlights" or symmetry gone wrong), three times or more is a design. If you repeat something 17 times, it was clearly deliberate! If you repeat a mistake in a stitch pattern often enough, it's a new stitch pattern!
2. If it looks like a mistake, embellish it to make a feature out of it.

These can be expressed so many ways. But I will tell you that my entire knitting career began because I crocheted over (to hide) a wonky side seam that had shifted to the front (because the stitch pattern had surprised me by being "oblique"). Everywhere I went someone wanted a version of this garment (because if it's asymmetrical, it's art, right?). I probably would not be here, or have the life I have, if I had ripped and reknit that garment.

Chapter 9

Patterns

A book with this instructional material doesn't actually need patterns, does it? After all, I am telling you to envision and draft your own. But here's what you might notice about—and take encouragement from— the garments in this chapter.

None of them are simple, basic shapes. I assume you can produce those pretty easily now. All the garments in this chapter have a combination of elements. The first three are the following: a set-in sleeve pullover + diagonal hem + side shaping; a saddle-shouldered, drop shoulder cardigan + side shaping; a raglan cardigan + short sleeves + collar. But all these patterns are intermediate!

In this book you are invited to combine elements. And just in case you thought it was too advanced and beyond your capabilities, take another look! These are not advanced garments, and they should soon be within your abilities. All that is required is a vision, a little study, a pencil (and eraser), a calculator, and some perseverance. After that, you'll put your yarn and needles together and create. I look forward to your results.   In the meantime, here are mine!

Three-Bow Pullover

This garment was based on a sweater I bought—with bows at the shoulder and hip. But after knitting my own version of it, I realized that I could give it a little hourglass with a third bow. (And three of something is always a better design than two.) The advantage of this third bow is not only the shape itself but that you are in control of how much shape you want, and you don't make that decision until after the piece is knit. Maybe there are other garments you have knit that could benefit from this treatment.

Skill Level
Intermediate

Sizes
S (M, L, 1X, 2X)
Finished circumference at hem (approximate) 53 (57, 61, 65, 69)″ (134.5 [145, 155, 165, 175] cm)
Finished circumference at bust 35½ (39, 43½, 47½, 51½)″ (90 [99, 110.5, 120.5, 131]cm)
Finished length (on long side, over weight 3 yarn) 27½ (28, 28½, 29, 29½)″ (70 [71, 72.5, 74, 75]cm). *Weight 4 yarn garment will be approximately 2″ (5cm) longer unless shortened.*
Finished shoulder width 14½″ (37cm)
Shoulders may stretch 2″ (5cm) wider than this measurement.
Finished sleeve length 28½ (29, 29½, 30, 30½)″ (72.5 [74, 75, 76, 77.5]cm)
Models are shown in size M.

Materials
- 1080 (1200, 1320, 1440, 1560) yd (988 [1098, 1207, 1317, 1426]m) / 10 (11, 12, 13, 14) skeins Koigu Kersti (100% merino wool, each approximately 1¾ oz [50g] and 114 yd [104m]), in color P700 **(3)** light
- 1080 (1200, 1320, 1440, 1560) yd (988 [1098, 1207, 1317, 1426]m) / 5 (5, 6, 6, 7) skeins Mountain Colors River Twist (100% merino wool, each approximately 3½ oz [100g] and 240 yd [220m]), in color Crazy Creek **(4)** medium
- One pair size 7 (4.5mm) needles, or size needed to obtain gauge

Gauge
18 stitches and 28 rows = 4″ (10cm) on weight 3 yarn, over stockinette stitch, after steam-pressing or washing
18 stitches and 27 rows = 4″ (10cm) on weight 4 yarn, over stockinette stitch, after steam-pressing or washing

Notes

- This garment is an A-line with a diagonal hem. The third bow—which gives an hourglass shape—is optional and added to the front as part of finishing.
- Because of the side tie, the hem measurement is approximate.
- Variegated yarns can create "pooling" of colors. You can deal with this by working from 3 balls of yarn, 1 row in each.

Front

Cable cast on 153 (162, 170, 180, 189) stitches.
Knit 1 RS row.

Shape Diagonal Hem + Right Edge

First WS short row P9. Turn.
If you prefer to wrap at short rows, you may do so; otherwise, be sure to pull yarn taut at the slip stitch.
Next RS row Sl 1, knit to the end.
When directions read "sl 1," always slip 1 purlwise with yarn to the wrong side.
WS short rows Purl to 9 stitches past the previous short row; turn.
Next RS decrease row Knit to the last 3 stitches, k2tog, k1: long-side decrease made.
Work 13 (14, 15, 16, 17) more WS short rows (adding 9 stitches each time), *at the same time* repeating RS decrease row every 3rd RS row.
Next WS row Bring the remainder of the stitches into working—approximately 148 (157, 164, 174, 183) stitches, depending on where you are with RS decreases.

Shape Left-Hip Tie + Right Edge

Continue in stockinette with a decrease every 3rd RS row, *at the same time* shaping left-hip tie as follows: at the beginning of RS rows, bind off 10 stitches once, 6 stitches once, 4 stitches once, 3 stitches once, 2 stitches twice, and 1 stitch 5 times—approximately 113 (121, 129, 139, 147) stitches.

Shape Right + Left Edges

Work in stockinette to the next scheduled long-side decrease row.
***Next RS decrease row** K1, ssk (or skp), knit to the last 3 stitches, k2tog, k1: short-side + long-side decrease made.
All WS rows Purl.
Knit 1 RS row.
Next RS decrease row K1, knit to the last 3 stitches, k2tog, k1.

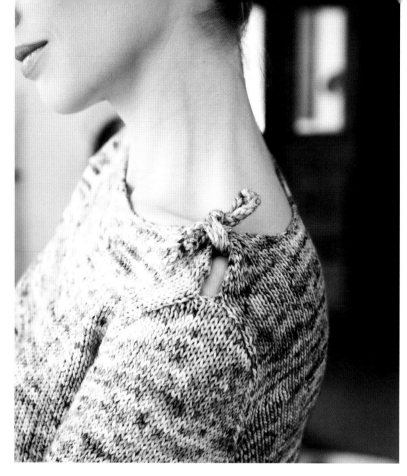

Next RS decrease row K1, skp (or ssk), knit to the end.
Next RS decrease row K1, knit to the last 3 stitches, k2tog, k1.
Knit 1 RS row.
It is easy to lengthen this garment by just working more rows before the armhole. But there is not much room to shorten unless you occasionally work fewer rows between decreases.
Repeat from * (decreasing on the short side every 3rd RS row and on the long side every alternate RS row) * until 82 (90, 100, 108, 118) stitches remain.
Stop decreasing when you reach this number of stitches, even though it means not decreasing at the end

of the last RS row or not finishing the 12-row repeat.

Continue in stockinette until the back measures 20″ (51cm) on the long side (measuring straight, not along the diagonal). End after working a WS row.

(Shorten or lengthen for finished length here.)

Shape Armholes

Bind off 2 (4, 6, 8, 10) stitches at the beginning of the next two rows—78 (82, 88, 92, 98) stitches.

Decrease row (RS) K1, skp (or ssk), knit to the last 3 stitches, k2tog, k1.

Purl 1 row.

Repeat the last 2 rows 4 (6, 9, 11, 14) times more—68 stitches. (Widen or narrow for shoulder width by working fewer or more decreases.)

Continue even until armhole measures 6½ (7, 7½, 8, 8½)″ (16.5 [18, 19, 20.5, 21.5]cm). End after working a WS row.

Shape Left Front Shoulder Tie + Neck

Next RS row Sl 1, knit to 20 stitches on the right needle, sl 1; turn.

The slips at the beginning and end of RS rows neaten the neck and tie edges.

Next WS row Bind off 3 stitches at the neck edge, purl to the end.

Next RS row Sl 1, knit to the last stitch, sl 1.

Next WS row Bind off 2 stitches at the neck edge, purl to the end—16 stitches.

***Next RS decrease row** Sl 1, skp (or ssk), knit to the last 3 stitches, k2tog, sl 1.

Next 3 rows Work even in stockinette, with slips at the beginning and end of RS rows.

Repeat from * 4 times more—6 stitches.

Work even in stockinette, with slips at the beginning and end of RS rows, for 1½″ (4cm). End after working a WS row.

Next RS row Sl 1, skp (or ssk), k2tog, sl 1.

Next WS row Bind off.

Shape Right Front Shoulder + Neck

Return to remaining stitches, RS facing.

Bind off 26 stitches, k21.

Next WS row Bind off 4 stitches, p16, sl 1.

Next RS row Bind off 3 stitches, k14.

Next WS row Bind off 4 stitches, p9, sl 1.

Next RS row Bind off 2 stitches, k8.

Next WS row Bind off 4 stitches, p3, sl 1.

Knit 1 RS row.

Next WS row Bind off 4 stitches.

Back

Cable cast on 153 (162, 170, 180, 189) stitches.

Shape Diagonal Hem + Right Edge

First RS short row K9; turn.

Next WS row Sl 1, purl to the end.

RS short rows Knit to 9 stitches past the previous short row; turn.

Next RS short row + decrease row K1, skp (or ssk), knit to 9 stitches past the previous short row: long-side decrease made; turn.

WS rows Sl 1, purl to end.

Work 12 (13, 14, 15, 16) more RS short rows (adding 9 stitches each

time), *at the same time* repeating RS decrease row every 3rd RS row.

Next RS row Bring the remainder of the stitches into working: some sizes will also decrease on this row—approximately 148 (157, 164, 174, 183) stitches.

Shape Left-Hip Tie + Right Edge

Continue in stockinette with a decrease every 3rd RS row, *at the same time* shaping left-hip tie as follows: at the beginning of WS rows, bind off 10 stitches once, 6 stitches once, 4 stitches once, 3 stitches once, 2 stitches twice, and 1 stitch 5 times—approximately 113 (121, 129, 139, 147) stitches.

Shape Right + Left Edges

Work in stockinette to the next scheduled long-side decrease row.

***Next RS decrease row** K1, ssk (or skp), knit to the last 3 stitches, k2tog, k1: short-side + long-side decrease made.

All WS rows Purl.

Knit 1 RS row.

Next RS decrease row K1, skp (or ssk), knit to the end.

Next RS decrease row K1, knit to the last 3 stitches, k2tog, k1.

Next RS decrease row K1, skp (or ssk), knit to the end.

Knit 1 RS row.

Repeat from *, (decreasing on the long side every alternate RS row and on the short side every 3rd RS row) until 82 (90, 100, 108, 118) stitches remain.

Stop decreasing when you reach this number of stitches, even though it means not decreasing at the end of the last RS row or not finishing the 12-row repeat.

Continue in stockinette until the piece measures the same as the front to the armhole. End after working a WS row.

Shape Armholes

Work as front to the end of the armhole shaping and to the same length between the armhole and the shoulder. End after working a WS row.

Shape Right Back Shoulder + Neck

Next RS row Bind off 4 stitches, knit to the end.
Next WS row Sl 1, purl to the end.
Next RS row Bind off 4 stitches, knit to 9 stitches on the right needle, sl 1; turn.
Next WS row Bind off 1 stitch at the neck edge, p9.
Next RS row Bind off 4 stitches, k4, sl 1.
Next WS row Bind off 1 stitch at the neck edge, p4.
Next RS row Bind off.

Shape Left Back Shoulder Tie + Neck

Return to the remaining stitches, RS facing.
Bind off 32 stitches, k18.
Next WS row Sl 1, p16, sl 1.
Next RS row Bind off 1 stitch at the neck edge, k17.
Next WS row Sl 1, p15, sl 1.
Next RS row Bind off 1 stitch at the neck edge, k16.
Next WS row Sl 1, p14, sl 1.
***Next RS decrease row** K1, skp (or ssk), knit to the last 3 stitches, k2tog, k1.
Next 3 rows Continue in stockinette, with slips at the beginning and end of WS rows.
Repeat from * 4 times more—6 stitches.
Continue in stockinette, with slips at the beginning and end of WS rows, for 1½″ (4cm). End after working a WS row.
Next RS row K1, skp (or ssk), k2tog, k1.
Next WS row Bind off.

Sleeves

Cable cast on 31 (31, 35, 35, 39) stitches.
Work 8 (8, 6, 4, 4) rows in stockinette.
Increase row (RS) K1, increase 1 in next stitch, knit to the last 2 stitches, increase 1 in the next stitch, k1.
Work all increases as lifted increases.
Work 7 (5, 5, 3, 3) rows even.
Repeat the last 8 (6, 6, 4, 4) rows 10 (13, 17, 20, 21) times more—53 (59, 71, 77, 83) stitches.
Work even until the piece measures 17″ (43cm). End after working a WS row.
(Shorten or lengthen for sleeve length here.)

Shape Sleeve Cap

Bind off 2 (4, 6, 8, 10) stitches at the beginning of the next 2 rows—49 (51, 59, 61, 63) stitches.
Decrease row (RS) K1, ssk, knit to the last 3 stitches, k2tog, k1.
Purl 1 row.

Repeat the last 2 rows 12 (13, 17, 18, 19) times more—23 stitches. End after working a WS row.

Bind off 2 stitches at the beginning of the next 2 rows, then 4 stitches at the beginning of the next 2 rows. Bind off remaining stitches.

Finishing

Sew the right shoulder seam.

Sew the right sleeve into the armhole.

Sew the left sleeve into the armhole, ignoring the ties. (Stop sewing to the back—and begin sewing to the front—when you reach the center of the sleeve cap, leaving the ties clear.)

After sewing and tying, there will be a slight space between the shoulder ties and the top of the left sleeve.

Sew the sleeve and right-side edge seams.

Sew the left-side edge seam, beginning at the armhole, and ending 1″ (2.5cm) above the end of the left hip ties.

Using the tail, close the beginning of the bound-off edges at the lower right corners of both front and back necks.

Front Ties

Try the garment on, tie the hip and shoulder ties, then mark a spot on the right front, in line with the bust and just above the waist, where you would like to center the front ties. Remove the garment, then find the stitch 2–2½″ (5–6.5cm) to the left of this marked spot.

The left is as you are looking at the garment, RS facing, not wearing it. The model's ties take 4–5″ (10–12.5cm) from the garment's width. If you wish to remove more width, go further than 2–2½″ (5–6.5cm).

Count up 6 rows from this stitch. With RS facing, slip needle through the edge of this stitch. Working down the garment's front, slip needle through the edge of the corresponding stitch for 11 more

rows. (Page 161 demonstrates this.) Do not turn your work until 12 stitches are picked up.

First RS row Sl 1, k11.

*WS row Sl 1, purl to the end.

Next RS decrease row Sl 1, skp (or ssk), knit to the last 3 stitches, k2tog, k1.

Repeat from * twice more—6 stitches remain.

Continue in stockinette, and with a slip at the beginning of all rows, for 2″ (5cm).

Repeat the decrease row—4 stitches.

Next WS row Bind off.

Find the stitch 4–5″ (10–12.5cm) to the right of the lowest stitch of tie just made.

With RS facing, slip the needle through the edge of the corresponding stitch and then for 11 rows above.

First RS row Sl 1, k11.

Repeat from *to the end as for previous tie.

Tie all ties to desired tightness.

three-bow pullover

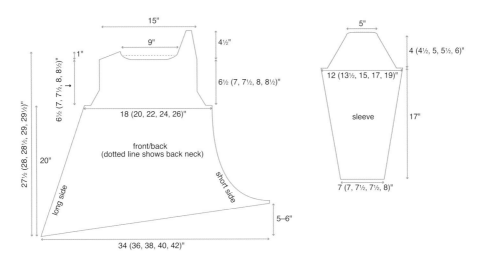

front/back
(dotted line shows back neck)

sleeve

Marsha's Top

I taught a class that a woman named Marsha attended. She had brought—and let us all try on—an unusual top. We all loved it, and many decided to draw a sketch from which to knit a version. As often happens, much was changed in mine: her top had no texture, and mine has a tumbling blocks motif; her top was a pullover, and mine is a cardigan; her top was a drop shoulder, and mine is saddled—illustrating how the saddle shoulder is best used—with plain sleeves framing a textured body.

Skill Level
Intermediate

Sizes
S (M, L, 1X, 2X)
Finished circumference at bust 35 (40, 44, 49, 54)″ (89 [101.5, 112, 124.5, 137]cm)
Finished length (at front sides) 20 (20½, 21, 21½, 22)″ (51 [52, 53.5, 54.5, 56]cm)
Finished length (at center back) 24 (24½, 25, 25½, 26)″ (61 [62, 63.5, 65, 66]cm)
Finished sleeve length 28 (28½, 29½, 30, 31)″ (71 [72, 75, 76, 79]cm)
Model is shown in size M.

Materials
- 990 (1100, 1210, 1320, 1430) yd (905 [1006, 1107, 1207, 1308]m) / 6 (6, 7, 8, 8) skeins Tahki Donegal Tweed (100% wool, each approximately 3½ oz [100g] and 183 yd [168m]), in color 846 Wheat ❹ medium
- One pair size 8 (5mm) needles, or size needed to obtain gauge
- One pair size 7 (4.5mm) needles, or size needed to obtain gauge
- One circular needle, size 6 (4mm), any length
- 3 buttons, 2″ (5cm) wide
- *Optional:* one dpn, same size as smallest needle, for neck edging

Gauge
17 stitches and 24 rows = 4″ (10cm), over stockinette stitch on middle-size needles, after steam-pressing or washing
16 stitches and 24 rows = 4″ (10cm), over tumbling blocks pattern on largest needles, after steam-pressing or washing

Tumbling Blocks Stitch Pattern
(over a multiple of 10 stitches and 20 rows)
See chart on page 174.
Row 1 (RS) *P1, k1; repeat from *.
Row 2 P2, (k1, p1) 3 times, k2.
Row 3 P3, (k1, p1) twice, k3.
Row 4 P4, k1, p1, k4.
Rows 5 and 6 P5, k5.
Row 7 K1, p4, k4, p1.
Row 8 P1, k1, p3, k3, p1, k1.
Row 9 K1, p1, k1, p2, k2, p1, k1, p1.
Row 10 *P1, k1; repeat from *.

Row 11 *K1, p1; repeat from *.
Row 12 P1, k1, p1, k2, p2, k1, p1, k1.
Row 13 K1, p1, k3, p3, k1, p1.
Row 14 P1, k4, p4, k1.
Rows 15 and 16 K5, p5.
Row 17 K4, p1, k1, p4.
Row 18 K3, (p1, k1) twice, p3.
Row 19 K2, (p1, k1) 3 times, p2.
Row 20 *K1, p1; repeat from *.
note Stitch pattern as written does not include selvedge stitches. These are written into the pattern.

Notes

- This garment has an unshaped front, which could be knit to your balance point (see page 22). The back falls to a wide, droopy A-line, and you'd want the center back to end mid-backside.
- The finished circumference at bust is approximate because it will depend on how tightly you button it.
- The finished circumference at hem is not possible to estimate because the back is longer and naturally folds.
- Finished sleeve length is 1½″ (4cm) longer than the schematic suggests, because the piece will stretch this much or more.
- The neck is knit to 6″ (15cm) wide but may stretch to almost 8″ (20.5cm).
- The color I used has been discontinued. But this yarn has a wide range of alternatives.

Back

With largest needles, cable cast on 122 (132, 142, 152, 162) stitches.
Row 1 (RS) K1, work stitch pattern to the last stitch, k1.
Row 2 P1, work stitch pattern to the last stitch, p1.

Work stitch pattern, with k1 at each end of RS rows and p1 at each end of WS rows, until piece measures 7″ (18cm). End after working a WS row.

Shape Sides

Maintain the stitch pattern through shaping.
Decrease row (RS) K1, skp (or ssk), work to the last 3 stitches, k2tog, k1.
WS row P1, work to the last stitch, p1.
Repeat the last 2 rows 24 times more—72 (82, 92, 102, 112) stitches. Work even for 6 (6½, 7, 7½, 8)″ (15 [16.5, 18, 19, 20.5]cm) and until the piece measures approximately 21½ (22, 22½, 23, 23½)″ (54.5 [56, 57, 58.5, 59.5]cm) at center, ending with row 9 or 19.
(Shorten or lengthen for finished back length here.)
Next WS row Bind off purlwise.

Left Front

With largest needles, cable cast on 42 (47, 52, 57, 62) stitches.
Begin with row 1 of the chart and work as follows:
RS Rows K1, beginning at the right edge of chart on page 174, work the stitch pattern over 40 (45, 50, 55, 60) stitches, ending at the left edge of the chart (chart center, left edge of chart, chart center, left edge of chart), k1.
WS rows P1, begin at the left edge of the chart (chart center, the left edge of the chart, chart center, left edge of chart), work 40 (45, 50, 55, 60) stitches to the last stitch, p1.
Repeat these 2 rows until the piece measures approximately 17½ (18, 18½, 19, 19½)″ (44.5 [45.5, 47, 48, 49.5]cm), ending with row 9 or 19.

(Shorten or lengthen for finished front length here.)
Next WS row Bind off purlwise.

Right Front

Decide where you would place 3 buttons on the left front.
Model has buttonholes worked at approximately 6, 10, and 14″ (15, 25.5, and 35.5cm) from hem.
Work right front as left, but at appropriate places make buttonholes as follows:
Make buttonhole (RS) K1, work 1 (1, 2, 2, 3) stitch(es), yf, sl 1 p-wise, yb, *sl 1, pass previous slip stitch over, repeat from * 3 times more—4 stitches bound off; put final slip stitch back onto the left needle; turn,

cable cast on 5 stitches; turn, work 1 stitch, pass the 5th cast-on stitch over the stitch just worked—4-stitch, 1-row buttonhole completed.
Work to the same length as left front, and bind off purlwise.

Left Sleeve
Reverse Stockinette Edging
With middle-size needles, long-tail cast on 27 (29, 31, 33, 35) stitches.
Purl 1 (RS) row, then knit 1 row.

Body
*Increase row (RS) K1, increase in the next stitch, knit to the last 2 stitches, increase in the next stitch, k1.
Work all increases as lifted increases.
Continue in stockinette for 5 (5, 3, 3, 3) more rows.
Repeat from * 14 (15, 16, 17, 18) times more—57 (61, 65, 69, 73) stitches.
Work even until piece measures 17½ (17, 16½, 16, 15½)″ (44.5 [43, 42, 40.5, 39.5]cm). End after working a WS row.
(Shorten or lengthen for sleeve length here.)

Shape Saddle
Bind off 18 (20, 22, 24, 26) stitches at the beginning of the next two rows—21 stitches.
Work even until the saddle measures 6 (7, 8½, 9½, 11)″ (15 [18, 21.5, 24, 28]cm) after bind-off. End after working a WS row.

Shape Left Back Neck
Next row (RS) K10; turn.
Shape back neck by binding off 1 stitch at the next 2 neck edges—8 stitches.
Work the remaining 8 stitches until the back neck measures

approximately 3″ (7.5cm). Put these stitches onto a holder.

Shape Left Front Neck
Return to the remaining 11 stitches, RS facing.
Shape the front neck by binding off at the neck edge—4 stitches once,

2 stitches once, then 1 stitch 3 times—2 stitches.
Bind off on the next WS row.

Right Sleeve
Work as left sleeve to the end of Shape Saddle.

Shape Right Front Neck

Next row (RS) K11. Turn.
Shape the front neck by binding off at the neck edge—4 stitches once, 2 stitches once, then 1 stitch 3 times—2 stitches.
Bind off on the next RS row.

Shape Left Back Neck

Return to the remaining 10 stitches, RS facing.
Shape the back neck by binding off 1 stitch at the next 2 neck edges—8 stitches.
Work the remaining 8 stitches until the back neck measures approximately 3″ (7.5cm). Put these stitches onto a holder.

Finishing

Sew the sleeve saddles to the front and back: directions for assembly of the saddle shoulder are on page 119.
Graft the center back necks together (adding or subtracting rows, if needed).
Sew sleeve seams.
Sew side seams, leaving 7″ (18cm) of backs and 3″ (7.5cm) of fronts open at the lower edge.

Front + Neck Band

You will find this easier to do with a circular needle. And you may wish to introduce a dpn for the corners: once you turn the corner, you can slip these stitches back onto the circular needle.

With the smallest needle, RS facing, and beginning at the lower edge of right front, pick up and knit up the right front, around the neck, and down the left front as follows:

- 2 stitches for every 3 rows along the front edges
- (k1, yo, k1) in the corner stitch of the front and front neck

marsha's top

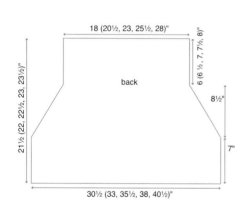

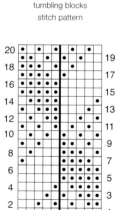

tumbling blocks
stitch pattern

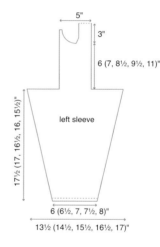

[10–stitch repeat]

☐ RS knit, WS purl
⊡ RS purl, WS knit

bold line shows chart center

- 1 stitch for every bound-off stitch and 1 stitch in every stair step between bound-off stitches around the front and back neck shaping
- 3 stitches for every 4 rows across the back neck

Knit 1 WS row (knitting corner yo's to twist them), then purl 1 RS row. Bind off knitwise.

Try the garment on, and decide how tightly you wish to close it.
Mark places for buttons on left front, then sew buttons to match.

Uptown Jacket

This tidy little jacket was based on one I bought in New York (hence the name). Like the original, it is a raglan with a little half-hourglass shaping, short full sleeves, a wide front band, and a collar. Unlike the original, it has texture!

Its closed measurements make it quite snug, but I prefer to wear it with only the top one or two buttons closed. This gives it a jaunty asymmetry—plus extra girth.

Skill Level
Intermediate

Sizes
S (M, L, 1X, 2X)
Finished circumference at hem (closed) 32 (38½, 44, 50½, 56)″ (81 [97, 112, 127.5, 142] cm)
Finished circumference at bust (closed) 33½ (40, 45½, 52, 57½)″ (84.5 [101.5, 114.5, 132, 146]cm)
Finished length 20 (20½, 21½, 22, 23)″ (51 [52, 55, 56, 58.5]cm)
Finished sleeve length 16 (16½, 17½, 18, 19)″ (40.5 [42, 44.5, 45.5, 48.5]cm)
Model is shown in size M.

Materials
• 745 (820, 900, 985, 1065) yd (682 [750, 823, 901, 974]m) / 6 (6, 7, 8, 8) skeins Manos del Uruguay Wool Clasica Semi-Solid (100% wool, each approximately 3½ oz [100g] and 138 yd [126m]), in color 29 Steel (5) heavy
• One pair size 9 (5.5mm) needles, or size needed to obtain gauge
• One pair size 8 (5mm) needles
• One pair size 7 (4.5mm) needles
• Stitch holder
• 10 buttons, 7/8″ (22mm) wide
• 1 utility button, ¾″ (19mm) wide (for inside closure)

Gauge
14 stitches and 22 rows = 4″ (10cm) over garter rib, on largest needles and after steam-pressing or washing

Garter rib
(over a multiple of 4 + 2 stitches and 2 rows)
RS rows Knit.
WS rows *P2, k2; repeat from * to the last 2 stitches, p2.

Notes
• You could make this jacket's finished length to your balance point (see page 22).
• This garment has a slight half-hourglass shaping in the back—wider at the hem than the bust. This is clear in the measurements. And this is also what allows it to be worn open without looking terribly wide at its hem. But it does make it snug at the waist if it's closed all the way.

- As with all raglans, for your garment to work out as mine does, your stitch and row gauges must match.

Back
Bottom band
With middle-size needles, cast on 54 (66, 78, 94, 106) stitches.
Work 2x2 rib, beginning and ending RS rows with k2 and WS rows with p2, to 2″ (5cm). End after working a WS row.

Body
Change to the largest needles, and work garter rib for 8 rows.
Increase row (RS) K1, increase 1 in next stitch, knit to the last 2 stitches, increase 1 in the next stitch, k1.
Maintain stitch pattern through all shaping.
Work 7 rows even.
Repeat the last 8 rows twice more—60 (72, 84, 100, 112) stitches.
Eventually all WS rows begin and end with p1.
Work even until piece measures 8″ (20.5cm). End after working a WS row.
(Shorten or lengthen for finished length here.)

Shape Armholes
Bind off 2 (2, 4, 6, 8) stitches at the beginning of the next 2 rows—56 (68, 76, 88, 96) stitches.
Work RS decrease and WS rows as written below. The pattern for how often to work decreases follows.
Decrease row (RS) K2, skp (or ssk), knit to the last 4 stitches, k2tog, k2.
WS rows P3, work to the last 3 stitches, p3.
*Work the decrease row 3 (1, 3, 3, 4) of every 8 (2, 5, 4, 5) RS rows.

Repeat from * until 32 stitches remain.
End after the next WS row.

Shape Right Back Neck
Next RS row K1, skp (or ssk), k1; turn.
Bind off 1 stitch at the beginning of the next WS row—2 stitches.
Knit 1 row, then bind off on the next WS row.

Shape Left Back Neck
Put the center 24 stitches on a holder—4 stitches on the left needle.
Next RS row K1, k2tog, k1.
Work 1 WS row.
Bind off 1 stitch at the beginning of the next RS row, then bind off on the next WS row.

Right Front
Bottom band
With middle-size needles, cast on 23 (27, 31, 35, 39) stitches.
Work 2x2 rib, beginning RS rows with k3 and ending WS rows with p3.
Work the right front bottom band as established to the same height as the back bottom band. End after working a WS row.

Body
Change to largest needles, and work garter rib—with p3 at the end of all WS rows—until the piece measures the same length as the back to armhole. End after working a RS row.

Shape Armhole

Bind off 2 (2, 4, 6, 8) stitches at the beginning of the next row—21 (25, 27, 29, 31) stitches.

Work RS decrease and WS rows as written below. The pattern for how often to work decreases follows.

RS Decrease row Knit to the last 4 stitches, k2tog, k2.

WS rows P3, work to the last 3 stitches, p3.

*Work the decrease row 3 (1, 1, 1, 5) of every 8 (2, 2, 2, 9) RS rows. Repeat from * until 9 stitches remain. End after the next WS row.

Shape Neck

Next RS row Bind off 2 stitches at the neck edge, knit to the last 4 stitches, k2tog, k2—6 stitches.

Work WS rows even.

Next RS row Bind off 1 stitch at the neck edge, k2tog, k2.

Next RS row Bind off 1 stitch at neck edge, k2tog.

Bind off on the next WS row.

Left Front
Bottom band

With middle-size needles, cast on 23 (27, 31, 35, 39) stitches.

Work 2x2 rib, beginning RS rows with k2, ending RS rows with k3, and beginning WS rows with p3. Work the left front bottom band as established to the same height as back bottom band. End after working a WS row.

Body

Change to the largest needles, and work garter rib—with p3 at the beginning of all WS rows—until the piece measures the same length as the back to armhole. End after working a WS row.

Shape Armhole

Bind off 2 (2, 4, 6, 8) stitches at the beginning of the next row—21 (25, 27, 29, 31) stitches.

Work RS decrease and WS rows as specified below. The pattern for how often to work decreases follows.

Decrease row (RS) K2, skp (or ssk), knit to the end.

WS rows P3, work to the last 3 stitches, p3.

*Work the decrease row 3 (1, 1, 1, 5) of every 8 (2, 2, 2, 9) RS rows. Repeat from * until 9 stitches remain. End after working a RS row.

Shape Neck

Next WS row Bind off 2 stitches at the neck edge, work to the end— 7 stitches.

Next 2 RS rows K2, skp (or ssk), knit to the end.

Next 2 WS rows Bind off 1 stitch at the neck edge, work to the end.

Next RS row Skp (or ssk), k1.

Bind off on next WS row.

Sleeves
Cuff

With middle-size needles, cast on 43 (45, 47, 49, 51) stitches.

RS rows (K2, p2) 3 times, (k1, p1) 9 (10, 11, 12, 13) times, k1, (p2, k2) 3 times.

WS rows (P2, k2) 3 times, p1, (k1, p1) 9 (10, 11, 12, 13) times, (k2, p2) 3 times.

Work band to 8 rows.

Body

Change to largest needles.

Increase row (RS) K12, increase in each of the next 19 (21, 23, 25, 27) stitches, k12—62 (66, 70, 74, 78) stitches.

Work garter rib for 1 WS row. (Lengthen for sleeve length by working more rows here.)

Shape Cap

Bind off 2 (2, 4, 6, 8) stitches at the beginning of the next 2 rows—58 (62, 62, 62, 62) stitches.

Work RS and WS rows as specified below. The pattern for how often to work decreases follows.

Decrease row (RS) K2, skp (or ssk), knit to the last 4 stitches, k2tog, k2.

WS rows P3, work stitch pattern to the last 3 stitches, p3.

*Work the decrease row 7 (5, 3, 3, 2) of every 9 (6, 4, 4, 3) RS rows. Repeat from * to 6 stitches.

End after working the next WS row.

Decrease row (RS) K1, k2tog, skp (or ssk), k1.

WS row P4.

Decrease row (RS) Skp (or ssk), k2tog—2 stitches.

Bind off on the next WS row.

Finishing
Left Front Band

Along the left front edge,** with the smallest needles, and RS facing, pick up and knit 5 stitches for every 6 rows.

Count stitches. Decrease as needed over the next row to a multiple of 4 while working the stitch pattern as follows.

Work the band in 2x2 rib; begin WS rows with sl 1, p2; end WS rows with p3; begin RS rows with sl 1, k2; and end RS rows with k3.

Always slip purlwise and with yarn to WS.

The slip stitch edge tidies the edges of the bands, although it will make picking up and knitting for the collar a little trickier.

Work band to 5″ (12.5cm). End after working a WS row.**

Next RS row (make 1 utility buttonhole) Sl 1, k2, p1, yo, k2tog, work to the end.

On the next row, purl yo so as not to twist it.

Continue front band to 6″ (15cm), then bind off in pattern.

Right Front Band

Working along the right front edge, work as left front band from ** to **.

On the left front band, determine the spacing for 5 buttons. (Begin near the top, and leave more space at the bottom, if needed, to space buttons evenly and in p2s.)

Next RS row (make 5 buttonholes) *Work to spot for buttonhole, ending after k2; p1, yo, k2tog, k1; continue rib with p2 to next buttonhole; repeat from * 4 times more, then work to the end.

On the next row, purl yo's so as not to twist them.

Continue front band to 6″ (15cm), then bind off in pattern.

Steam-press front bands as needed to hang straight.

Sew buttons to the left front band to match the placement of buttonholes. Sew 5 more buttons, 1″ (2.5cm) from the first row of the left front band.

Sew sleeves into the armholes, adjusting as needed (you may not have exactly the same number of rows between sleeves and the front/back pieces).

Try the garment on, closing as many buttons as desired. Mark placement, then sew utility button to WS of right front band to match placement of inside buttonhole on the left front band.

Sew sleeve and side seams. Sewing up the center of the edge knit stitches—taking half a stitch into each seam allowance—will make neat side seams.

Collar

With the smallest needles, RS facing, beginning 3″ (7.5cm) from the bound-off edge of the right front band, and ending 3″ (7.5cm) from the bound-off edge of the left front band, pick up and knit as follows: *Remember that the band has a slip-stitch edge, so 1 slip- stitch = 2 rows.*

- 3 stitches for every 4 rows (along edge of bands)

- 1 stitch for every bound-off stitch and 1 stitch for every stair step between bound-off stitches (around front and back neck shaping)
- 1 stitch for every stitch on hold (across the back neck)— approximately 88 stitches. (Increase or decrease across the next row to achieve 88 stitches.)

Row 1 (RS) Sl 1, *k2, p2; repeat from * to the last 3 stitches, k3.
Always slip purlwise and with yarn to WS.
First row is a RS row, even though WS of garment is showing, because collar will turn over.
Row 2 (WS) Sl 1, p2, M1 purlwise, *k2, p2; repeat from * to the last 5 stitches, k2, M1 purlwise, p3.

Row 3 (RS) Sl 1, k3, p2, *k2, p2; repeat from * to the last 4 stitches, k4.
Row 4 (WS) Sl 1, p2, M1 purlwise, p1, *k2, p2; repeat from * to the last 6 stitches, k2, p1, M1 purlwise, p3.
Row 5 (RS) Sl 1, k4, p2, *k2, p2; repeat from * to the last 5 stitches, k5.
Row 6 (WS) Sl 1, p2, M1 knitwise, *p2, k2; repeat from * to the last 5 stitches, p2, M1 knitwise, p3.
Row 7 (RS) Sl 1, k2, p1, *k2, p2; repeat from * to the last 6 stitches, k2, p1, k3.
Row 8 (WS) Sl 1, p2, M1 knitwise, k1, *p2, k2; repeat from * to the last 6 stitches, p2, k1, M1 purlwise, p3.
Repeat the last 8 rows once more, then bind off in rib on the next WS row.

Steam-press collar as needed.

uptown jacket

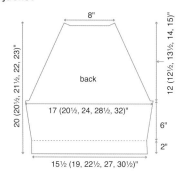

back

20 (20½, 21½, 22, 23)″

12 (12½, 13½, 14, 15)″

8″

17 (20½, 24, 28½, 32)″

6″

2″

15½ (19, 22½, 27, 30½)″

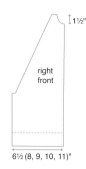

right front

1½″

6½ (8, 9, 10, 11)″

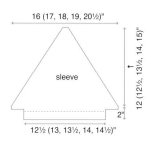

sleeve

16 (17, 18, 19, 20½)″

12 (12½, 13½, 14, 15)″

2″

12½ (13, 13½, 14, 14½)″

Lace-Paneled Top

If you want a dressy top, you might pick a precious yarn (hence my choice of a sequined silk). If you purchase a precious yarn, you'd want to knit a garment that is flattering (as this shape certainly is) and that can be worn many ways (sleeveless or over a top). And you'd want to use as little as possible of that precious yarn (which the lack of sleeves also allows you to do) while still doing something special with it (which the shaped hem and center lace panel certainly do). And the good news doesn't end there: for those who have never knit a lace garment, have no fear: there is no shaping in the lace panel!

Skill Level
Intermediate

Sizes
S (M, L, 1X, 2X)
Finished circumference at hem 39 (43, 47, 51, 55)" (99 [109, 119.5, 129.5, 139.5]cm)
Finished circumference at bust 36 (40, 44, 48, 52)" (91.5 [101.5, 112, 122, 132]cm)
Finished length (at side seam) 23 (23½, 24, 24½, 25½)" (58.5 [59.5, 61, 62, 65]cm)
Finished length (at center back) 24½ (25, 25½, 26, 27)" (62 [63.5, 65, 66, 68.5]cm)
Finished length (at center front) 19½ (20, 20½, 21, 22)" (49.5 [51, 52, 53.5, 56]cm)
Finished shoulder width 12" (30.5cm)
Model is shown in size M.

Materials
- 610 (675, 745, 810, 900) yd (558 [618, 682, 741, 823]m) / 3 (3, 4, 4, 4) skeins Tilli Thomas Disco Lights (90% spun silk, 10% petite sequins, each approximately 3½ oz [100g] and 225 yd [206m]), in color 249 Parchment (4) medium
- One pair size 7 (4.5mm) needles, or size needed to obtain gauge
- One pair size 8 (5mm) needles
- One circular needle, size 6 (4mm), 16–20" (40.5–51cm) long
- Stitch holder (or spare needle)

Gauge
20 stitches and 26 rows = 4" (10cm) over stockinette stitch, on middle-size needles

Lace Pattern
(over 33 stitches and 14 rows)
See chart on page 186.
Rows 1, 3, 5 K1, *k1, skp (or ssk), k2, yo, k1, yo, k2, k2tog; repeat from * twice more, k2.
WS rows Purl.
Row 7 K1, *k1, yo, skp (or ssk), k5, k2tog, yo; repeat from * twice more, k2.

Row 9 K1, *k2, yo, skp (or ssk), k3, k2tog, yo, k1; repeat from * twice more, k2.

Row 11 K1, *k3, yo, skp (or ssk), k1, k2tog, yo, k2; repeat from * twice more, k2.

Row 13 K1, *k4, yo, s2kp, yo, k3; repeat from * twice more, k2.

Notes

- This garment has an A-line back, with a straight front which could land at your balance point (see page 22).
- To open up the lace, it is knit on one size larger needles—and so will get a slightly different gauge from stockinette. It is difficult to

measure stitch gauge in lace, but the panel should be 7–7½" (18–19cm) wide (including selvedge stitches). Its row gauge does not matter, but it will get a different row gauge from the stockinette pieces. Therefore, this piece is knit separately and then seamed to the right and left fronts.

- Shoulder width may be slightly wider for some sizes.

Right Front

With middle-size needles, long-tail cast on 32 (37, 42, 47, 52) stitches.

Shape Reverse Shirttail Hem

First WS short row P8; turn.
If you prefer to wrap at short rows, you may do so: this is not written into the pattern. Otherwise, be sure to pull the yarn taut at the slip stitch.
All RS rows Sl 1, knit to the end.
When directions read "sl 1," always slip 1 purlwise with yarn to the wrong side.
Next WS short row Purl to 4 stitches past the previous short row; turn.
Next 4 (5, 6, 7, 8) WS short rows Purl to 3 stitches past the previous short row; turn.
Next 3 (4, 5, 6, 7) WS short rows Purl to 2 stitches past the previous short row; turn.
Next WS row P32 (37, 42, 47, 52). Work even in stockinette until the side edge measures 16½" (42cm). End after working a RS row. (Shorten or lengthen for finished length here.)

Shape Armhole

Bind off 2 (4, 6, 8, 10) stitches at the beginning of the next WS row—30 (33, 36, 39, 42) stitches.
Work RS decrease and WS rows as

specified below. The pattern for how often to work decreases follows.
Decrease row (RS) Knit to the last 3 stitches, k2tog, k1.
WS rows Purl.
*Work the decrease row 5 (9, all, all, all) of every 6 (10, all, all, all) RS rows. Repeat from * until 14 stitches remain (but read through the following italicized note).
(Widen for shoulder width by working decreases every RS row to the desired shoulder width then work even.)
Work even (if necessary) until the armhole measures 6 (6½, 7, 7½, 8½)" (15 [16.5, 18, 19, 21.5]cm). End after working a RS row.
If your armhole is the length you want, and you have more than 14 stitches, just stop with the next RS row and bind off the extra stitches (instead of 3) at the beginning of the next WS row.
Bind off 3 stitches at the beginning of the next WS row, purl to the end. Put the remaining 11 stitches onto a holder.

Left Front

With middle-size needles, long-tail cast on 32 (37, 42, 47, 52) stitches.

Shape Reverse Shirttail Hem

Purl 1 row.
First RS short row K8; turn.
All WS rows Sl 1, purl to the end.
Next RS short row Knit to 4 stitches past the previous short row; turn.
Next 4 (5, 6, 7, 8) RS short rows Knit to 3 stitches past the previous short row; turn.
Next 3 (4, 5, 6, 7) RS short rows Knit to 2 stitches past the previous short row; turn.
Next RS row K32 (37, 42, 47, 52). Work even in stockinette until the side edge measures the same as the

right front. End after working a WS row.

Shape Armhole

Bind off 2 (4, 6, 8, 10) stitches at the beginning of the next RS row—30 (33, 36, 39, 42) stitches.

Work RS decrease and WS rows as specified below. The pattern for how often to work decreases follows.

WS rows Purl.

Decrease row (RS) K1, skp (or ssk), knit to the end.

*Work the decrease row 5 (9, all, all, all) of every 6 (10, all, all, all) RS rows.

Repeat from * until 14 stitches (or number of stitches for right front) remain.

Work even (if necessary) until

armhole measures the same as the right front. End after working a WS row.

Bind off 3 stitches at the beginning of the next RS row, knit to the end. *If you bound off more than 3 for the right front shoulder, do the same here.* Put the remaining 11 stitches onto a holder.

Back

With middle-size needles, long-tail cast on 98 (108, 118, 128, 138) stitches.

Shape Shirttail Hem

First WS short row P68 (78, 88, 98, 108); turn.

First RS short row Sl 1, k37 (47, 57, 67, 77); turn.

Next 8 short rows Sl 1, work to 6 stitches past the previous short row; turn.

Next RS short row Sl 1, k91(101, 111, 121, 131).

Next WS row P98 (108, 118, 128, 138).

Next RS row Knit.

Shape A-Line

*Work 11 rows even.

Decrease row (RS) K1, skp (or ssk), knit to the last 3 stitches, k2tog, k1. Repeat from * 7 times more—82 (92, 102, 112, 122) stitches.

Work even until the piece measures the same as the right front at the side edge. End after working a WS row.

Shape Armholes

Bind off 2 (3, 5, 7, 9) stitches at the beginning of the next 2 rows—78 (86, 92, 98, 104) stitches.

Work RS decrease and WS rows as specified below. The pattern for how often to work decreases follows.

Decrease row (RS) K1, skp (or ssk), knit to last 3 stitches, k2tog, k1.

WS rows Purl.

*Work the decrease row 1 (3, 2, 4, 5) of every 2 (5, 3, 5, 6) RS rows. Repeat from * until 60 stitches remain (but read to the end of this section). Work even (if necessary) until armhole measures the same as the right front. End after working a WS row.

If your armhole is the same length as the right front, and you have more than 60 stitches, stop decreasing and read to the end of this section. Bind off 3 stitches at the beginning of the next 2 rows—54 stitches. *Bind off the same number of stitches as you bound off for the front shoulders. If you have more than*

lace-paneled top

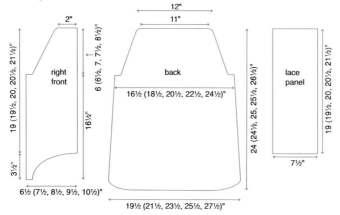

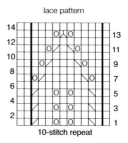

lace pattern

- ☐ knit on RS, purl on WS
- ◺ skp (or ssk)
- ◿ k2tog
- �◯ yo
- ◪ s2kp (slip 2 knitwise, k1, pass both slipped stitches over, together)

---

54 stitches remaining, just put what remains into the back neck.
Put stitches onto the smallest needle.

Front Lace Panel

With largest needles, long-tail cast on 33 stitches.
Purl 1 row.
Beginning with row 1, work lace stitch pattern until the piece measures approximately 19 (19½, 20, 20½, 21½)″ (48 [49.5, 51, 52, 54.5]cm), ending with row 6 or 14.
Put stitches onto a holder.

Finishing

Count the number of rows along the length of the lace panel.
Count the number of rows along the right front center edge.
Divide the smaller number by the larger, then go to the chart on page 219) for directions on how to sew the length of the lace panel to the right and left fronts.

Neck Edging

Sew shoulder seams.
With WS facing, slip all neck stitches onto the smallest (circular) needle so that all pieces are in order and you are at the right shoulder seam, ready to work the neck edging in the round, over WS rows—approximately 11 + 33 (lace panel) + 11 + 54 (back neck) = 109 stitches.
If your back neck has more than 54 stitches, your totals will be different and the spacing of the following decreases will be different. Read the following italicized note.
Next WS decrease row K2tog tbl, k7, k2tog; k2tog tbl, (k8, k2tog) 2 times, k9, k2tog; k2tog tbl, k7, k2tog; k2tog tbl, (k7, k2tog) 5 times, k5, k2tog—94 stitches.
Work k2tog's at shoulder seams to reduce extra stitches: k2tog tbl (through the back) aligns decrease appropriately.
If you have more than 109 stitches, you will have more than 94 remaining, which is fine.
Knit 2 more WS rounds, then bind off loosely.

Front Lower Edging

With the circular needle and RS facing, pick up and knit along the front hem

- 1 stitch in every cast-on stitch
- 1 stitch in every short-row turn space

—approximately 111 (125, 139, 153, 167) stitches.
While a reverse shirttail with such a minimal edging does not need extra stitches, I chose to add them to give the front more width at the hem.
Knit 1 WS row, purl 1 row, knit 1 row, then bind off purlwise.

Back Lower Edging

With the circular needle and RS facing, pick up and knit along the back hem

- 1 stitch in every cast-on stitch
- 1 stitch in every short-row turn space

—approximately 108 (118, 128, 138, 148) stitches.
Again, I chose to add extra stitches to make sure the back maintains its A-line shaping through its hem.
Knit 1 WS row, purl 1 row, knit 1 row, then bind off purlwise.
Sew side seams.

Escher-Inspired Vest

I love two-color knitting (sometimes wrongly referred to as fairisle). And when I do it, I prefer something with a simple shape and chart—like this one. But I don't do the one thing most knitters find daunting in this technique: the steeking and cutting. This is avoided in this pattern by working back and forth, producing pieces that are seamed. Since I learned to purl with one color around the neck (and the second in my working hand), I find purling with two colors very easy and very addictive. If you don't know how to do this, go to my book *The Purl Stitch* or look it up online. It's a wonderful trick!

Skill Level
Intermediate

Sizes
S (M, L, 1X, 2X)
Finished circumference at bust (closed) 41½ (45½, 49½, 54, 58)″ (105.5 [115.5, 125.5, 137, 147.5] cm)
Finished length (longer version) 23 (23½, 24, 24½, 25)″ (58.5 [59.5, 61, 62, 63.5]cm)
Finished length (shorter version) 20½ (21, 21½, 22, 22½)″ (52 [53.5, 54.5, 56, 57]cm)
Finished shoulder width 16½″ (42cm)
Models are shown in size M.

Materials
- Manos del Uruguay Silk Blend Semi-Solid (70% merino wool, 30% silk, each approximately 1¾ oz [50g] and 150 yd [137m]) (3) light

For Longer, Two-Color Version
- 785 (870, 960, 1045, 1130) yd (718 [796, 878, 956, 1034]m) / 6 (6, 7, 7, 8) skeins MC, in color 300G Coffee
- 395 (440, 485, 530, 575) yd (361 [403, 444, 485, 526]m) / 3 (3, 4, 4, 4) skeins CC, in color 3068 Citric

For Shorter, Five-Color Version
- 475 (525, 575, 630, 680) yd (434 [480, 526, 576, 622]m) / 4 (4, 4, 5, 5) skeins MC1 (used for edgings), in color 300M Bing Cherry
- 240 (265, 290, 320, 345) yd (219 [242, 265, 293, 315]m) / 2 (2, 2, 3, 3) skeins MC2, in color 300U Rust
- 130 (145, 160, 175, 190) yd (119 [133, 147, 160, 174]m) / 1 (1, 2, 2, 2) skein(s) in each of the following 3 colors: CC1, in color 3202 Tomato; CC2, in color 3069 Hibiscus; CC3, color 3203 Zinnia
- Small amount of waste yarn
- One crochet hook, size E-4 (3.5mm)
- One pair size 5 (3.75mm) needles
- One needle, smaller than size 5 (3.75mm)
- One pair size 6 (4mm) needles, or size needed to obtain gauge
- Stitch holder
- One button, 1½–2″ (3.8–5cm) wide
- *Optional:* One snap

Gauge

22 stitches and 28 rows = 4″ (10cm) over 2-color chart, on larger needles and after steam-pressing or washing

Notes

- I offer 2 versions. One is longer and worked in only two colors: one main color (MC) and one contrast color (CC). The other is shorter, and worked in five colors: two main colors (MC1 and MC2) and three contrast colors (CC1, CC2, and CC3). The pattern covers both lengths, and the chart covers both color options.
- It is difficult to define either bust circumference or length, because the piece is buttoned to hang asymmetrically and to fit as you wish.
- For all increases, I recommend the lifted increase.

Back

Hem

With middle-size needles, crochet hook, and waste yarn, crochet cast on 82 (92, 102, 112, 122) stitches. **With MC (or MC1 for 5-color version), and beginning with a knit row, work stockinette to 1½″ (4cm). End after working a knit row—back hem completed.

Knit 1 (turn) row.

Continue in stockinette, beginning with a knit row, until the second side of the hem is 1½″ (4cm). End after working a purl row—front hem completed.

Hook up the hem as follows.

- Slip the smallest needle through stitches of the cast-on edge (being sure to be in and not between stitches).
- Remove waste yarn.

- Fold the front and back hems together (wrong sides together), with the front hem to front of the work.
- With RS facing, k2tog across the row (1 stitch from each needle).
- There will be 1 less stitch on the smallest needle, so in the middle of the row k1 from the front hem.

Increase row (WS) Purl across, increasing in each 5th stitch**—98 (110, 122, 134, 146) stitches.

Body

Change to the largest needles.

Next row (RS) K1, work (with two colors) row 3 from the chart and to the last stitch, k1.

Next row (WS) P1, work (with two colors) row 4 from the chart and to the last stitch, p1.

When working fairisle back and forth, it is essential to bring each color to the edge on every 2-color row. So, if you end a row with 1 CC stitch, begin the next row with 1 MC stitch. (These selvedge stitches will go into the seam allowance.)

Continue with selvedge stitches and from the chart until the piece measures 9½ (10, 10, 10½, 10½)″ (24 [25.5, 25.5, 26.5, 26.5]cm) for shorter version—or 12 (12½, 12½, 13, 13)″ (30.5 [32, 32, 33, 33]cm) for the longer version. End after working a WS row.

(Shorten or lengthen for finished length here.)

Shape Armholes
Bind off 4 (6, 8, 10, 12) stitches at the beginning of the next 2 rows—90 (98, 106, 114, 122) stitches.
Decrease row (RS) K1, skp (or ssk), work to the last 3 stitches, k2tog, k1. Work 1 WS row.
Repeat the last 2 rows 4 (8, 12, 16, 20) times more—80 stitches.

(Widen or narrow for shoulder width by working fewer or more decreases.)

Continue with selvedge stitches and from the chart until the armhole measures 10 (10, 10½, 10½, 11)″ (25.5 [25.5, 26.5, 26.5, 28]cm). End after working a WS row.

Shape Shoulders
Bind off 2 stitches at the beginning of the next 10 rows—60 stitches. Put stitches onto a holder.

Right Front
Hem
With middle-size needles, crochet hook, and waste yarn, crochet cast

on 52 (57, 62, 67, 72) stitches. Work as back hem from ** to **—62 (68, 74, 80, 86) stitches.

Body
Change to the largest needles.
Next row (RS) K1, work (with two colors) row 3 from the chart to the last stitch, k1.
Next rwo (WS) P1, work (with two colors) row 4 from the chart and to the last stitch, p1.
Continue with selvedge stitches and from the chart until the piece measures the same as the back to armhole. End after working a RS row.

Shape Armhole
Bind off 4 (6, 8, 10, 12) stitches at the beginning of the next row—58 (62, 66, 70, 74) stitches.
Decrease row (RS) Knit to the last 3 stitches, k2tog, k1. Work 1 WS row.
Repeat the last 2 rows 4 (8, 12, 16, 20) times more—53 stitches.
(Widen or narrow for shoulder width by working fewer or more decreases.) Continue with selvedge stitches and from the chart until the armhole measures the same length as the back. End after working a RS row.

Shape Shoulder
Bind off 2 stitches at the beginning of the next 5 WS rows—43 stitches. Put stitches onto a holder.

Left Front
Work as right front to Shape Armhole. End after working a WS row.

Shape Armhole

Bind off 4 (6, 8, 10, 12) stitches at the beginning of the next row—58 (62, 66, 70, 74) stitches.
Work 1 WS row.
Decrease row (RS) K1, skp (or ssk), work to the end.
Work 1 WS row.
Repeat the last 2 rows 4 (8, 12, 16, 20) times more—53 stitches.
(Widen or narrow for soulder width by working fewer or more decreases.) Continue with selvedge stitches and from the chart until the armhole measures the same length as the back. End after working a WS row.

Shape Shoulder

Bind off 2 stitches at the beginning of the next 5 RS rows—43 stitches.
Put stitches onto a holder.

Finishing

Sew shoulder seams.

Armhole Edgings

With MC (or MC1 for 5-color version), middle-size needles, and RS facing, pick up and knit around the armhole edge as follows: 1 stitch for each bound-off stitch and 3 stitches for every 4 rows.
Purl 1 WS row.
Next RS decrease row K4 (6, 8, 10, 12), s2kp, knit to the last 7 (9, 11, 13, 15) stitches, s2kp, knit to the end.
Work 2 rows stockinette.
Knit 1 WS (turn) row, then work 2 rows stockinette.
Next RS increase row K4 (6, 8, 10, 12), work lifted increase in the next stitch, knit to the last 5 (7, 9, 11, 13) stitches, work lifted increase in the next stitch, knit to the end.
Purl 1 row, then bind off, leaving a long tail.

With the tail, sew the bound-off edge of the band to the selvedge stitch around the armhole edge.
Sew side seams.

Front Bands

With MC (or MC1 for 5-color version), middle-size needles, and RS facing, pick up and knit along the front edges as follows: 2 stitches for every 3 rows along the edge of the hem, 3 stitches for every 4 rows along the 2-color edge.
*Next row E-wrap cast on 1 stitch at the beginning of the row, knit to the end, with the tail e-wrap 1 stitch at the end of the row onto the left needle, knit this stitch.
The extra stitches are for selvedges of the front bands.
Work stockinette until the band measures 2″ (5cm). End after working a knit row.
Knit 1 WS (turn) row, then work stockinette until the back of the band is one row shorter than the front of the band.
Bind off, leaving a long tail.*
Sew the bottom of the band closed, taking 1 stitch from each edge into the seam allowance.
With the long tail, sew the bound-off

edge of the band to the selvedge stitch of the front edge.

Neck Band

With MC (or MC1 for 5-color version), middle-size needles, and RS facing, pick up and knit for neck band as follows:

- 3 stitches for every 4 rows along the edge of the front bands
- k5, k2tog across stitches on the holder for the front and back necks
- k2tog on both sides of both shoulder seams

—approximately 140 stitches. Work as front bands from * to *. Sew the front edges of the neck band closed, taking 1 stitch from each edge into the seam allowance.

With a long tail, sew the bound-off edge of the band to the base of the neck edge. Try the garment on, and decide where you'd like the button. Mark the spot at edge of the right front band where a matching buttonloop should be attached. With MC (or MC1 for 5-color version) and crochet hook, draw yarn through the edge of the right front band at the marked spot, then crochet a 3″ (7.5cm) chain. Sew the chain down to the same spot. Sew a button onto the left front. *Optional:* Sew a snap where desired (to RS of left front neck band and WS of right front band) to close the neck band.

escher-inspired vest

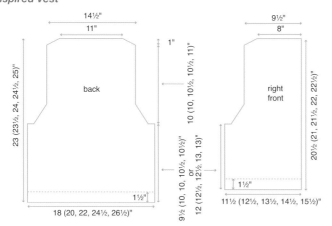

back shows longer version, right front shows shorter version

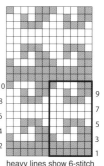

heavy lines show 6-stitch and 10-row repeat

▨ with MC, knit on RS, purl on WS

☐ with CC, knit on RS, purl on WS

For 2-color version, work chart as shown For 5-color version, use 2 MC's and 3 C(change MC after 2 solid rows of CC; change CC after 2 solid rows of MC.

Bordered Lace

This garment was designed to illustrate the principles of having a change of stitch pattern define the balance point (page 24). A garment with this definition is versatile, as is its shallow V-neck, which can be worn at the front or the back. Its other features contribute toward a slimming silhouette: length to the widest point of the hip, tight set-in sleeves, and hourglass shape.

Skill Level
Intermediate

Sizes
S (M, L, 1X, 2X)
Finished circumference at hem 39 (42, 45, 49, 55)″ (99 [106.5, 114.5, 124.5, 139.5]cm)
Finished circumference at waist 33 (37, 41, 43, 50)″ (84 [94, 104, 109, 127]cm)
Finished circumference at bust 36 (39, 43, 46, 51)″ (91.5 [99, 109, 117, 129.5]cm)
Finished length 23½ (24, 24½, 25, 25½)″ (59.5 [61, 62, 63.5, 65]cm)
Finished waist length 15½ (16, 16½, 17, 17½)″ (39.5 [40.5, 42, 43, 44.5]cm)
Finished shoulder width 14½″ (37cm)
Finished sleeve length 18 (19, 20, 21, 22)″ (45.5 [48, 51, 53.5, 56]cm)
Model is shown in size M.

Materials
- 695 (770, 850, 925, 1000) yd (636 [704, 778, 846, 915]m) / 6 (7, 8, 8, 9) skeins Rowan Summer Tweed (70% silk, 30% cotton, each approximately 1¾ oz [50g] and 118 yd [108m]), in color 542 Mango (4) medium
- One circular needle, size 8 (5mm), 20–24″ (51–61cm) long or size needed to obtain gauge
- One pair size 9 (5.5mm) needles, or size needed to obtain gauge
- Stitch holder
- *Optional:* Three (decorative) buttons, ½″ (1.5cm) wide

Gauge
15½ stitches and 24 rows = 4″ (10cm), over stockinette stitch, on smaller needles and after steam-pressing or washing
15 stitches and 23 rows = 4″ (10cm), over lace pattern, on larger needles and after steam-pressing or washing

Lace Pattern
(over a multiple of 6 + 3 stitches and 8 rows)
See chart on page 198.
Row 1 K2, *yo, skp (or ssk), k1, k2tog, yo, k1; repeat from * to the last stitch, k1.
All WS rows Purl.

Row 3 K2, *yo, k1, s2kp, k1, yo, k1; repeat from * to the last stitch, k1.

Row 5 K2, *k2tog, yo, k1, yo, skp (or ssk), k1; repeat from * to the last stitch, k1.

Row 7 K1, k2tog, *k1, yo, k1, yo, k1, s2kp; repeat from * to the last 6 stitches, k1, yo, k1, yo, k1, skp (or ssk), k1.

Notes

- Finished length could occur at the widest point of your hips (page 23).
- The change of stitch pattern is made to occur at 1″ (2.5cm) shorter than your balance point (page 23). This will allow the garment to stretch with wear.
- The cuffs on this garment are tight, but the yarn stretches out. However, you could wrap a cast-on edge around your arm, just above the elbow (where your sleeve fits) to be sure you are casting on a large enough cuff.
- The shoulders may stretch wider than the measurements and schematic indicate.
- The garment is shaped with a shallow V-neck. This can be worn to the back (as the model shows) or to the front (as the pattern is written). The buttons are optional.
- The sleeves are meant to end just above the armhole. (This yarn will distort at the elbow if made longer).

Back

Lace Border

With larger needles, cable cast on 75 (81, 87, 93, 105) stitches.
Begin with row 1 of the lace pattern. Work the lace for 7 rows.

Decrease row (WS) P1, p2tog, purl to the last 3 stitches, ssp, p1.
Maintaining the lace pattern through shaping, repeat the last 8 rows twice more—69 (75, 81, 87, 99) stitches.
Work even until the piece measures approximately 5″ (12.5cm). End after working row 4 or row 8.
(Shorten or lengthen for finished length here.)

Next RS row Change to smaller needle, and purl to make the border between stitch patterns.
Sizes S (M, 2X) only: **next WS row** P69 (75, 99).
Sizes L (1X) only: **next WS row** Purl, increasing 2 stitches evenly across the row—83 (89) stitches.

Stockinette Body

Beginning with a RS row, work 69 (75, 83, 89, 99) stitches in stockinette to 8 rows.

Decrease row (RS) K1, skp (or ssk), knit to the last 3 stitches, k2tog, k1.
Work 7 rows even.
Repeat the last 8 rows once more— 65 (71, 79, 85, 95) stitches.
Work 2″ (5cm) even. End after working a WS row.

Increase row (RS) K1, increase in the next stitch, knit to the last 2 stitches, increase in the next stitch, k1.
Work 11 rows even.
(Shorten or lengthen for waist length by working fewer or more rows between decreases.)

Repeat the last 12 rows twice more—71 (77, 85, 91, 101) stitches. Work even until the piece measures 16½" (42cm) from the beginning. End after working a WS row.

Shape Armholes

Bind off 2 (4, 6, 7, 8) stitches at the beginning of the next two rows—67 (69, 73, 77, 85) stitches.
Decrease row (RS) K1, skp (or ssk), knit to the last 3 stitches, k2tog, k1.
Purl 1 row.
Repeat the last 2 rows 4 (5, 7, 9, 13) times more—57 stitches.
(Widen or narrow for shoulder width by working fewer or more decreases, but end with a multiple of 6 + 3 stitches.)
Work even until the armhole measures 3 (3½, 4, 4½, 5)" (7.5 [9, 10, 11.5, 12.5]cm). End after working a WS row.
Next RS row Purl to make the border between stitch patterns.
Purl 1 WS row.

Lace Yoke

Change to larger needles.
Beginning with row 1, work the lace pattern until the armhole measures 6 (6½, 7, 7½, 8)" (15 [16.5, 18, 19, 20.5] cm). End after working a WS row.

Shape Back Neck and Shoulders

Maintain the lace pattern through shaping.
Bind off 4 stitches at the beginning of the next RS row, work to 12 stitches on the right needle; turn.
*Bind off 1 stitch at the neck edge, work to the end.
Bind off 3 stitches at the armhole edge, work to the end.
Repeat the last 2 rows once—4 stitches.*

Purl 1 row, then bind off on next RS row.
Return to the remaining 41 stitches, and put the center 25 stitches on a holder (for the back neck).
Next RS row K16.
Bind off 4 stitches at the beginning of the next WS row, purl to the end.
Repeat from * to * above.
Bind off on the next WS row.

Front

Work as back, from cast-on through 8 rows of the lace yoke. End after working a WS row.

Shape Front Neck and Shoulders

Next RS row K28; turn.
Maintain the lace pattern through shaping.
**Bind off 3 stitches at the next 4 neck edges, then 2 stitches at the next neck edge—14 stitches.

bordered lace

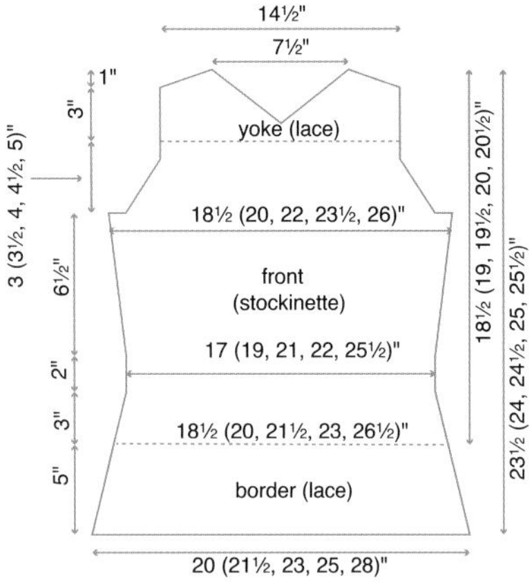
14½"
7½"
1"
3"
yoke (lace)
3 (3½, 4, 4½, 5)"
18½ (20, 22, 23½, 26)"
6½"
front
(stockinette)
17 (19, 21, 22, 25½)"
2"
3"
18½ (20, 21½, 23, 26½)"
5"
border (lace)
20 (21½, 23, 25, 28)"
18½ (19, 19½, 20, 20½)"
23½ (24, 24½, 25, 25½)"

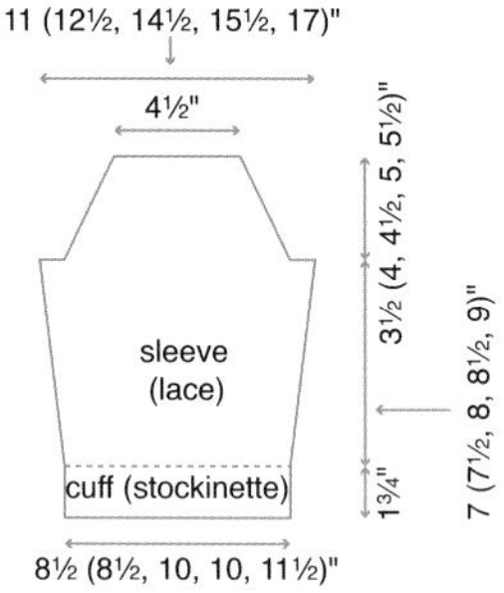
11 (12½, 14½, 15½, 17)"
4½"
sleeve
(lace)
cuff (stockinette)
8½ (8½, 10, 10, 11½)"
3½ (4, 4½, 5, 5½)"
1¾"
7 (7½, 8, 8½, 9)"

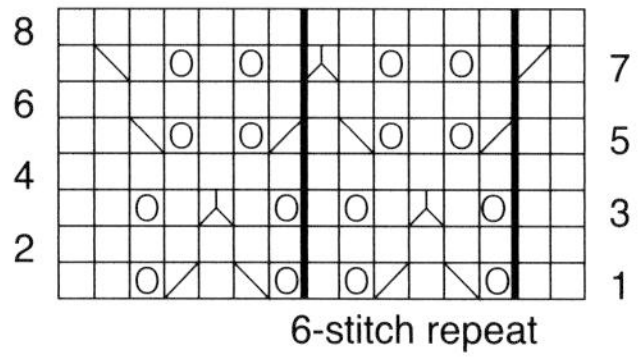
8
6
4
2
7
5
3
1
6-stitch repeat

☐ knit on RS, purl on WS

⧅ skp (or ssk)

⧄ k2tog

◻ yo

☐ s2kp (slip 2 knitwise, k1, pass both slip stitches over, together)

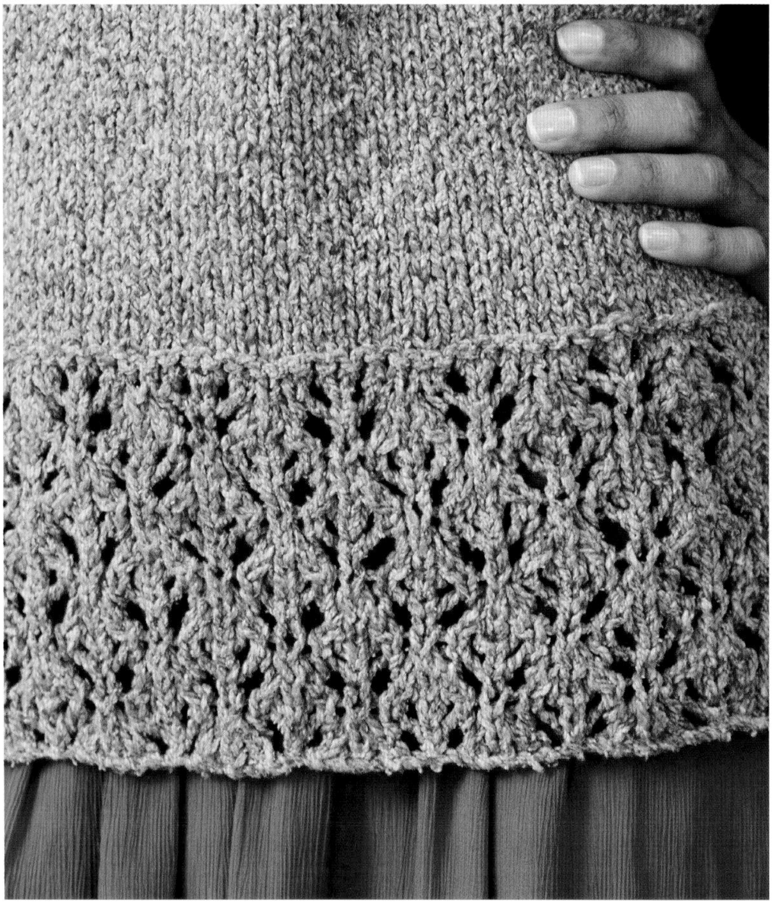

Work even until the armhole measures the same as back.

At the armhole edge, bind off 4 stitches once, 3 stitches twice, then 4 stitches once.**

Return to the remaining 29 stitches, and put 1 center stitch on a holder.

Beginning with a RS row, work 2 rows even.

Work as ** to ** above.

Sleeves

Stockinette Cuff

With smaller needle, cable cast on 33 (33, 39, 39, 45) stitches.

Beginning with a knit row, work stockinette until the cuff measures 1¾″ (4.5cm). End after working a WS row.

Next RS row Purl to make a fold line.

Purl 1 WS row.

Lace Body

Change to larger needles, and purl 1 more row.

This extra purl row makes what should have been a RS row into a

WS row, so the cuff folds up.
Beginning with row 1, work the lace pattern for 5 rows.
Increase row (WS) P1, increase in the next stitch, purl to the last 2 stitches, increase in the next stitch, p1.
Work 5 (5, 3, 3, 3) rows even.
Repeat the last 6 (6, 4, 4, 4) rows 3 (6, 7, 9, 8) times more—41 (47, 55, 59, 63) stitches.
Work even until the piece measures 7 (7½, 8, 8½, 9)″ (18 [19, 20.5, 21.5, 23]cm) above the fold line. End after working a WS row.
(Shorten or lengthen for sleeve length here.)

Shape Sleeve Cap
Bind off 2 (4, 6, 7, 8) stitches at the beginning of the next two rows—37 (39, 43, 45, 47) stitches.
Decrease row (RS) K1, skp (or ssk), knit to the last 3 stitches, k2tog, k1.
Purl 1 row.
Repeat the last 2 rows 9 (10, 12, 13, 14) times more—17 stitches. End after working a WS row.
Bind off 2 stitches at the beginning of the next 2 rows, then bind off the remaining stitches.

Finishing
Sew shoulder seams.

Neck Edging
With the smaller needle, begin at the left shoulder seam and, with RS facing, pick up and knit as follows:
- 3 stitches for every 4 rows (along straight row edges)
- 1 stitch for every bound-off stitch and 1 stitch for every stair step (around front and back neck shaping)
- 1 stitch for every stitch on holders—approximately 86 stitches.

Working in the round, purl 1 RS row, then bind off knitwise.
Sew sleeves into armholes.
Sew side seams.
Sew cuffs, then turn cuffs inside out to sew the remaining sleeve seams.

Fold cuff to RS. (You may sew the inside of the cuff to the sleeve to secure it.)
Optional: Sew 3 buttons below the V-neck, with the first 1″ (2.5cm) below the lace yoke, and the next 2 each 1¼″ (3cm) below the previous one.

Carrie's Wrap

My daughter called one day very excited. "Mom, you gotta come over and watch *Sex and the City* with me!" This was nothing new, and I was happy to oblige. But what she wanted me to see was not Carrie meeting her Russian, but the garment she was wearing—a long, gray, shawl-collared cardigan with a V in the back hem. Caddy wanted to produce something similar.

This was the first test of the book. Caddy took the relevant pages (set-in sleeve, diagonal hem, shawl collar) and got to work. The good news is that she passed the test, which means that so will you!

Skill Level
Intermediate

Sizes
XS (S, M, L, 1X)

Finished circumference at hem (closed) 43 (48, 53, 58, 63)″ (109 [122, 134.5, 147.5, 160] cm)

Finished circumference at bust (closed) 34 (39, 44, 49, 54)″ (86.5 [99, 112, 124.5, 137]cm)

Finished length at center back 27 (28, 29, 30, 32)″ (68.5 [71, 73.5, 76, 81]cm)

Finished length at center front 21 (22, 23, 24, 25)″ (53.5 [56, 58.5, 61, 63.5]cm)

Finished shoulder width 16″ (40.5cm)

Finished sleeve length 29 (29½, 30, 30½, 31)″ (73.5 [75, 76, 77.5, 79]cm)

Model is shown in size S.

Materials
- 705 (780, 860, 940, 1015) yd (645 (713, 786, 860, 928]m) / 12 (13, 15, 16, 17) balls Berocco Blackstone Tweed Chunky (65% wool, 25% kid mohair, 10% angora, each approximately 1¾ oz [50g] and 60 yd [55m], in color 6602 (**5**) heavy
- One pair size 10 (6mm) needles, or size needed to obtain gauge
- stitch holder
- 2 stitch markers

Gauge
12 stitches and 19 rows = 4″ (10cm) over stockinette, after steam-pressing or washing

Notes
- This garment has a center-back seam, to ensure that it holds its shape.
- It has no front closure and is meant to be secured with a shawl pin. This also means that the finished circumferences are approximate.
- The shoulders may stretch 2″ (5cm) when worn. And the sleeves may stretch 1″ (2.5cm) in length with wear. This is reflected in the finished measurements.
- Short rows are written as "slip 1 purlwise (with yarn to wrong side)." If you wish to

- work wraps, you may do so.
- The cuffs for this garment are tight. Wrap a cast-on edge around your wrist to be sure the suggested number of stitches will allow your hand to pass through.
- This garment is show in the same yarn and in color 6646 on page 120.

Right Back
Ribbed Band
Cable cast on 30 (34, 38, 42, 46) stitches.
Row 1 (RS) K2, *p2, k2; repeat from *.
Row 2 P2, *k2, p2; repeat from *.
Work 2 more rows rib.
Row 5 K1, work lifted increase in the next stitch, work rib to the last 3 stitches, k2tog, k1.
Row 6 P2, k1, *p2, k2; repeat from * to the last 3 stitches, p3.
Work 2 rows rib as established.

Row 9 K2, work lifted increase in the next stitch, work rib to the last 3 stitches, k2tog, k1.
Row 10 P2, *p2, k2; repeat from * to the last 4 stitches, p4.
Work 2 rows rib as established.
Row 13 K1, kf&b, work rib to the last 3 stitches, k2tog, k1.
Row 14 P1, *p2, k2; repeat from * to the last 5 stitches, p2, k1, p2.
Work 2 rows rib as established.
Row 17 As row 13.
Row 18 P2, *k2, p2; repeat from *.
Work 4 rows rib as established.

Shape Hem
Next RS increase row Knit, increasing 2 stitches in the row—32 (36, 40, 44, 48) stitches.
***Next WS short row** P4; turn.
Next 7 (8, 9, 10, 11) RS rows Slip 1 purlwise (with yarn to WS), knit to the end.
Next 6 (7, 8, 9, 10) WS short rows Purl to 4 stitches past the previous short row; turn.
Next WS row P32 (36, 40, 44, 48) stitches.

Shape Body
Beginning with a RS row, work stockinette for 6 rows.
Decrease row (RS) K1, skp (or ssk), knit to the end.
Work 5 rows even.
Repeat the last 6 rows 7 times more—24 (28, 32, 36, 40) stitches.
Work even until the piece measures 17″ (43cm) at the side seam. End after working a WS row.
(Shorten or lengthen for finished length here.)

Shape Armhole
Bind off 3 (4, 5, 6, 7) stitches at the beginning of the next RS row—21

(24, 27, 30, 33) stitches.
Purl 1 WS row.
Decrease row (RS) K1, skp (or ssk), knit to the end.
Repeat the last 2 rows 0 (3, 6, 9, 12) times more—20 stitches.
(Widen or narrow for shoulder width by working fewer or more decreases.)
Work even until the armhole measures 6 (6½, 7, 7½, 8)″ (15 [16.5, 18, 19, 20.5]cm). End after working a WS row.

Shape Shoulder
Bind off 4 stitches at the beginning of the next RS row, knit to 8 stitches on the right needle; turn.
Next WS row P8.
Shape shoulder by binding off 4 stitches at the beginning of the next 2 RS rows.
Purl WS rows.
Put remaining 8 stitches onto a holder for the right back neck.

Left Back
Ribbed Band
Cable cast on 30 (34, 38, 42, 46) stitches.
Row 1 (RS) K2, *p2, k2; repeat from *.
Row 2 P2, *k2, p2; repeat from *.
Work 2 more rows rib.
Row 5 K1, skp (or ssk), work rib to the last 2 stitches, work lifted increase in the next stitch, k1.
Row 6 P3, *k2, p2; repeat from * to the last 3 stitches, k1, p2.
Work 2 rows rib as established.
Row 9 K1, skp (or ssk), work rib to the last 3 stitches, work lifted increase in the next stitch, k2.
Row 10 P2, *p2, k2; repeat from * to the last 4 stitches, p4.
Work 2 rows rib as established.

Row 13 K1, skp (or ssk), work rib to the last 3 stitches, kf&b, k2.

Row 14 P2, k1, *p2, k2; repeat from * to the last 3 stitches, p3.

Work 2 rows rib as established.

Row 17 K1, skp (or ssk), work rib to the last 4 stitches, kf&b, p1, k2.

Row 18 P2, *k2, p2; repeat from *.

Work 4 rows rib as established.

Shape Hem

Next RS increase row Knit, increasing 2 stitches in the row—32 (36, 40, 44, 48) stitches.

*Purl 1 row.

Next RS short row K4; turn.

Next 7 (8, 9, 10, 11) WS rows Sl 1 purlwise, purl to the end.

Next 6 (7, 8, 9, 10) RS short rows Knit to 4 stitches past the previous short row; turn.

Next RS row K32 (36, 40, 44, 48) stitches.

Shape Body

Beginning with a WS row, work stockinette for 5 rows.

Decrease row (RS) Knit to the last 3 stitches, k2tog, k1.

Work 5 rows even.

Repeat the last 6 rows 7 times more—24 (28, 32, 36, 40) stitches. Work even until the piece measures the same length as the right back to armhole. End after working a RS row.

Shape Armhole

Bind off 3 (4, 5, 6, 7) stitches at the beginning of the next WS row—21 (24, 27, 30, 33) stitches.

Decrease row (RS) Knit to the last 3 stitches, k2tog, k1.

Purl 1 row.

Repeat the last 2 rows 0 (3, 6, 9, 12) times more—20 stitches.

(Widen or narrow for shoulder width by working fewer or more decreases.)

Work even until armhole measures the same length as the right back. End after working a RS row.

Shape Shoulder

Bind off 4 stitches at the beginning of the next WS row, purl to 8 stitches on the right needle; turn.

Next RS row K8.

Shape shoulder by binding off 4 stitches at the beginning of the next 2 WS rows, knit RS rows.

Put remaining 8 stitches on a holder for left back neck.

Right Front

Ribbed Band

Cable cast on 31 (35, 39, 43, 47) stitches.

Work as right back ribbed band BUT with an extra k1 at the beginning of all RS rows and p1 at the end of all WS rows.

Shape Hem

Next RS increase row Knit, increasing 1 stitch in the row—32 (36, 40, 44, 48) stitches.

Work short rows as Right Back,

carrie's wrap

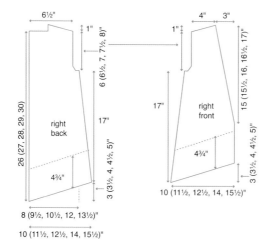

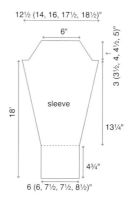

Shape Hem, from * to end of final RS short row.
Next WS row P32 (36, 40, 44, 48) stitches.

Shape Body and V-neck
Side-decrease row (RS) Knit to the last 3 stitches, k2tog, k1.
Work 5 rows even.
V-neck + side-decrease row (RS)
K1, skp (or ssk), knit to the last 3 stitches, k2tog, k1.
Work 5 rows even.
Repeat the last 6 rows 5 times more—19 (23, 27, 31, 35) stitches.
Continue working the side even until the side measures the same as the right back to armhole after working a RS row, then shape armhole as specified below. *At the same time* continue to decrease at the front, V-neck edge every 6th row 3 times more, then work the front edge even to the end. End after working a RS row.

Shape Armhole
Bind off 3 (4, 5, 6, 7) stitches at the beginning of the next WS row.
Decrease row (RS) Knit to the last 3 stitches, k2tog, k1.
Purl 1 row.
Repeat the last 2 rows 0 (3, 6, 9, 12) times more.
After completion of the armhole + V-neck shaping, 12 stitches remain. Work even until the armhole measures the same length as the right back. End after working a RS row.

Shape Shoulder
Bind off 4 stitches at the beginning of the next 3 WS rows.

Left Front
Ribbed Band
Cable cast on 31 (35, 39, 43 47) stitches.
Work as left back ribbed band BUT with an extra k1 at the end of all RS rows and p1 at the beginning of all WS rows.

Shape Hem
Next RS increase row Knit, increasing 1 stitch in the row—32 (36, 40, 44, 48) stitches.
Work short rows as Left Back, Shape Hem from * to end of final WS short row.
Next RS row K32 (36, 40, 44, 48) stitches.

Shape Body and V-neck
Purl 1 WS row.
Side decrease row (RS) K1, skp (or ssk), knit to the end.
Work 5 rows even.
V-neck + side decrease row (RS)
K1, skp (or ssk), knit to the last 3 stitches, k2tog, k1.
Work 5 rows even.
Repeat the last 6 rows 5 times more—19 (23, 27, 31, 35) stitches.
Continue working the side even until the side measures the same as the left back to armhole after working a WS row, then shape the armhole as specified below. *At the same time* continue to decrease at the front V-neck edge every 6th row 3 times

more, then work the front edge even to the end.
End after working a WS row.

Shape Armhole
Bind off 3 (4, 5, 6, 7) stitches at the beginning of the next RS row.
Purl 1 row.
Decrease row (RS) K1, skp (or ssk), knit to the end.
Repeat the last 2 rows 0 (3, 6, 9, 12) times more.
After completion of the armhole + V-neck shaping, 12 stitches remain. Work even until the armhole measures the same length as the left back. End after working a WS row.

Shape Shoulder
Bind off 4 stitches at the beginning of the next 3 RS rows.

Sleeves
Ribbed Band
Cable cast on 18 (18, 22, 22, 26) stitches.
Row 1 (RS) K2, *p2, k2; repeat from *.
Work rib as established to 4¾″ (12cm). End after working a WS row.

Body
Work stockinette to 4 rows.
Increase row (RS) K1, work lifted increase in the next stitch, knit to the last 2 stitches, work lifted increase in the next stitch, k1.
Work 5 (5, 5, 3, 3) rows even.
Repeat the last 6 (6, 6, 4, 4) rows 9 (11, 12, 14, 14) times more—38 (42, 48, 52, 56) stitches.

Work even until the sleeve measures 18″ (45.5m). End after working a WS row.
(Shorten or lengthen for sleeve length here.)

Shape Cap
Bind off 3 (4, 5, 6, 7) stitches at the beginning of the next 2 rows—32 (34, 38, 40, 42) stitches.
Decrease row (RS) K1, skp (or ssk), knit to the last 3 stitches k2tog, k1.
Purl 1 row.
Repeat the last 2 rows 6 (7, 9, 10, 11) times more—18 stitches.
Bind off 2 stitches at the beginning of the next 2 rows, then bind off 14 stitches.

Finishing
Sew center back seam.
Sew shoulder seams.
Sew sleeves into armholes.
Sew side and sleeve seams.

Shawl Collar
Beginning at the lower right front edge, pick up and knit around the entire front and neck edges as follows:
- 3 stitches for every 4 rows (along row edges)
- 1 stitch for every stitch on the holder
- k2tog on each side of center back seam

Count stitches. Increase or decrease (as needed) over the next row to a multiple of 4 + 2 stitches.
Next row (WS) P2, *k2, p2; repeat from *.
***Decrease row (RS)** K1, skp (or ssk), work rib to the last 3 stitches, k2tog, k1.
Work 3 rows rib as established.
Repeat the decrease row.
Work 1 row rib as established.
Repeat from * 3 times more. End after working a WS row.
Band measures approximately 4½″ (11.5cm).
Next RS short row Rib to 18 stitches on the right needle; place marker; rib to 18 stitches from the end of the row; place marker; turn.
Next WS short row Slip 1 purlwise with yarn to WS, rib to marker on the right front; turn.
Subsequent short rows will simply read "Sl 1"; always slip purlwise and with yarn to WS.
Next RS short row Sl 1, rib to 6 stitches from marker on the left front; turn.
Next WS short row Sl 1, rib to 6 stitches from marker on the right front; turn.
Next 10 short rows Sl 1, rib to 6 stitches from previous short row; turn—band measures 7½″ (19cm).
Cut yarn. Slip stitches to beginning of RS row.
Bind off in pattern.
To close holes that may appear at short rows, increase 1 at each short row at the same time as binding off.

Cee-Cee Wrap

My fashionista friend Mel tells me that this kind of thing is very au courant, so she encouraged me to continue with what was a bit of a risk (because it was a new silhouette for me).

The *Cee-Cee* stands for Collared and Cuffed: it also has an easy, but fun to knit stitch pattern. But this is not the first incarnation of this piece. The first one was all rectangles—without shaping at the sides—and it was too much knitting, plus it looked rather aging (an effect that too much fabric can have). This shaped version is a huge improvement—using less yarn and offering a more flattering silhouette.

Skill Level
Intermediate

Sizes
XS–S (M–L, 1X–2X)
Finished width at back hem 22½ (24½, 28½)″ (57 [62, 72]cm)
Finished length 21½ (22½, 23½)″ (54.5 [57, 59.5]cm)
Finished sleeve length (after stretching, without allowance for blousing) 33½″ (85cm)
Model is shown in size M–L.

Materials
- 1140 (1330, 1530) yd (1042 [1216, 1399] m) / 6 (7, 8) balls Brown Sheep Lamb's Pride Worsted (85% wool, 15% mohair, each approximately 4 oz [113g] and 190 yd [174m]), in color M191 Kiwi (4) medium
- One pair needles, size 7 (4.5mm)
- One circular needle, size 8 (5mm), 30″ (76cm) or longer, or size needed to obtain gauge
- One stitch holder
- One stitch marker
- Three split markers
- 3 buttons, 2″ (50mm) wide
- *Optional* 2 snaps, ¾″ (2cm) wide

Gauge
16 stitches and 24 rows = 4″ (10cm) over stitch pattern, after steam-pressing or washing

Notes
- You want this piece to land mid-backside. The garment will slide to the back a bit, so back length may be 1″ (2.5cm) longer than finished measurement.
- Because the neck stretches out, the sleeve length will be 3″ (7.5cm) longer than the schematic suggests. This is reflected in the finished sleeve length.
- The side snaps help hold it in place, but are optional.
- The stitch pattern is easy but changes immediately with side increases. A large swatch will help you understand and maintain it through shaping.

Easy-Over-Under Stitch Pattern

(over a multiple of 8 + 6 stitches and 8 rows)

See chart on page 211.

Row 1 Knit.

Row 2 Purl.

Row 3 K1, *p4, k4; repeat from * to the last 5 stitches, p4, k1.

Row 4 P1, *k4, p4; repeat from * to the last 5 stitches, k4, p1.

Row 5 K1, purl to the last stitch, k1.

Row 6 P1, knit to the last stitch, p1.

Row 7 As row 3.

Row 8 As row 4.

Back

Edging

With smaller needles, cable cast on 76 (92, 108) stitches.

Work edging, as follows, for 4 rows.

RS rows K3, *p2, k2; repeat from * to the last stitch, k1.

WS rows P3, *k2, p2; repeat from * to the last stitch, p1.

Shape Body

Change to larger needles.

Knit 1 row.

Increase row (WS) P1, work lifted increase in the next stitch, purl to the last 2 stitches, work lifted increase in the next stitch, p1—78 (94, 110) stitches.

Next RS row Beginning with row 3, work stitch pattern.

Continue in stitch pattern *at the same time* working the increase row for all WS rows—56 (48, 40) increases on each side, 190 stitches. *Maintain the stitch pattern through shaping. After all increases, you will have a full pattern repeat.*

Work even until the piece measures 20½ (21½, 22½)" (52 [54.5, 57]cm) after steam-pressing. End after working a WS row, preferably row 6.

The shoulder seam is invisible if you end with row 6, so the following directions include instructions for this preference.

(Shorten or lengthen for finished length here.)

Shape Right Back Neck

Next RS row (row 7) Work 80 stitches; turn.

Continue with the stitch pattern while shaping the neck as follows.

Next 2 WS rows (rows 8 and 2) Bind off 1 stitch at neck edge—78 stitches.

Continue in pattern for 3 more rows (to the end of row 5). Bind off, knitwise, on the next WS row.

Shape Left Back Neck

Put center 30 stitches on a holder (for the back neck).

With RS facing, and beginning with the same row as the right back neck (row 7), work 2 rows over 80 stitches.

Next 2 RS rows (rows 1 and 3) Bind off 1 stitch at the neck edge—78 stitches.

Continue in pattern for 2 more rows (to the end of row 5). Bind off, knitwise, on the next WS row.

Right Front

Edging

With smaller needles, cable cast on 28 (36, 44) stitches.

Work edging, as follows, for 4 rows:

RS rows K3, *p2, k2; repeat from * to the last stitch, k1.

WS rows P3, *k2, p2; repeat from * to the last stitch, p1.

Shape Body

Change to larger needles.

Knit 1 row, increasing 1 stitch in the middle of the row—29 (37, 45) stitches.

Increase row (WS) P1, work lifted increase in the next stitch, purl to the end—30 (38, 46) stitches.

Next RS row Beginning with row 3, work stitch pattern.

Continue in stitch pattern *at the same time* working the increase row for all WS rows—56 (48, 40) more increases.

Maintain the stitch pattern through shaping. After final increase, you will have a full pattern repeat.

At the same time, when the piece measures 11 (12, 13)″ (28 [30.5, 33] cm) after steam-pressing and after working a WS row, shape the neck as follows.

Shape V-Neck

Decrease row (RS) K1, skp (or ssk), work the stitch pattern to the end.

Work 5 rows even at the neck edge.

Repeat the last 6 rows 7 times more.

At the end of the neck decreases and side-edge increases, the piece has 78 stitches.

Work even to the same length as the back at shoulder seam, ending with the same row as the back (row 5).

Bind off, knitwise, on the next WS row.

Left Front

Edging

With smaller needles, cable cast on 28 (36, 44) stitches.

Work edging, as follows, for 4 rows:

RS rows K3, *p2, k2; repeat from * to the last stitch, k1.

WS rows P3, *k2, p2; repeat from * to the last stitch, p1.

Shape Body

Change to larger needles.

Knit 1 row, increasing 1 stitch in the middle of the row—29 (37, 45) stitches.

Increase row (WS) Purl to the last 2 stitches, work lifted increase in the next stitch, p1—30 (38, 46) stitches.

Next RS row Beginning with row 3, work the stitch pattern.

Continue in stitch pattern *at the same time* working the increase row for all WS rows—56 (48, 40) more increases.

After all increases, you will have a full pattern repeat.

At the same time, when the piece measures the same length as the right front to V-neck, shape the neck as follows.

Shape V-Neck

Decrease row (RS) Work stitch pattern to the last 3 stitches, k2tog, k1.

Work 5 rows even at neck edge.

Repeat the last 6 rows 7 times more.

At end of the neck decreases and side-edge increases, the piece has 78 stitches.

Work even to the same length as the back at shoulder seam, ending with the same row as the back (row 5). Bind off, knitwise, on the next WS row.

Finishing

Steam-press pieces.

Right Side Edging + Cuffs

Wrap a cast-on edge around your fist to find the minimum number of stitches for your cuff. Make this a multiple of 4 + 2 stitches, then divide this number by 2.

Sew the right shoulder seam.

Row 1 (RS) With larger needles, pick up and knit 3 stitches for every 4 rows along the right front and back side edges.

Count stitches. You need a multiple of 4 + 2 stitches, so decrease across the next row as needed.

Row 2 (WS) P2, *k2, p2; repeat from * to the end.

Work 2 more rows of 2x2 rib as established.

Next row (RS) Bind off in pattern until half the stitches you need for your cuff (as determined above) remain before the shoulder seam. (It's also important for your cuff to begin with a k2, so stop binding off after a p2 that is as close as possible to this spot.)

It's okay if your cuff isn't centered exactly over your shoulder seam.

Work 2x2 rib over the number of stitches you need for your cuff, then continue binding off in pattern to the end. Cut yarn.

Change to smaller needles, and continue in 2x2 rib over the stitches of your cuff until it measures 7″ (18cm).

(Shorten or lengthen for sleeve length by making the cuff shorter or longer.)

Bind off in pattern, leaving a long tail to sew the cuff.

Steam-press the edging and cuff. Sew the cuff, taking 1 knit stitch from each edge into the seam allowance.

Left Side Edging + Cuff

Sew the left shoulder seam. Working along the left front and back side edges, work as Right Front Side Edging + Cuff from Row 1 to end.

Shawl Collar

Row 1 (RS) Beginning at the right front edge and using larger needles, pick up and knit around the entire front edge as follows:

- 2 stitches for every 3 rows between the lower edging and the point of the V-neck
- (k1, yo, k1) at the point of the V-neck
- 3 stitches for every 4 rows between the point of the V-neck and the shoulder seam
- 6 stitches around the back neck shaping
- 1 stitch for every stitch on the holder

Count stitches. You need a multiple of 4 + 2 stitches, so decrease across the next row as needed.

Row 2 P2, *k2, p2; repeat from * to the end.

Work in rib until the collar measures 2″ (5cm). End after working a WS row.

Use split markers to mark spots for buttonholes as follows: All buttonholes are placed in purl troughs. The top buttonhole is placed 1½–2″ (4–5cm) below the beginning of the V-neck shaping; bottom buttonhole is placed 2½–3″ (6.5–7.5cm) from lower edge; the

cee-cee wrap

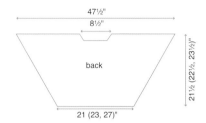

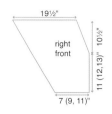

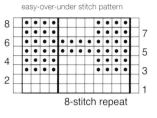

easy-over-under stitch pattern

8-stitch repeat

☐ RS purl, WS knit
☐ RS knit, WS purl

3rd buttonhole is placed an even distance between them.

What follows is an enlarged version of the 3-row buttonhole to accommodate really big buttons.

Next row, begin 3 buttonholes (RS) Work row of rib as established, working each buttonhole as follows: rib to each buttonhole, ending after working a p2 and ready to work the k2 that precedes the buttonhole, and then working the 6 stitches of each buttonhole as follows; k1, skp (or ssk), yo twice, k2tog, k1.

Next row, continue 3 buttonholes (WS) Work rib as established, working the 2 WS knit stitches of each buttonhole as follows: make 1 yo, drop 1 yo, knit remaining yo.

Next row, finish 3 buttonholes (RS) Work rib as established, working the 2 RS purl stitches of each buttonhole as follows: p1, then purl through the buttonhole itself; drop the remaining threads from the left needle before working the following k2.

Continue in 2x2 rib until the rib measures 4″ (10cm). End after working a WS row.

Next RS row Work rib to 1½–2″ (4–5cm) below the point of the right front V-neck, ending after k2; place marker; rib to 1½–2″ (4–5cm) past the point of the left front V-neck, ending after p2; turn.

Next WS short row Sl 1 purlwise, k1, work rib to marker; turn.

RS short rows Sl 1 purlwise, p1, work rib to 4 stitches short of the previous short row; turn.

WS short rows Sl 1 purlwise, k1, work rib to 4 stitches short of the previous short row; turn.

Repeat the last 2 rows until 40 stitches have been left behind at each side. End after the final WS short row.

Next RS row Sl 1 purlwise, k1, work rib to center back neck. Cut yarn. Slip to the beginning of the WS row (at the lower left front). Bind off in pattern on the WS row, and work as follows to fill the space at the short-row turn: at each space of the "turns," work a knitwise lifted increase into the edge of the stitch below the slipped stitch, then bind it off.

Steam-press the shawl collar and band.

Sew buttons to match placement of buttonholes.

Optional: Sew snaps to WSs of side edgings, 2½″ (6.5cm) from the lower edge, so that the side edgings are attached at their WSs; they do not overlap.

APPENDIX

ESSENTIAL SKILLS what follows is a list of the skills I think are essential for every knitter. I have included what I believe to be the salient characteristics or uses for each one, but I did not include directions on how to do them: these are available, with illustrations, in most knitting manuals or online. (If they aren't readily available, as with some of the buttonhole options, I give you instructions.)

CAST-ONS

Long-tail

- It needs a tail 2½ times the length of the cast-on edge plus a length of tail to sew down or seam with.
- It is just the e-wrap with a row of knitting attached (so the next row has the purl side facing).
- This row of knitting is helpful if you are working circularly (because it helps you see that the row is not spiraled around the needle). But this row of knitting is not helpful if you need to purl a WS row before beginning a stitch pattern (like lace, which usually begins with a RS row).
- It's not beautiful, so I would not use it if it will be visible.
- It is not usable when you need to cast on in the middle of a piece.

E-wrap (or half-hitch or backwards loop)

- It is important *not* to do this cast-on backwards—off the left thumb rather than the right index finger. (Doing it backwards makes it difficult

to maneuver and opens up the twist of your yarn.)
- It is loose, reversible, and can be done in the middle of a piece.
- Do not separate your needles as you work your 1st row, or you'll produce long loops.
- If you're picking up and knitting against it, always insert your needle so as to see 2 threads on the needle.

Knit Cast-on

- I rarely use this because it is not a particularly attractive way to begin a piece: I prefer the cable cast-on instead. But I did use it for the no-turn bobble (page 139).

Cable

- This is a gorgeous, heavy, ropey cast-on—a wonderful alternative to the knit cast-on. The difference between it and the knit cast-on is that for this one the right needle is inserted behind, rather than into, the leading stitch on the left needle.
- To loosen it, insert your needle for the next stitch

before tightening the yarn from the previous stitch.
- It is commonly used for buttonholes (to oppose a bound-off edge).
- This cast-on is usually shown as if to knit, but you can produce a 1x1 rib cable cast-on by inserting the needle for alternate stitches as if to purl.

Crochet

- This cast-on mirrors the basic (chain) bind-off.
- It's also useful as a provisional (that is, temporary) cast-on. To execute that, you will cast on with a smooth waste yarn, cut it, introduce the garment's yarn, and knit the garment piece. When ready to remove the waste yarn, undo the last cast-on stitch, and the waste yarn will rip right off. Open stitches will present.

INCREASES

Kf&b (knit into the front and back of the next stitch)

- This is the best increase in garter.

- It leaves a bump in stockinette unless, instead of knitting into the back of the stitch, you simply slip what remains off the left needle purlwise.
- But if you are increasing in rib—and the bumpy stitch can be a RS purl—this increase is wonderful!

M1 (make 1 by twisting and knitting into the thread before the stitch on the left needle)

- This increase is good in all stitch patterns but somewhat visible.
- It's also important to understand that it happens between stitches rather than in a stitch (so it can pucker your knitting if you need many increases along a row).

Lifted increase (knit into the right leg of the stitch below the next stitch on the left needle, then knit the stitch on the left needle)

- This is considered the best increase in stockinette.

Yo (yarn-over)

- It doesn't matter which way a yarn-over is executed: what matters is how you treat it on the next row.
- If you want a hole (as in lace or a buttonhole), you must not twist the yarn-over.

- If you want an increase, you must twist it—and it will look like an M1.
- To not twist a yarn-over, work through its leading edge—the part of the yarn-over closest to the tip of the left needle. (This could be the back or the front, depending upon how your formed your yo.)

DECREASES

K2tog (knit 2 together—usually on a knit row)

P2tog (purl 2 together—usually on a purl row)

- These two decreases reduce 1 stitch with a right-leaning result (when viewed on the RS of stockinette).

Ssk (slip1 knitwise, slip 1 knitwise, knit both together—usually on a knit row)

Skp (slip1 knitwise, k1, pass slip stitch over—usually on a knit row)

Ssp (slip1 knitwise, slip1 knitwise, pass both back onto the left needle, purl 2 together through the back—usually on a purl row)

- These three decreases reduce 1 stitch with a left-leaning result (when viewed on the RS of stockinette).

K3tog (knit 3 together—usually on a knit row)

- This reduces 2 stitches with a right-leaning result and is rarely used.

Sk2p (slip1, knit 2 together, pass slip stitch over—usually on a knit row)

- This reduces 2 stitches with a left-leaning result. It is not my preferred double decrease (see the following).

S2kp (slip2 knitwise and together, knit 1, pass both slip stitches over—usually on a knit row)

- This reduces 2 stitches with a centered result. This is my favorite double decrease because I like the strong vertical it produces.

BIND-OFFS

There are two places at which we bind off:
- some stitches that will go into a seam
- some stitches that will be on public view.

In the former case, working the stitches in stockinette gives the easiest edge to seam. In the latter case, it's important to bind off in pattern unless you have a compelling reason to do otherwise.

Basic (chain) bind-off

- This bind-off is used so often that it's never referred to by

name—except to just say "bind off." (It's the one where we work 2, *pass 1 over, work 1, repeat from *.)
- It's a helpful skill to learn how to tighten this bind-off (page 159).

Sewing-needle bind-offs
- There are many versions of this, and I recommend that you check them out. (Sometimes they're given this name; sometimes they're called *tubular bind-offs*.)
- The one I know is sometimes called the *stem stitch bind-off*. I don't use it very often, but it mirrors the long-tail or e-wrap cast-on. (This is helpful when you shorten something and need to finish that edge with a bind-off that looks like your long-tail cast-on edge.)

Three-needle bind-off
- This is actually a seaming method, but it seems best placed in the bind-off section.
- I don't use this at the shoulders because I prefer the firmness of a sewn seam.
- I will use it, turned to the right side, when I want a decorative stitch-to-stitch join of 2 pieces, to assemble the pieces of an afghan, for example.

SEAMING
There are 3 seaming situations we face:
- row-to-row (side seams,

underarm-to-cuff sleeve seams, and many of the sleeve-cap-to-garment seams of a set-in sleeve or raglan).
- stitch-to-stitch (shoulder seams, the underarm bind-offs of a set-in sleeve or raglan, and the center back seam of a saddle shoulder).
- stitch-to-row (sleeve-to-garment seams of a drop or saddle shoulder, the yoke-to-garment seams of a saddle shoulder, and the final-sleeve cap-to-garment seams of a set-in sleeve).
For all seams, use the yarn of the garment unless it has not been plied or has bits that will get stuck.

Mattress (sometimes called kitchener) stitch seams
- This is the best seaming method to master.
- It is always done with RS facing.
- It produces a seam allowance—taking one selvedge from each side of row-to-row seams (although with bulky yarns you may only take ½ stitch) and the bind-off edge from each side of stitch-to-stitch seams.
- Its motion works for all three seaming situations (as specified above), but do read what follows for exceptions.

Row-to-row seams
Stockinette and other related stitch patterns:

- For the seam allowance, work a stockinette selvedge on each edge of each piece.
- In stockinette, which rolls to the back, these mattress stitch seams are invisible.
Garter stitch:
- In garter stitch, a mattress stitch seam is not appropriate because garter lies flat and doesn't take a seam allowance very easily.
- For seams in garter stitch, one choice is to work garter stitch at all edges, and then work a butted version of the mattress stitch. (This isn't a technical term: it just means using the same motion of the mattress stitch but working right at, rather than 1 stitch in from, the edge.) There will be no seam allowance.
- Another option in garter is to work a slip-stitch selvedge, then take half the slip stitch of each piece into the seam allowance, using the motion of a mattress stitch seam.
Rib:
- In ribbing, you'll get the best seams if the stitches at the edges of the ribbing are knit stitches (reacting like stockinette).
- In 1x1 rib, begin and end each piece with 1 RS knit stitch (working the band over an odd number of stitches). Work a mattress stitch seam up the center of each edge's knit stitch (taking only 1/2 stitch into the seam allowance).

- In 2x2 rib, begin and end each piece with 2 RS knit stitches. Work a mattress stitch seam between the 2 knit stitches (taking 1 knit stitch from each piece into the seam allowance).

Reverse stockinette:
- In reverse stockinette, mattress-stitch row-to-row seams are painful, because the fabric is rolling the wrong way. If your garment's stitch pattern will allow this, the best way to counteract it is with 2 RS knit stitches at the edge of each piece. Work a mattress. stitch seam between the 2 knit stitches. You'll have a beautiful seam and a frame to your work.

Stitch-to-stitch seams

Stockinette and related stitch patterns:
- If my bind-off edge will go into a seam, I bind off in stockinette and use the motion of mattress stitch seams. These stockinette stitches are easy to see, but the roll of stockinette makes the seam awkward. However, I just do what it takes to turn the bound-off edge to the wrong side.
- If the bind-off edge is stair-stepped (as it is in the shoulders), I just bind off and sew as usual, right over the little jogs that present.

Reverse stockinette:
- If the garment is knit in reverse stockinette, a stitch-to-stitch seam will be invisible (which reminds us again that it's all about the roll!).

Grafting or three-needle bind-off:
- I don't find the 3-needle bind-off or grafting strong enough for the shoulders of garments.
- But grafting (live stitches) is the best method for the back yoke of a saddle shoulder, where we don't want a seam allowance on a sensitive spine.
- If you don't like the result of your grafting, or if your grafting line is distorted by oppositional stitch patterns, graft anyway, but pull your grafting line tight—for a seam with no seam allowance.

Stitch-to-row seams
- Even though you will continue to use the motion of mattress stitch seaming, the difficulty here is that numbers often don't match up well. Go to the chart on page 219) for assistance in dealing with the numbers you find.

BUTTONHOLES

General principles for buttonholes
- Most buttonholes will stretch to accommodate a larger button than you'd think.

- Buttons should be in scale to the fabric—smaller on finer knit, larger on coarser.
- There should be more buttons on a fitted garment, and you might begin placement with one at the bust—where the band will experience the greatest stress.
- If you have a choice, buttonholes should be placed closer to the garment body, rather than right at the band's center. (The buttons will pull to the center of the band.)
- To place buttonholes, make the button band first. (This means making a V-neck band in 2 parts and with a center back seam.) Decide how many buttons you need and where they should go on this band. As you make the buttonhole band, make buttonholes to correspond.
- Odd numbers of buttons are considered more appealing, but once you exceed 7, who's counting?
- For a V-neck cardigan, place the first button just slightly below the point of the V. (If you place it right at the V, it will tend to come undone.)

Eyelet buttonhole
- This is the simplest buttonhole in which a yo (yarn-over) is paired with a decrease. The yo is then, usually, not twisted on the next row (although in some bulky yarns and with

some loose knitters it might need to be twisted or else the buttonhole will be too big).

- To not twist a yarn-over, work through its leading edge (the front or back—whichever is closest to the tip of the left needle).
- To make the buttonhole bigger, work through the buttonhole on the next row and drop the stitch you should have worked (the stitch that was the yo two rows before).
- Although good in all fabrics, it is especially nice in the purl ditch of ribbing.
- Its instructions are in the Uptown Jacket (page 180).
- I've developed a larger version of this buttonhole in 2x2 rib: complete instructions for it are in the Cee-Cee Wrap (page 211).

One-row buttonhole

- This buttonhole can be used over any number of stitches and is much neater than the buttonhole in which you bind off in 1 row and then cast on in the next.
- Its security makes it the best choice for buttonholes made in less-dense fabric.
- To not have a thread that cuts the buttonhole in half, bring yarn to the front between the 2 needles before putting the final cast-on stitch onto the left needle.
- Its complete instructions are in Marsha's Top (page 172).

3-B (Between-the-Band-and-the-Body) buttonhole

- This is a solution for buttonholes in minimal bands—by making spaces between the band and the body.
- Work this as follows: where you want a buttonhole, turn the work and cast on some stitches (rather than picking up and knitting); skip an appropriate number of spaces in which you should have picked up and knit before continuing to pick up and knit.

common abbreviations

k	knit
p	purl
RS	right side
sl 1	slip one
tbl	through back of stitch
WS	wrong side
yb	with yarn in back (the side of the knitting not facing you)
yf	with yarn in front (the side of the knitting facing you)

CYCA *standard yarn weight system*

	① Super fine	② Fine	③ Light	④ Medium	⑤ Bulky
Yarn Weight	Lace, Fingering, Sock	Sport	DK, Light Worsted	Worsted, Aran	Chunky
Avg. Knitted Gauge over 4" (10cm)	27–32 sts	23–26 sts	21–24 sts	16–20 sts	12–15 sts
Recommended Needle in US Size Range	1-3	3-5	5-7	7-9	9-11
Recommended Needle in Metric Size Range	2.25–3.25mm	3.25–3.75mm	3.75–4.5mm	4.5–5.5mm	5.5–8mm

Adapted from the Standard Yarn Weight System of the Craft Yarn Council of America (www.yarnstandards.com).

needle and hook sizes

US	MM	HOOK
0	2	A
1	2.25	B
2	2.25	C
3	3.25	D
4	3.5	E
5	3.75	F
6	4	G
7	4.5	–
8	5	H
9	5.5	I
10	6	J
10 ½	6.5	K
10 ¾	7	–
11	8	L
13	9	M
15	10	N

HOW TO USE THIS CHART

- *Decrease* means to reduce by 1 stitch.
- If you are decreasing at both armholes, divide the total number of stitches to be decreased by the total number of rows for decreasing. Go to the nearest result: you will decrease as noted at each end of your decrease rows.
- If you are decreasing at only one armhole (for a cardigan front), divide the number of stitches to be decreased at one armhole by the number of RS rows for decreasing. Go to the nearest result: you will decrease as noted at only one end of your decrease rows.

ratios for decreasing

0.2 = 1/5	decrease 1 of every 5 RS rows
0.25 = 1/4	decrease 1 of every 4 RS rows
0.3 = 3/10	decrease 3 of every 10 RS rows
0.33 = 1/3	decrease 1 of every 3 RS rows
0.375 = 3/8	decrease 3 of every 8 RS rows
0.4 = 2/5	decrease 2 of every 5 RS rows
0.43 = 3/7	decrease 3 of every 7 RS rows
0.5 = 1/2	decrease 1 of every 2 RS rows
0.55 = 5/9	decrease 5 of every 9 RS rows
0.57 = 4/7	decrease 4 of every 7 RS rows
0.6 = 3/5	decrease 3 of every 5 RS rows
0.625 = 5/8	decrease 5 of every 8 RS rows
0.66 = 2/3	decrease 2 of every 3 RS rows
0.71 = 5/7	decrease 5 of every 7 RS rows
0.75 = 3/4	decrease 3 of every 4 RS rows
0.77 = 7/9	decrease 7 of every 9 RS rows
0.8 = 4/5	decrease 4 of every 5 RS rows
0.83 = 5/6	decrease 5 of every 6 RS rows
0.857 = 6/7	decrease 6 of every 7 RS rows
0.875 = 7/8	decrease 7 of every 8 RS rows
0.9 = 9/10	decrease 9 of every 10 RS rows
1 = 1/1	decrease all RS rows
1.12 = 9/8	decrease 8 RS rows, then decrease on the next WS row
1.14 = 8/7	decrease 7 RS rows, then decrease on the next WS row
1.16 = 7/6	decrease 6 RS rows, then decrease on the next WS row
1.2 = 6/5	decrease 5 RS rows, then decrease on the next WS row
1.25 = 5/4	decrease 3 RS rows, then decrease on the next WS row
1.3 = 4/3	decrease 4 RS rows, then decrease on the next WS row
1.4 = 7/5	decrease 3 RS rows, then decrease the next WS row, decrease the next 2 RS rows, then decrease on the next WS row
1.5 = 3/2	decrease 2 RS rows, then decrease on the next WS row
2 = 2/2	decrease all rows

HOW TO USE THIS CHART

- Count to find both the number of stitches and the number of rows for the area you will seam.
- Divide the smaller number by the larger one. (The number of rows will always be the larger number.)
- Go to the nearest result, and seam as specified (remembering that a row is a single "bar" or thread, and a stitch is a "V").
- Sometimes (as in a raglan), you can find yourself seaming one number of rows against a different number of rows. Again, divide the smaller number by the larger one, go to the nearest result, and seam as specified. (In that case, you will most likely find your result at the bottom of this chart, and that's why it includes seaming rows to rows.)

ratios for seaming

0.5 = 1/2	seam 1 stitch for every 2 rows
0.6 = 3/5	seam 3 stitches for every 5 rows
0.63 = 5/8	seam 5 stitches for every 8 rows
0.67 = 2/3	seam 2 stitches for every 3 rows
0.71 = 5/7	seam 5 stitches for every 7 rows
0.75 = 3/4	seam 3 stitches for every 4 rows
0.8 = 4/5	seam 4 stitches (or rows) for every 5 rows
0.83 = 5/6	seam 5 stitches (or rows) for every 6 rows
0.88 = 7/8	seam 7 stitches (or rows) for every 8 rows
0.9 = 9/10	seam 9 stitches (or rows) for every 10 rows
0.95 = 19/20	seam 19 stitches (or rows) for every 20 rows

HOW TO USE THIS CHART

- On page 147, I offer pick-up-and-knit ratios that work for me. You may start by working a trial 4" (10cm) piece of your edging with that ratio. If you have too many stitches, your trial piece will flare: if you have too few, it will flip open. If one of these has occurred, look on this chart to find the ratio that didn't work, then go to a tighter, or looser, ratio—whichever you think will remedy the situation. (The chart begins with the tightest ratio then proceeds through the looser ones.)
- But remember: if you pick up and knit too many stitches, you can easily fix that by tightening the bind-off row (page 160).

ratios for picking up and knitting

0.5 = 1/2	pick up and knit 1 stitch for every 2 rows
0.6 = 3/5	pick up and knit 3 stitches for every 5 rows
0.63 = 5/8	pick up and knit 5 stitches for every 8 rows
0.67 = 2/3	pick up and knit 2 stitches for every 3 rows
0.71 = 5/7	pick up and knit 5 stitches for every 7 rows
0.75 = 3/4	pick up and knit 3 stitches for every 4 rows
0.83 = 5/6	pick up and knit 5 stitches for every 6 rows
0.8 = 4/5	pick up and knit 4 stitches for every 5 rows
0.88 = 7/8	pick up and knit 7 stitches for every 8 rows

Resources

Berroco, Inc.

1 Tupperware Drive, Suite 4
North Smithfield, RI USA 02896-6815
401-679-1212
www.berroco.com

Brown Sheep Company Inc.

100662 County Road 16
Mitchell, NE USA 69357
800-826-9136
www.brownsheep.com

Cascade Yarns Inc.

1224 Andover Park East
Tukwilla, WA USA 98188
206-574-0440
www.cascadeyarns.com

Fairmount Fibers (for Manos del Uruguay)

P. O. Box 2082
Philadelphia, PA USA 19103
888-566-9970
www.fairmountfibers.com

Fiesta Yarns

5401 San Diego Ave. NE
Albuquerque, NM USA 87113
505-892-5008
www.fiestayarns.com

Koigu Wool Designs

Box 158
Chatsworth, ON CA N0H 1G0
888-765-wool
www.koigu.com

Misti International

P.O. Box 2532
Glen Ellyn, IL USA 60138-2532
888-776-9276
www.mistialpaca.com

Mountain Colors

P.O. Box 156
Corvallis, MT USA 59828
406-961-1900
www.mountaincolors.com

Tahki Stacy Charles, Inc. (for Donegal Tweed)

70-60 83rd St., Building #12
Glendale, NY USA 11385
718-326-4433
www.tahkistacycharles.com

Tilli Tomas

Boston, MA USA 02130
617-524-3330
www.tillitomas.com

Westminster Fibers (for Rowan)

165 Ledge St.
Nashua, NH USA 03060
800-445-9276
www.westminsterfibers.com

Acknowledgments

This book was a long time in the works, with many contributors and events. What follows is a short and imperfect list.

First, I am grateful to my mother, who knew enough to help me knit but not enough to measure gauge or tell me how to achieve it. Because I could do neither, I began to draft my own patterns. What followed were years of trial and error, and I thank my father for his lessons in patience.

I've had great teachers along the way, but I am very grateful that they couldn't answer the questions I didn't know to ask. So my most persistent teacher was failure—a subject best studied in solitude. And then what failure didn't teach, my students did. I am grateful for their patience and intelligence and generosity.

And speaking of generosity, I must thank yarn companies for yarn, plus the many yarn shop owners who support both my teaching and my yarn habit. Many of you have become cherished friends whose wisdom and advice I trust.

On the technical side, thanks to Shannon Moore (who answered Illustrator questions while on vacation), Stasia Bania (a fine and proficient knitter), my agent Beverley Slopen (who keeps cool through dumb questions), Lynne Moore (who found her editor's mind), and the staff at Potter Craft (especially Betty Wong, a voice of calm).

On the personal side, I have friends and family who offer humor, patience, and forbearance, and who shine light when days seem dark. The brightest of these is Jeremy. I won't list the rest—and risk omissions—but please assume that if I did include a list you'd be on it!

Finally, and above all, to my daughter Caddy . . . forever love and thanks. I cannot find words to express my gratitude and admiration. You read this book with meticulous care and fierce intelligence. When I was wrong, you were right. When I was right, you were happy! I share this work with you.

P.S. Dear Ivy, may you climb high!

Index